OCCULT CONNECTION II: THE HIDDEN RACE

BY
KEN HUDNALL

Omega Press
El Paso, Texas

Other Works by Ken Hudnall

FICTION

Manhattan Conspiracy
Blood On The Apple
Capital Crimes
Angel of Death

The Darkness Series
When Darkness Falls
Fear the Darkness

Even Paranoids Have Enemies

NON-FICTION

The Occult Connection
UFO's, Secret Societies and Ancient Gods
The Hidden Race

Spirits of the Border
The History and Mystery of El Paso Del Norte
The History and Mystery of Fort Bliss, Texas

Occult Connection II: The Hidden Race

OMEGA PRESS
An imprint of Omega Communications

For Information Address:

Omega Press
5823 N. Mesa, #823
El Paso, Texas 79912
Or
http://www.kenhudnall.com

FIRST EDITION

Printed in the United States of America

DEDICATION

To Sharon, who never ceases to be supportive and understanding. She is the reason for my success.

TABLE OF CONTENTS

PROLOGUE

Just as I did in the Occult Connection: UFOs, Secret Societies and Ancient Gods[1], I am going to be discussing a rather far out theory. I originally theorized that there was an alien race that predated our own that came to earth to exploit the resources of this planet. As a result of an internal struggle, a civil war erupted which sapped the capabilities of these visitors. Due to the destruction of a good portion of their resources, the survivors were marooned here on earth, waiting for reinforcements that may never come.

I have also come to believe that members of this race of early visitors to our world have continued to influence things through the cooperation of human agents. However, as I began to watch international events and some of the various activities that have gone on in our own country, I began to wonder if this alien race was as helpless as I had presupposed.

What if this alien race that had once walked among us lesser mortals as gods wanted to be gods once again? Clearly, we must outnumber them millions to one, but I would submit that to control the vast majority of the human population, an invader would only have to control a handful of influential leaders. Could it be that there has been a well developed plan to keep us fighting among ourselves so that we never notice what "the man behind the curtain is doing?[2]" I would submit that the facts bear this out.

Join me for this second journey into the unknown as we look for signs of this mysterious Hidden Race. First we see if there seems be a plan to divide and conquer the Human Race, perhaps keeping us in the dark in so far as learning is concerned and then we see if there is evidence of a major advanced race moving

---

[1] Hudnall, Ken, The Occult Connection: UFOs, Secret Societies and Ancient Gods, Omega Press, El Paso, Texas 1996.

[2] In the movie, The Wizard of Oz, when Toto pulled back the curtain to reveal the wizard was human, the wizard instructed Dorothy and her friends to ignore the man behind the curtain.

amongst us. Take off the blinders and you never know what you can find.

PART ONE

THE OBVIOUS

CHAPTER ONE

WHY?

"Treason doth never prosper, what's the reason?
For if it prosper, NONE DARE CALL IT TREASON."
Sir John Harrington (1561-1612)

When I wrote the first book in this series, I had the germ of a new theory regarding alien visitation to this planet. At first my theory revolved solely around the mystery of the Unidentified Flying Objects that so many people seemed to be seeing in our night skies. Since, at the time, I was doing a nightly radio show I was being inundated with data from my many listeners regarding these mysterious lights in the sky. This put me in a unique position to be able to get a fairly good picture of what was happening in the so-called "fringe areas" such as alleged UFO landings, mysterious disappearances and similar events.

As I gathered the (almost daily) reports that dealt with these strange objects, I also began to hear about an area of this mystery that I had previously heard little about, that of human abductions. As a result of interviewing several of the more famous abductees, I began to see that there was much more to the story than what the average person knew about. Upon making this discovery, I began to delve deeper into the stories told by the abductees. I found that what they reported had a striking similarity with stories told by people in past ages who had allegedly been abducted by fairies and other such way out creatures. I found it hard to believe what I was finding.

The trail led me deeper and deeper into what our modern world calls myths and the supernatural. I found that, while the trappings changed (i.e. flying saucers instead of broomsticks) much of the behavior exhibited by these mysterious, unexplainable "creatures" who periodically interacted with the human race remained fairly constant.

The United States military sought to explain all of this away by discrediting the witnesses rather than investigating the occurrence. Could all of these bizarre happenings be the results of swamp gas and hoaxes as our ivory tower inhabiting scientists were fond of saying? I tried to talk to some of the better known researchers in this field but found that, in many cases, they were having trouble seeing past their own egos. In fact, after an interview on my show, I had one U.F.O. researcher that I had considered a friend until this point, call me at my office and proceed to read me the riot act for not showing him what he felt was the proper deference as befitted his station as a “famous” UFO expert.

In fact a great deal of what I found in this somewhat unusual field of research seemed to consist of various people trying to twist the known facts to fit their own pet theories rather than really seeking the truth. It also became very clear that a great deal of the data being put out by several supposedly serious sources seemed to be about fifty percent disinformation (an intelligence term meaning information designed to confuse the reader) and twenty-five percent lies. Therefore, I resolved to do a book about the matter as I saw it. However, I vowed to avoid the paranoia that seemed to pervade the field.

Unfortunately, as I began to put some flesh on the bare bones of my theory, I began to come across some of the most unbelievable information that I had ever seen. From researching Unidentified Flying Objects and the so-called abductions, I found that I had to delve into various religious teachings, as much of what the so-called aliens seemed to be saying had a religious bent. While studying religion, I found that I was constantly running across references to various secret societies and cults that were known to be operating in the shadows to influence the activities of the Human Race. A study of these little known organizations led me back through history to the ancient Gods and Goddesses.

Trying to put it all together, I found, as an inadvertent result of my other research, that in many cases, contemporary reports by little known writers painted an entirely different picture of historical events than did the accepted sources. As a result I was coming up with an entirely different picture of what had actually happened at various turning points in history rather than what accepted history told us had happened. This, naturally, led me into taking a closer look at the various accepted historical reports.

To my utmost surprise, I found that much of what I had been taught in school about the history of this country and many other topics was not anywhere close to being correct. Much of history seems to have been rewritten to suite the whims of the powers that be.

As an example, I could not find anyone, except a few confused researchers like myself, who had ever heard or read anything about the Czar of Russia sending troops and ships to help Abraham Lincoln fight the American Civil War. After all, Russia was now our enemy and there could be nothing to admire among such evil people.

After coming across several of these similar historical omissions, I began to see that, perhaps, history books had been intentionally changed to benefit some person or persons unknown or perhaps some political group. From this monumental discovery, it was only a short step to finding myself neck deep in what the liberal media laughingly calls the Conspiracy Theory of History.

What did this have to do with a study of Unidentified Flying Objects? Maybe nothing, but then again, maybe a great deal. Having spent several years working for the Government in one capacity or another, I was well aware of how facts could be distorted to make embarrassing events simply disappear. Therefore, I had to wonder whether or not there was a great deal more to some of the abductee reports and landings than was being revealed. Then I began to wonder if perhaps some of the more paranoid U.F.O. researchers might not be correct and information on UFOs was being covered up by our Government. In other words, was there a conspiracy that was attempting to cover-up information regarding UFO cases?

THE CONSPIRACY THEORY OF HISTORY

I found that as I researched the material that became the first volume of *THE OCCULT CONNECTION,* that the Conspiracy Theory of History had a great deal of support when one took the trouble to check the facts. Unfortunately for society in general, those in education and government who should be checking the historical facts taught in our schools to ensure that they are accurate are too busy espousing the position of the Conspirators, since they have everything to gain and nothing to lose by siding with those in power.

For example, what would orthodox historians do to an individual, or even one of their own, who tried to prove that Franklin D. Roosevelt actually knew of and looked forward to the attack on Pearl Harbor or that Woodrow Wilson had made a deal with the British before his re-election in 1916 to ensure that we would enter World War I on the side of the British Empire?

In fact, while researching material for another book, I discovered that President Franklin Roosevelt actually goaded the Japanese into attacking Pearl Harbor. At this time in our nation's history, many of those of influence considered Roosevelt to be a socialist and a traitor and there was actually a coup in the making led by such people as Joseph Kennedy. There is every possibility that if the Japanese had not attacked our fleet at Pearl Harbor, that Roosevelt would have been overthrown and the world in which we live would have been much different that we know it.

I also found, to my surprise, that many otherwise intelligent people were ready to dismiss my book as ridiculous without bothering to even check my source material. I made very public challenges on the radio for anyone who desired to do so to appear on my program and debate me. I dared anyone who wanted to do so to come and prove me wrong. No one took me up on my challenge. However, the station was bought and the format changed so that the station only played Lawrence Welk music. Was this end to my very popular radio talk show just coincidence or conspiracy? Whatever may have been the case, so much for my show.

AN UNNECESSARY DEFENSE

Seldom do I feel it necessary to defend my actions, I generally take the position that a friend is going to believe that my intentions were good and an enemy is never going to be convinced that I did not act with evil intentions. However, in this particular instance, I will break my usual rule and explain the reasons I wrote the first volume of *THE OCCULT CONNECTION: U.F.O.S, SECRET SOCIETIES AND ANCIENT GODS*[3]

In spite of what some of my critics have had to say, first, I had no intention of trying to make anyone believe that there is no GOD. Nor did I have any intention of attacking anyone's religious beliefs. Let me say for the fourth or fifth time that I do believe in GOD, however, believing in GOD does not (and should not) forbid one from exploring the legends and stories that clutter up the religious landscape.

I was, and am, making a valid attempt to examine certain aspects of world history from a purely common sense point of view. Much of our knowledge of the ancient world and the basis of many of our religious beliefs come from our history books and the ancient Sumerian writings. Therefore, I felt that in examining some of those writings, I could get an idea of the reality of some of our "Ancient Gods". I was correct, however, this examination appears to, inexplicably, have upset many people. What upset me was that I found that the historical text books that I felt I could rely on were turning out to be incorrect if the original translations of the Sumerian tablets could be relied upon. Once again I had to ask why the "true" facts put forth by contemporary Sumerian writers were being ignored for theories concocted by modern day historians.

Next, I must point out that what I created in Book One of this series was a theory or a series of theories, if you prefer. Before one can arrive at any valid truth, there must be a theory, or a starting point from which to start any research. I will be the first to admit that my theory may sound outlandish to some, but simply because something sounds outlandish, doesn't mean it isn't true. I would suggest that to Americans living in 1934, the idea that in 35 years, men from America would walk on our Moon would have sounded just as outlandish.

So I began a study to try and answer several questions at one time. First, to

---

[3] Hudnall, Ken, The Occult Connection: UFOs, Secret Societies and Ancient Gods, Omega Press, El Paso, Texas 1996.

try and make some sort of sense out of the UFO mystery, at the same time examines the impact that advanced beings may have had on the human race and then to delve into the question of whether or not these same advanced beings may not be manipulating us today.

For those who have not as of yet read Book One of this series, and at the risk of boring those who have read the first volume, I think it would be of value to repeat within this volume my theory in its entirety, the theory around which this entire series is built.

EMOTIONAL BASKET CASES

In my travels and research, I have met quite a number of the so-called abductees and those who claim to have come in contact with the unexplained. While I have found them, for the most part, to be truthful sincere people, I have noticed one thing that they all have in common. They all seem to have some sort of mental or emotional problems. Does it mean that all of those so-called abductees and those who have come in contact with the unexplained are just crazy, or does it perhaps mean that as a result of their pre-existing problems they are somehow more sensitive to the unexplained than the rest of us? Only time will tell.

THE WORST SCENARIO

There is, of course, a dark side to this theory that I have only recently realized. The hidden race that I theorize exists on our planet alongside us once ruled this planet with a firm hand. Then something happened and they lost the absolute power that they once enjoyed. Now, our technology, while in all likelihood primitive compared to their own as well as our huge numbers makes it very unlikely that they could once again exert their ruler ship over the human race. That is, unless some worldwide catastrophe so reduced our numbers and our level of sophistication that they could once again simply overawe us with their power and glory.

There was once a Star Trek episode that proposed that the gods of pre-history were aliens who had decided that they once again wanted to rule over mankind. This would only be possible if humans gave up all freewill to obey with no questions asked regarding the dictates of the gods. Could this be true? Only time will tell, but as you read these pages, a very real possibility will present itself, that this unknown band of survivors are working behind the scenes to actually destroy the human race.

CHAPTER TWO

A NEW LOOK AT THE OCCULT CONNECTION

For those who have not as of yet read Book One of this series, I think it would be of value to repeat within this first chapter of this Second Volume, the theory around which this entire series is built.

MY THEORY[4]

(Reprinted in its' entirety from the first volume of this series)

I am sure that you have wondered up to this point, exactly where I am going with this book. Well, I aim to show, at least, circumstantially, that it is entirely possible that this planet was colonized by a small group of settlers from another planet. I don't think that they planned on staying as long as they have, but they were marooned here. Where that other planet might be shall be addressed as we progress. However, allow me to present my case.

First I want to list my main reference books. While I am sure that the skeptics among you will scoff that I am using third hand information, I want to challenge them to at least read the works that I am about to list. The problem with most skeptics is that they generally have absolutely no idea what they are talking about when they denigrate a theory. It appears that they just like to flap their gums.

The authors of the modern works I have carefully researched. I have the greatest respect for their credentials. The ancient works that I use have been vouched for by literary minds much greater than mine, so I shall give respect to the works until they can be proven wrong.

Now one point that you must remember, as I remarked in the Preface to

---

[4] Ibid, Chapter 9, Page 155

this work, I DO BELIEVE IN GOD, I just question whether some of the things attributed to HIM were performed by HIM. I find the idea of the GOD who created this marvelous planet being as petty as recorded in the Old Testament and in some of the legends as being unpalatable. I would also point out that during World War II primitive tribes in the South Pacific came to worship the "Gods" that rode through the clouds. In fact, an entire religion, called The Cargo Cult, sprang up complete with priests and prays to the gods of the air to deliver benefits to the people. The gods of the air were the very human pilots that flew the planes that dropped supplies to our troops on the ground. Winds blew some of these drops into the hands of the worshipers. I would submit that compared to the primitive tribesmen, we were gods. That does not mean that this lessens the reality of the existence of GOD.

So before deciding that I am attacking your faith and therefore throw this book in the trash, at least do me the courtesy of hearing my theory in its' fullest.

References:

Works by Zecharia Sitchin
The 12th Planet
The Stairway To Heaven
The Wars of Gods and Men
The Lost Realms

Works by Christian O'Brien
The Megalithic Odyssey
The Genius of the Few

The King James Version of the Holy Bible

Translations of the Original Greek version of the Holy Bible

Translations of the Original Hebrew version of the Holy Scriptures

The Book of Mormon

The Book of Enoch
The Book of the Secrets of Enoch

As you can see there are numerous works that I have used as references in compiling my theory. You might be surprised that not one of these works even came close to opposing my theory. So without further ado, I present Hudnall's Theory of History.

Now understand, I am not an archeologist, nor an anthropologist. I have used reports written by the ancient scribes, so I may be wrong in details, but I believe that my overall picture is accurate.

1. I believe it entirely possible that at some point, estimated to be some one half million years ago, a small band of colonists came to this planet.

DATA: The arrival of the colonists pre-dated the earliest of man's written records. Zecharia Sitchin places their arrival at approximately 450,000 years ago, based on writings of the ancient Sumerians[5]. It is theorized that these visitors from another world came in search of silver and gold that was needed on their home world for scientific purposes. There is, of course, always the possibility that they were sent here to prepare this planet for resettlement by the rest of their race. For if their race is in dire trouble on their home planet, and this planet is suitable for them to survive on, then it would make since to prepare a new home for their race.

Other records of Sumerians call these visitors, the Annanaki or Annanagi depending on which theory you subscribe to, the Lords of Cultivation, since they first established farming as a task for man[6]. It is theorized that the Garden of Eden, of Biblical fame, was a colony established when they first arrived on this planet. The Garden was an area where food was grown for consumption. History does seem to support the belief that the particular area of the Middle East was barren when the Annanaki first arrived.

2. These colonists built an earth base, called Eden, from which they began to survey the planet.

DATA: Christian O'Brien in his book, THE GENIUS OF THE FEW, refers to the Book of Enoch for the name of the Garden. He states that "At Kharsag, where Heaven and Earth met, the Heavenly Assembly, the Great Sons of Anu, descended--the many wise Ones[7].

As is pointed out by Sitchin in his works, ANU was the name, or title, of the Supreme Ruler of the Annanaki. Baalbek was built in his honor, as an Earth base for him.

3. The concept of Heaven, in reality, referred to Eden, the Annanaki mountain base.

DATA: The word from the original Hebrew that has been translated as 'the heavens' was ha'shemin. This Hebrew word is a plural form that actually means the skies. (3) The Hebrew word SHEM also means heights. SHM was also the root of a word

---

[5] Sitchin, Zecharia, THE WARS OF GODS AND MEN. Avon Books, New York. 1985.

[6] O'Brien, Christian, THE GENIUS OF THE FEW, Turnstone Press Limited, Wellingborough, Northamptonshire, G.B. 1985.

[7] *Ibid*

meaning plant. Based on these clues, it is felt that the word ha'shemin actually meant the highlands, the location of the Garden of Eden.

4. The colonists were physically bigger and stronger than earth man. Primitive man, less sophisticated than modern homo sapien, viewed these beings with awe.

DATA: Using the story of the early Hebrews wandering in the desert, being led by YAHWEH ELOHIM, or JEHOVAH, as he has come to be known, it is possible to get some idea of the size of the ANNANAKI. From the construction of the tent that was built by Moses, (as a "home" for YAHWEH ELOHIM) it appears that YAHWEH ELOHIM was approximately eight feet tall.

As a result of the power demonstrated by these beings, early man followed them in child-like awe. The counsel and guidance of these beings gave rise to the first and most glorious civilization in history, the Sumerian Civilization.

5. The colonists had some characteristic that made them give off a shine or glow from their skin.

DATA: The Hebrew word EL is translated as God. However, GOD is referred to as ELOHIM, the plural form, meaning Gods. The Hebrew word EL came from the Sumerian word EL which translates as brightness or shining. As a matter of fact, the Akkadians, the Babylonians, the Old Welsh, the Old Irish, the English and the Old Cornish all had words that were variations of the original EL and each of these variations meant shining or brightness. This gives rise to the theory that the ancient writers were trying to describe a being that gave off a glow or a brightness.

6. These colonists had the ability to fly, whether individually or by a craft.

DATA: Almost every ancient writer talks of the Angels or the Annanaki being able to fly. Enoch talks of being taken up by them and taken to Heaven[8]. It has been said that early artists painted wings on Angels merely to show that they can fly.

7. The colonists were divided into two classes, the autocrats and the technicians.

DATA: The ancient Sumerian writings refer to the Annanaki who were laboring to carry out the orders of the Heavenly Council[9]. Other of the Annanaki were later sent to the lowlands to teach mankind.

---

[8] The Book of Enoch

[9] Sitchin, Zecharia, THE WARS OF GODS AND MEN, Avon Books, New York. 1985.

8. The colonists are very long lived, but also have the ability to extend their normal life spans to something approaching immortality.

DATA: The patriarchs of the Bible all lived several hundred years. This infers one of two things. Either man was originally genetically designed to live extended periods or that there was some artificial way of extending life. The later seems the more probable.

In fact there is reference to the existence of a life extending substance both in the Bible[10] and in the ancient Sumerian Texts[11]. I might also point out that there is reference to this same substance in the legends of almost every civilization that existed on this earth. In Europe it was called ambrosia, the Nectar of the Gods. In the legends from India, Gilgamesh set off to ask for Immortality from the Supreme God. The implication is that this substance would also extend the life of man. If man and the Annunaki are genetically similar as we shall discuss later, then this would be quite likely.

A prime example of the existence of this substance came from one of the Sumerian Texts, from which the later Book of Genesis was taken. In this text, the wording is as follows:

[Then did the Deity Yahweh say: "Behold, the Adam has become as one of us, to know good from Evil. And now might he not put forth his hand and partake also of the Tree of life, and eat, and live forever?" And the Deity Yahweh expelled the Adam from the orchard of Eden.][12]

This scene took place after Adam and Eve ate from the Tree of Knowledge. It would appear that the promise of eternal life was intended to be a physical eternal life and not a spiritual eternal life.

It also shows that the Annunaki had reason to fear man if man should be given the opportunity for eternal life. Could it be that the "gods" of the ancient world were not as all powerful as they would have it appear?

9. The colonists established several bases throughout the Middle East.

DATA: The ancient Sumerians write of the head of the Gods, called ENLIL, as establishing several centers. The "gods" established the cities of Eridu, Larsa, Nippur, Bad-Tibira, Larak, Sippar, Shuruppak, and Lagash. Each of these cities

---

[10] Holy Bible, The King James Edition, The Book of Genesis.
[11] Sitchin, Zecharia, THE WARS OF GODS AND MEN, Avon Books, New York. 1985.
[12] O'Brien, Christian, THE GENIUS OF THE FEW, Turnstone Press Limited, Wellingborough, Northamptonshire, G.B., 1985.

served a certain function[13].

10. The class made up of the autocrats, which included the scientists, manipulated the weather to give them a longer growing season for crops.

DATA: The ancient writers speak of the "gods" making the rains come and causing crops to grow. This has been a belief of almost every race on this planet. After all, ENLIL was also known as the Lord of Cultivation[14].

11. The technician class was forced to do all the heavy labor. This resulted in a mutiny[15]. The head of the science team was ordered by the mission commander to see if it was possible to train indigenous man to work in place of the technicians. It was found that ape-man was not a suitable worker.

DATA: Both Sitchin and O'Brien report on the Sumerian writings regarding the unhappiness of the Annunaki who were forced to do manual labor. It is interesting to note that while the two researchers differ on how they view what they found in the ancient records, their overall interpretations arrive at the same point.

The ancient Sumerian writings, the Epic of Creation, point to this mutiny of the lesser Annunaki as being the reason for the creation of man. Mankind was designed and created to serve the masters, the Annunaki.

12. On orders of the mission commander, which the approval of the overall commander, a program of genetic manipulation was undertaken, to find a suitable worker drone.

DATA: Many researchers have puzzled over the statements attributed to GOD in the Bible, such as "Let us make man in our image." The basic question is, if there is and was only one God, then who was God talking to? According to the Sumerian writings, the Annunaki had to finally mix the sperm of an Annunaki with the ova of an ape-woman and then had it placed in the womb of female Annunaki volunteers. Eventually, man was created.

13. Several genetic programs were undertaken to find the perfect worker. One involved taking the egg of a reptile, but this was found not to be suitable. The resulting creature was turned out of Eden.

DATA: There have been several articles written by anthropologists theorizing what

---

[13] Sitchin, Zecharia, THE WARS OF GODS AND MEN, Avon Books, New York. 1985.

[14] O'Brien, Christian, THE GENIUS OF THE FEW, Turnstone Press Limited, Wellingborough, Northamptonshire, G.B., 1985.

[15] Sitchin, Zecharia, THE WARS OF GODS AND MEN, Avon Books, New York. 1985.

a reptilian humanoid would look like. Eventually several skeletons were found that confirmed the theories. These skeletons were dated as being as old, if not more so, than the oldest human skeleton[16].

14. It was found that mammals, the ape specifically, were best suited to genetic manipulation.

DATA: It is apparent that the Annunaki were, themselves, mammalian in genetic make-up since they could breed with human females.[17] "And the sons of God saw the daughters of man and took them to wife."

15. Ape man, Neanderthal, and Cro-Magnon man were all results of these genetic manipulation programs. None of these species were entirely suitable.

DATA: The theories of Charles Darwin propose that modern man is the result of changes in the makeup of various stages of human development such as Ape man to Neanderthal. However, science has discovered that at one point in history, several different "models" of human existed at the same time. Therefore, it appears to be improbable that one developed from the other. The most probable answer would be a genetic manipulation program. Such a genetic manipulation program could also explain how the various racial differences came into being.

16. Finally, it was decided to take the sperm of one of the colonists and mix it with the eggs of a Cro-Magnon woman. The fertilized ovary was then implanted in the womb of a colonist female. The result was homo-sapien.

DATA: This is thoroughly explained in the Epic of Creation, one of the Sumerian Epics[18].

17. Man being a hybrid was sterile. However, in order not to have to waste precious genetic material, man was given the ability to procreate. This ability to procreate was perhaps unauthorized, but once the damage was done, the commander accepted it.

DATA: This is also touched on in the Epic of Creation and other Sumerian and Akkadian writings[19].

18. Man, being genetically close to the colonists is able to have his life extended in the same manner as the colonists.

---

[16] Weekly World News, Tabloid.

[17] The Book of Enoch and The Holy Bible, The Kings James Edition.

[18] Sitchin, Zecharia, THE WARS OF GODS AND MEN, Avon Books, New York. 1985.

[19] Ibid.

DATA: Already discussed in #8 above.

19. Man originally began life as a servant in Eden, farming the "Garden".

DATA: The original twelve couples who were the patriarchs of the Bible were placed in the Garden according to both the Scriptures and the Sumerian Texts. It was only when Adam and Eve disobeyed that they were turned out of the Garden. Later when the Human Race became too many to comfortably fit in the Garden, that many, the excess if you will, were resettled onto the plains nearby[20].

20. When the number of humans became too many to be comfortably held in Eden, tribes, or settlements, were established on the plains below the mountains in which Eden lay.

DATA: According to the Sumerian Texts, the Gods established the cities of the Sumerian Civilization. Each "God" had his, or her, own city state, all loosely under the control of the Heavenly Assembly.

21. The technician class was becoming rebellious and caused certain of the plans of the autocrats to go awry. For example, it is recorded in the Sumerian legends that it was one of the Watchers (See 23) that tempted Eve. It appears that he tempted her to eat the material that resulted in mind expansion, i.e., the knowledge of good and evil, and perhaps, extended life. An act strictly against the rules.

DATA: According to the Book of Enoch, the "junior gods" were sent out from Eden to teach and watch the developing human race. These teachers or the Watchers as they were called (the IGIGI in the original Sumerian) were apparently all male and were tempted by the Human females. As a result, the Watchers broke their orders of non-interference and took human females as wives. They also proceeded to teach the human race ideas that they were not intended to know.

It is also interesting to know that the Watchers were called Serpents. Thus was Eve tempted by a Serpent, a man of the Serpent Order, not literally a talking reptile.

22. Eating the material that extended life also seems to have had the effect of sharpening mental powers, making Adam and Eve aware of their nakedness. The numerically smaller colonists rightly feared man's awakening mental state and exiled the two transgressors to the outside world. The guards had orders not to let

---

[20] O'Brien, Christian, THE GENIUS OF THE FEW, Turnstone Press Limited, Wellingborough, Northamptonshire, G.B., 1985.

them back into the Garden.

DATA: If Eden was a colony, it had an entrance. Once Adam and Eve were exiled from the Garden, or the colony, the security guards had orders not to let them back inside the colony. It was probably feared that they would "contaminate" the rest of the human race[21].

23. The technicians were sent down to the plains to study the development of man and to make sure that everything went according to plan. Such an act also kept them from causing mischief in Eden.

DATA: It was the Watchers, or the technician class, who had earlier rebelled against the senior Annunaki[22]. Therefore, the safest course of action would have been to have sent the more aggressive of the Watchers out into the world to keep an eye on the burgeoning human race. It would also serve double duty in that it would keep the Watchers from being able to plot amongst themselves and cause more trouble in Eden[23].

24. These technicians, called the Watchers by Enoch since their job was to watch the human race, were lonely and took human females as wife. These unions produced monstrous children.

DATA: This is verified in the Bible, the Book of Enoch, the Sumerian and the Akkadian Writings. The Sons of God saw that the daughters of man were fair and took them to wife[24]. From these unions children were born who became man of renown in days of old. It is recorded that these children grew into monsters who proceeded to rape and pillage the land[25].

25. Certain humans were taken and trained to be agents of the colonists among the developing tribes. Enoch was one.

DATA: Several times in the Bible, it is recorded that certain of the patriarchs did not die, but were taken up by God to walk with God. Among these were Elisah and Enoch[26]. It is also possible that Moses was so taken.

In the Book of Enoch, the true story of what happened to one of these who was taken by God is told. Enoch was trained to be a scribe and a liaison from the

---

[21] Ibid

[22] Sitchin, Zecharia, THE WARS OF GODS AND MEN, Avon Books, New York. 1985.

[23] O'Brien, Christian, THE GENIUS OF THE FEW, Turnstone Press Limited, Wellingborough, Northamptonshire, G.B., 1985.

[24] The Holy Bible, The King James Edition

[25] The Book of Enoch

[26] Ibid

Heaven Assembly. What is told in the Book of Enoch is the tale of a primitive man who is taken up by an advanced race of beings and trained to be their servant.

26. Angered at the actions of the technicians, the autocrats sent a human emissary, Enoch, to inform them of their punishments.

DATA: In the Book of Enoch, Enoch talks of the anger of the Gods at the acts of the Watchers. He is sent to tell the Watchers of their punishments. The Watchers try and get Enoch to be their defense attorney in their upcoming trial in absentia[27].

27. Colonial law enforcement personnel were sent to arrest the Watchers. The offending colonists were imprisoned in underground caverns.

DATA: The area around Eden was rift with several ravines and caverns. Since these Watchers were almost immortal as a result of their extended life spans, the best that the Annunaki Council could do would be to imprison them until they could be transported to the home planet for trial[28].

28. In order to protect the gene pool of the developing Human Race, the colonial commander had all the human families of the offending Watchers killed. This served the double duty of stopping the spread of advanced technological information that the Watchers had revealed and also stopped the disruption of the normal development of the gene pool of the Human Race[29].

DATA: The head of the Annunaki seemed unusually angry at the action of the Watchers. More than such a transgression would appear to warrant. Granted, it might appear to be similar to the way that we would view bestiality, since they appeared to view the developing Human Race as something to be used or as a tool, but certainly it would not be something that should warrant such treatment. It seems that the Annunaki were willing to be unmerciful to anything that would effect the genetic structure of the new race.

Therefore, it had to be a transgression that was considered extremely serious to warrant the mass death and destruction that took place in order to wipe out the human families of the offending Watchers.

29. A sympathetic technician working in the scientific section helped the imprisoned Watchers plan a jail break. It was planned that the break would be covered by an artificially generated storm.

---

[27] Ibid
[28] Ibid
[29] Ibid

DATA: According to the information presented in Christian O'Brien's work, THE GENIUS OF THE FEW, Eden was destroyed by a storm such as this planet had never seen[30]. During the Vietnam War, the CIA experimented with weather control in order to cause flooding in the North. It backfired and resulted in flooding that threatened to cause harm in the South. It was also the reason that the P.O.W. camp that was raided at Son Tay was evacuated by the North Vietnamese.

Several of the written works by the Sumerians make it evident that the Annunaki were able to affect the weather.

30. The storm allowed the Watchers to escape, but the technician who generated the covering storm miscalculated and the ensuing storm totally destroyed Eden and resulted in a major flood that covered most of the surrounding area.

DATA: See #29 above[31].

31. The Watchers escaped, swearing revenge for the death of their families.

DATA: It is evident that the Watchers escaped for their remains have never been found in the areas where they were imprisoned. It would suppose the need for revenge as it would be a natural feeling after having your family destroyed for no good reason. The Annunaki seemed to exhibit much of the same moods as we Humans show.

32. The two competing groups, the autocrats and the Watchers are locked in a struggle for control of the planet.

DATA: This is supposition, but some of the names of the Watchers given in the Book of Enoch are the same of similar as the names of some of the followers of Satan. This would explain the battle between "Good and Evil" and the "Sons of the Light against the Powers of the Dark". The prize seems to be either the control of men in some physical manner or else control of this planet as a whole[32].

33. The Watchers have become known as the Legions of Satan .

DATA: As pointed out above, the names of Satan's demons are the same or similar as names of the Watchers. The Watchers were also "thrown out of Heaven" so to speak, in that they were first more or less exiled to the plains and then forced to

---

[30] O'Brien, Christian, THE GENIUS OF THE FEW, Turnstone Press Limited, Wellingborough, Northamptonshire, G.B., 1985.

[31] Ibid

[32] Prophet, Elizabeth Clare, FORBIDDEN MYSTERIES OF ENOCH, Summit University Press, Livingston, MT. 1983.

escape[33].

34. The autocrats have become known as the Angels of the Lord.

DATA: According to the writings of the ancient Sumerians, such names as Michael and Gabriel were senior members of the Host who served God. Therefore, we can identify the senior Annunaki as those who are considered to be the power of light[34].

35. Over the ensuing eons of time, both groups have lost their ability to support interstellar travel and can, at best, move around the solar system.

DATA: The ancient writings also talk of a war that broke out between two factions of the "good gods". The prize was allegedly the space base located in the Sinai. One side is supposed to have used a mighty weapon that sounds suspiciously like a nuclear bomb to destroy the base so that the other side could not gain control of it. I would venture to guess that this destroyed a lot of irreplaceable equipment and may have marooned them here[35].

36. The Watchers have established bases on, and in, the Earth.

DATA: Many of the legends of earlier times maintain that such things as Imps, Trolls, Dwarfs and Fairies lived underground in caves and caverns. I would be willing to bet that these creatures were the Watchers, mutated by the radiation fields of this Planet. These levels of radiation were in all likelihood different from what they were accustomed to. I would venture to guess that the Tree of Life in the Garden helped offset this problem. Without the benefits of this Tree, they may have begun to mutate.

37. The autocrats, and probably the Watchers as well, have established bases in other parts of the solar system.

DATA: I would point to the giant face and the ruined city on Mars as reported by Richard C. Hoagland in his book, The Monuments of Mars: A City on the Edge of Forever as partial proof of the existence of a much earlier race within our solar system. Some unknown race built a massive face and a city that consisted of architecture similar to that found in ancient Egypt[36]. In addition, several

---

[33] Ibid

[34] Ibid

[35] Sitchin, Zecharia, THE WARS OF GODS AND MEN, Avon Books, New York. 1985.

[36] Hoagland, Richard C., THE MONUMENTS OF MARS: A CITY ON THE EDGE OF FOREVER, North Atlantic Books, Berkeley, CA. 1987.

photographs of the surface of the Moon have shown what appear to be structures on the Moon's surface[37].

38. Originally, both groups controlled man through the establishment of religions. As man become more sophisticated, this control method lost its usefulness.

DATA: I am not sure that religion was the original reason behind the establishment of the priesthood. I would assume that such powerful beings as the Annunaki showed themselves to be that they have massive egos as well. For this reason, I would suppose that the Annunaki felt it necessary to have many servants. These servants would be trained in the proper care and feeding of Gods. It would only be natural to use the servants as a method of talking to the common men. This later became modified, once the "Gods" no longer wished to rule directly, to the demi-god priest kings. Then later became the rule of the strongest with the Priests dealing only with the words of the gods[38].

39. Originally, half-breed offspring of the "Gods" were set up as the secular rulers of man.

DATA: Historically, Demi-gods, half man-half god, ruled prior to the dawn of modern history. Demi-gods were allegedly the off-spring of the union of God and Human.

40. Secret societies were established, where certain initiated individuals were given directions by the "gods" in how to manipulate their fellow men.

DATA: There is little doubt that the first secret societies were the priests, who were taught much "secret" knowledge by the Gods. The later secret societies were probably made up of the followers of the various Dark Gods or those who gave allegiance to the Watchers.

41. For some reason, between roughly A.D. 200 and A.D. 1990, the "gods" were unable to remain among us as rulers.

DATA: It is theorized that sometime around 2,000 B.C. a nuclear war took place between two groups of Gods. This event is recorded in the writings of many civilizations of the ancient world. Even descriptions of the destruction of Sodom and Gomorrah appear to be the result of a rocket attack[39].

It is also theorized that the fallout cloud from the destruction of the space port was carried by the wind to Sumeria where it killed many. It is also reported

[37] Steckling, Fred, WE DISCOVERED ALIEN BASES ON THE MOON.
[38] Sitchin, Zecharia, THE WARS OF GODS AND MEN, Avon Books, New York. 1985.
[39] Ibid

that the Gods fled the fallout. This would imply that they were not totally immortal since they could apparently die from radiation[40].

During this period, according to Sitchin's work, The Lost Realms[41], some of the Gods of the ancient world turned up in the Americas where they proceeded to establish civilization. The original architects of civilization in South America appear to be white, human appearing, men. This original civilization was destroyed by barbarians after the "Gods" left for their homelands.

42. Through certain artificially created beings, the "gods" have continued to carry out the genetic experiments that began with the creation of early man.

DATA: Several abductees who have had close contact with the "Greys", as well as, several prominent researchers have come to the conclusion that these creatures may be genetic constructs designed to operate in our environment. It is evident from their controlled jerky almost choreographed movements that they do not have the same type of free will that Humans demonstrate.

It is also evident from abductee reports that the "Greys" either conduct limited procedures in the bedroom or take the abductee to ships or bases where other, more expert personnel, perform more complicated medical procedures. Perhaps the "Greys" are sophisticated androids that can follow simple programming, but have to contact higher headquarters if faced with unexpected resistance.

43. Through these same artificially created beings, the "gods" have been making "deals" with various world governments in order to pave the way for their return.

DATA: Again, this refers to the alleged treaty between the aliens and the U.S. Government. It is alleged that members of the U.S. Air Force met with the Aliens at Holloman Air Force and signed a treaty[42].

44. Certain financially powerful humans have assisted the "gods" in creating their desired world order in return for promises of power.

DATA: Refers to the secret societies that have assisted in trying to create a one world government, an apparent requirement of the "Gods"[43]. More on this in a later

---

[40] Ibid

[41] Sitchin, Zecharia, THE LOST REALMS, Avon Books, New York. 1989.

[42] Cooper, Milton William, OPERATION MAJORITY.

[43] Allen, Gary and Larry Abrahamson, NONE DARE CALL IT CONSPIRACY, Double A Publications, Seattle, Washington.

chapter.

45. Each side of this "War of the Immortals" is attempting to mass a human following for a final confrontation. Only one side of this war will survive.

DATA: According to reports from several abductees, the aliens are now starting to conduct dialogues with their victims. Such terms as "Will you follow us?" are used in the discussions. Religion is brought into the situation more and more. Even the final "confrontation" has been mentioned[44]. The major question is who are the good guys?

A DISCUSSION OF MY THEORY

So now you have seen the basis of my theory. I believe that these Annunaki have come down to us reported as ancient Gods. The glowing characteristics of the entities, reported in the Book of Enoch, and elsewhere, are identical to those reported in such instances as the miracle at Fatima. Alleged miracles, such as the one at Fatima, have been used down through the ages to influence the direction in which civilization has been moving. When it appears that mankind is moving in a way that the "Gods" do not approve of, then along comes a "miracle", or a very charismatic leader that takes mankind back into the path approved of by these "Gods".

Due to the small number of these Annunaki that originally came here, they aren't strong enough to dominate a sophisticated race; they can openly dominate only primitive tribes. As an example, when mankind and civilization was in its' infancy, the "Gods" moved among us openly as our direct rulers. As mankind became more sophisticated, then the "Gods" became more distant. Obviously, these "Gods" fear us as much as we have come to fear them.

A prime example of their desire to keep civilization disrupted and the humans fighting among ourselves it the sage of the Tower of Babel. Allegedly, this tower was built to allow man to strive for the power and the same level as the "Gods". As a response, the "Gods" confused the languages of man so that they were no longer able to work as a cohesive whole. This confusing of languages has led to eternal bloodshed and wars. Hardly the acts of benevolent "Gods".

These so-called "Gods" fear us and our potential. They fear us so much that they no longer walk among us, but work from a distance with a kind of remote control. In addition to, or perhaps because of, the fear that they have for us, they are few in number. It was reported by the ancient Sumerian records that less than a thousand of these "Gods" came to this planet. With so few of their own race on this planet, it is no wonder that they began to interbreed with Homo Sapien man.

As a result, in order to control so many humans, the Annunaki found that it was necessary that they utilize human fifth columnists to make up for their small

---

[44] Fowler, Raymond, THE ANDREASSON AFFAIR, Bantam Books, New York. 1980.

numbers. The first of these human fifth columnists are those who have started the original secret society that gave rise to all of the others that are attempting to control the world.

I would believe, since the Sumerian records so report, that some of the Annunaki can pass among us without too much concern of detection by ordinary humans. These are the ones who act as liaison with the secret societies. Others, less "human looking" control the abduction crews that man the silver disks.

It is my contention that the small pasty white aliens who move in unison are actual genetic constructs that are under the mental control of the leader of the team. They are either genetic constructs or temporary bodies being operated by computer controlled intelligences. The implants, allegedly placed in each of the abductees, are probably a device to make mental control possible or easier.

The war between the Watchers and the Gods continues to this day. But instead of open combat, with pawn countries fighting in the name of religion or some other allegedly "holy" purpose, it is more like a behind the scenes war. Each side strives to build more followers for the big day when the next open warfare does breakout. All of these battles build up to what most religions call "The day of Armageddon" or what we call the Last Battle. For on this day, the Gods of the ancient world return.

In discussing these ancient Gods, there are certain questions that I am sure that you would like to ask. In fact, as I have talked to many people, they have all asked similar questions. The main questions have been:

(1) Where did the "Gods" go when they disappeared?

(2) Why did they leave? and

(3) What have they been up to over the last thousand of our years?

I touched on some of the answers to these questions when I discussed my original theory of the interaction of the alleged aliens with the Ancient Gods of history, with which was the basis of Volume I of this series[45]. In Volume I, I expanded the theory greatly and showed various common aspects between the U.F.O.s that seemingly fill out night skies, the above referenced secret societies and the Ancient gods of history. I pointed to several common threads of teachings promoted by all three. The reactions of the readers have been both gratifying and totally puzzling.

Most have said once they picked up the book and actually started to read it, they couldn't put it down. Some have bought more than one copy in order to given

---

[45] Hudnall, Ken, THE OCCULT CONNECTION: UFOs, Secret Societies and Ancient Gods, Omega Press, El Paso, Texas. 79912.

copies to their friends. Several have reported thefts of the book by their friends who couldn't put the book down. Such reports make any author feel good that people like his writing style. However as I said earlier, some reactions have puzzled me. Below are three of the puzzling reactions.

THEY ARE GOING TO GET YOU!

The reaction that most amuses me is the one where the reader is sure that because I am putting out what they feel is, or should be, classified information that the forces of silence are going to remove me. I submit that such a removal would be the best proof that what I am saying is true. Of course, it is always pointed out that such a method of proving my theory would not be conducive to a long career in writing, which is true.

I am not delving into classified files of any particular service and revealing information that would make it a certainty that we would all be speaking Russian by next Thursday. What I am doing is taking information that is released to the public, but not given wide coverage, together with information furnished me by various contacts and showing how it fits into a pattern. This pattern shows a plan that is worse for the human race than a mere conquering by a foreign power.

YOU REPRESENT THE FORCES OF SATAN!

Since the publication of the first book of this series, I have had many come to debate my theory, each all puffed up with his or her "God-given" power to banish the forces of darkness. It is amazing that if one merely raises questions regarding organized religion, then it is assumed that the one who raises the questions is anti-God. I find it puzzling that some of the same people, who make it a point to examine everything of every angle before making a decision, immediately yell anti-God when religion is questioned. There seems to be something wrong with this picture.

I have been no different from other authors of book of this type. I have been inundated by kooks and detractors of all description. My favorite was the little old lady with the flower in her hat. She was simply the nicest lady I have ever met. She reminded me so much of my own grandmother that even though she annoyed me no end, I simply couldn't get mad at her. Unfortunately, she was so sure that I was sent here by Satan to lead people from the "true" path that she couldn't really concentrate on my logic, but instead, sat with her back to the door and appeared ready to run at the first sign that I was changing into SATAN.

I debated with this little old lady for over an hour with her quoting scripture until she was totally out of breath. I think that it confused her that for every scriptural quote she gave me, I gave her one that proved my point. (For those fundamentalists who call and quote scripture over the phone and then hang up, I do know something about the Bible.)

After another hour of seriously discussing my theory with an open mind, she finally admitted that I raised some points that she couldn't find answers for in her Bible. I think that we parted as friends, but I'm not sure.

IF IT'S TRUE WHY DOESN'T OUR GOVERNMENT DO SOMETHING ABOUT IT?

Then there are the super patriots and the "let's not talk about bad things" groups. Both of these groups take the position that the U.S. Government can do no wrong and will always look out for its citizens. It is those who have this viewpoint that find it the hardest to adjust to the truth. These groups are also the ones who react the most violently when I answer their questions and then expound on my views in this area.

They simply find it impossible to believe that our government doesn't do something about the conspiracy because our government is part of it. In spite of their denials, the evidence is very convincing that our government has been infiltrated by the very forces that I write about. In fact it is to thoroughly examine this question that I have written this particular book in the series.
However, before moving on, let me once again answer the main questions of most:

1.) I do believe in God.

2.) I also believe that there is a major conspiracy underway.

3.) I do believe in our system of government, but not necessarily in the manner in which it is being operated.

4.) I will continue to believe in my theory until such time as someone can show me a fallacy in it.

AND I DO CHALLENGE ANYONE TO FIND A FLAW IN MY THEORY. IF I AM WRONG, SHOW ME!

THE CONSPIRACY

In Volume One of the Occult Connection, I had originally started out to write a book about Unidentified Flying Objects, but somehow in the midst of this endeavor, I stumbled across many other matters that seemed, at least to me, to be directly involved. Most have now heard about the MJ-12 scenario, where there is, allegedly, an organization that was put together by one of our earlier Presidents charged with dealing with the Aliens. From this, admittedly farfetched conspiracy of silence, I began to investigate many apparently unrelated areas. The result was a theory even more unbelievable than Aliens visiting this Planet and abducting females. I discovered, interconnected with various aspects of the UFO puzzle, what appeared, to me, to be a signs of a larger conspiracy that seemed to run back into the mists of time. It's goal, world domination.

Is such a thing possible, could there actually be a few families that have dedicated themselves to a centuries long program of domination and destruction? I had to find out. Therefore, I began to delve deeper and deeper into the various conspiracy theories that seemed to litter the landscape. To my amazement, I found that I could construct a logical conspiracy theory that would account for many, heretofore, puzzling aspects of world politics and also account for some extremely bizarre behavior exhibited by many of our politicians. Worst of all, it also seemed to account for the steady decline of our own great land.

Many people have no idea what is going on behind the scenes in this country. We have grown up being taught that our government is a government of the people, by the people and for the people. Once this was true, but in the early part of this century, this changed to read a government of the Conspiracy, by the Conspiracy and for the Conspiracy.

COINCIDENCE?

To really believe what I am about to write will make you a deadly enemy to the liberal media in this country. According to the national media, the written press especially, everything bad in the world just happens; there is no master plan to world events. In fact, if you want to make an enemy of a liberal, tell him or her that you subscribe to the conspiracy theory of history. Any liberal worth his salt will point out that a conspiracy such as this proposes would have to be world wide and span centuries. It will be quickly pointed out that such things just simply don't happen, then the tired old excuses of "It's all the fault of capitalism" or other such liberal tripe will fill your ears as he or she begins to warm to their favorite topic.

The liberal establishment wants you to believe that the mere fact that almost every ally that we have sworn to protect from the RED MENACE, (a former name for Communism, for those of you raised and educated by the liberal establishment) has eventually been taken over by Communists must be just a coincidence. I must admit, however, that I, for one, subscribe to the James Bond School of Reasoning.

WHERE IS JAMES BOND WHEN WE NEED HIM?

It was Ian Fleming's fictional character, James Bond who proposed the school of thought that I find the most logical.

"If it happens once it is happenstance. If it happens twice, it is coincidence. If it happens three times, it is enemy action."

The truth is that almost every time that our State Department tries to prop up or support a friendly government, said friendly government goes Communist. This has happened far more than three times; actually it has happened over forty times since World War II. Every small Communist country that we try to oppose suddenly receives a stream of money, technology and assistance from unknown sources. Allegedly this steady stream of resources and backing comes from the Soviet Union, but let's face it, the Soviet Union's economy has been such a shambles for several years that their empire finally collapsed. Where did the Soviet Union get the funds to support over a third of the world? This has also happened far more than three times. Can some other agency or entity be supporting the Soviet Union's conquests?

In order to give the reader a frame of reference for these happenings and in order to show the seriousness of these acts, in a later chapter we will discuss some of these "coincidences".

TREASON

I am sure that it has long been evident to the mysterious "controllers" who direct the conspiracy, that if the Conspiracy can control the United States then the Conspiracy can control the world. America seems to be a hard nut to crack for these "Controllers". For whatever reason, they have had to move very slowly in their conquest. It has been America and the strength of its people that have stopped the move for world domination in two world wars. So it soon became obvious that militarily, at least, America was a major problem for the one worlders. So other ways had to be found to control this country.

In spite of the liberal establishment's attempts to ignore the more obvious signs of a move afoot to control this country, a thorough study of history reveals very diligent efforts have actually been made to control this country. As was observed by Adam Weishaupt, the alleged founder of the Illuminati, to control an organization or a country, one does not have to use force of arms. A smarter, more subtle way is to control the leaders. As we progress, see if you don't agree with me that this appears to be what has happened to this Country.

In a later chapter, as we study some of our State Department's so-called errors in diplomacy, we can begin to get a glimpse of the "big picture" of treason and betrayal.

The effect of the treason is obvious. If our country can undermine the governments of our allies, then it is easier for agents of the Conspiracy to take these governments over. History shows that one after another we have, indeed, betrayed our allies and turned them over to the enemy. We do it so consistently that it couldn't be accidental, it can only be intentional. So then, why do our own elected leaders seek to work to our detriment? Is it intentional or accidental? Who are these leaders and what are their backgrounds? Could their actions be part of a much broader conspiracy? If there is a broad based conspiracy, than what is its' purpose?

As we try to answer these questions, let us first study some of the evidence that there really exists a conspiracy that has spanned eons. Can we really determine if there actually exist hidden "Masters" that work to keep mankind under control? Are we really being manipulated or are we just happily killing ourselves for nothing? As we try and answer these questions, settle back and get ready for the next installment of THE OCCULT CONNECTION as we try to look into the very real possibility of a HIDDEN RACE.

CHAPTER THREE

UPDATE

Over the intervening years since I wrote the first of this series, there has been new data that has been discovered impacting on Book One. For this reason, it is felt that an update is required. I have had many assure me that my theory of a multinational power group working behind the scenes to bring down civilization as we know it is absurd. However, if this is true, then why have many of our own government's policies added our enemies much more than they aided this country.

Along with the so-called "New Age" of new political world order, there is now newly available information regarding a parallel religious "New Age". It would seem that the forces of the conspiracy are not just content with changing the way we govern ourselves, but they also desire to control the way that we worship our God. There seems to be a move afoot to create a "New Religious Order" in much the same way that Himmiler attempted to create a newly formed pagan order worshipping the dark gods of history.

This religious "New Order" was addressed by Manley P. Hall in his book, *LECTURES ON ANCIENT PHILOSOPHY*[46], when he wrote:

"A new light is breaking in the east; a more glorious day is at hand. The rule of the philosophic elect - the dream of the ages - will yet be realized and is not too far distant."

Another writer, Alice Bailey, in her book, *THE EXTERNALISATION OF*

---

[46] Hall, Manley P., LECTURES ON ANCIENT PHILOSOPHY, The Philosophical Research Society, Inc. L.A. 1984.

THE HIERARCHY[47] wrote:

"*Eventually, there will appear the Church Universal, and its definite outlines will appear towards the close of this century.*"

I would point out that we have closed out the 20th Century, but one only has to look at the daily newspapers or listen to the news broadcasts to see the truth of these statements. There seem to be numerous new religions springing up all across the world as more and more people become dissatisfied with the old ways of worship and look for new ways of communicating with their creator.

Christianity seems to find itself in somewhat the same position as the pagan religions did thousands of years ago, as more and more former members defect for the promises of the new "Gods". Even Satan seems to have found a fertile recruiting ground for new members as Satanic Cults spring up in some of our most religious countries.

Some have even turned the teachings of Christianity, itself, into a basis for new orders, such as the Aryan Nations Groups and the so-called Christian Identity religions[48]. Once again, an organized religion is being used as the spring broad to breed hate and contempt for others.

A METHOD OF DIVISION

What do these new religions or orders accomplish? They do not have the broad based appeal that Christianity did, and their message is usually one of hate. So what is the attraction that they hold out for new members?

Historically, it is during the declining years of a civilization that men seek new gods and new beliefs and insanity seems to run rampant. Even the most hide bound scientist must now admit, based on the evidence that there have been many civilizations prior to our own. For example in the last days of the Roman Empire, numerous new religions sprang into existence, one of which was Christianity. In fact, this "new" religions was one of the contributing factors to the destruction of the old order. Today, we also have numerous "new" religions that want to tear down the existing order in order to install their own version of paradise. Will we go the way of the Roman Empire?

It is my belief that behind each and every one of the major changes of history has been this mysterious organization that I call the conspiracy. This group is just as active today as it were a thousand years ago. They have always been with us, manipulating things from behind the scenes, causing death and destruction to

---

[47] Bailey, Alice, THE EXTERNALISATION OF THE HIERARCHY, The Lucis Publishing Co. New York.

[48] Flynn, Kevin and Gary Gerhardt, THE SILENT BROTHERHOOD, Signet Books, New York. 1989.

untold millions in order to tighten their control a little here and there and to make a profit.

THE NEW RELIGION

What are the tenets of this New Age Faith? What will the new religion preach? What kind of God will the new religion member worship?

In her book, *THE HIDDEN DANGERS OF THE RAINBOW*[49] Constance Cumbey discussed the beliefs of this new religion. According to Mrs. Cumbey, the new religion will have the following tenets:

1. There will be a new Messiah, a World Government and a new world religion under the control of a Pope like figure named Maitreya. In support of this prediction there have been a number of figures aspiring to this exalted position, a few of whom have gathered many hundreds of thousands of followers[50].

2. Instead of a cash economy, there will be a universal credit card system. I really do not have to point out that the debit cards issued by most banks have replaced checks in most localities.

3. All the world's food supply will be consolidated under one authority.

4. The will be a world wide tax system. The United Nations does tax its member nations (it is called membership fees) and these fees are actually tax dollars obtained from the citizens of the member nations. So in actuality, there is a world wide tax system in place even as you read these words.

5. There will be a world wide draft. The United Nations Security forces are made up of soldiers from the various nations placed under United Nations command. These soldiers chosen to make up the UN Peacekeeping forces are required to obey the orders of the UN rather than their own military. Thus, there is a form of world wide draft in effect as I write these words.

6. Christianity will be stamped out and its adherents will be exterminated.

I would point out that there have been assaults on the Catholic Church for many hundreds of years. However, rather than examine each of these tenets here, as we progress through the book, keep these tenets in mind and see of there is not evidence that a move is afoot to put these into operation. You might be surprised regarding the identities of some of the supporters of these concepts.

However, keep in mind that the Conspiracy has long advocated the

---

[49] Cumbey, Constance, THE HIDDEN DANGERS OF THE RAINBOW, Huntington House, Inc. Shreveport, LA. 1983.

[50] Just look at Reverend Moon.

extermination of Christianity and the re-establishment of a Pantheistic Religion, which would be a religious counterpart to the collectivist type political environment that the Conspiracy desires. So it comes as little wonder that a new "Religious Age" is on the horizon.

CHAPTER FOUR

THE UNSEEN MASTERS

"*An invisible hand is guiding the populace.*" Lafayette

So in keeping with the basic premise of the Occult Connection Series, the question must be asked: where do Secret Societies fit into the scheme of things in so far as Unidentified Flying Objects are concerned? I have no intention to bore the reader, but a quick review is necessary at this point. My theory proposes the following points:

1. Advanced beings colonized this planet eons ago.

2. These advanced beings were looked at as "Gods" by various religions and were responsible for creating what became the human race.

3. These advanced beings taught us the rudiments of civilized living and directly ruled over human cities.

4. The humans who directly served the "Gods", called naturally, the Servants of God, acted as intermediaries between the "Gods" and the common man.

5. The "Gods" had a falling out among themselves and a civil war resulted. In this civil war, human pawns fought the battles of the "Gods". Nuclear weapons were used in these battles.

6. For some reason the "Gods" were forced to withdraw from direct contact with mankind. They left half breed offspring in their place as a new race of "demi-Gods" to rule over mankind, with the "Servants of the Gods" as

assistants.

7. The "demi-Gods " died out or left to join their parents. This left the "Priest-Kings" to rule over the human race as the direct representatives of the "Gods". The Priest Kings, in turn, were replaced by secular rulers. This began the struggle between religion (the priests) and government (the King). Behind the scenes were the "Gods" who have continued to try and direct events from the side-lines with humans as pawns. These humans were members of various secret societies that purported to have secret hidden information that would give the members the ability to rule over their neighbors.

Secret societies have been with us since the beginning of recorded history, after al,l everyone likes to know a secret that he thinks his friends do not know. I am sure that each one of us knows or has known someone who is a member of a secret society. Membership in these types of organizations is usually viewed as a harmless distraction for men and women to take part in as an amusement. However, this is actually far from being the truth. Secret Societies are neither for amusement nor a mere distraction, in fact they are, or can be, the worst threats to freedom that exist.

WHAT ARE WE LOOKING FOR?

So in order to prove my theory, we must look for and find a secret society that has the following characteristics:

1. Is world wide in scope.

2. Can trace its history back for thousands of years.

3. Has as its goal and is working to dominate the world and establish a one world government.
4. Has been responsible for wars and revolutions throughout history.

5. Has worked hard to suppress knowledge.

6. Has as its members leading political figures of the day.

7. Has members who place the goals of the secret society above the well being of the citizens of any one country.

If we can show that there is such an organization existing today, then a large art of my theory will have been proven. I am sorry to say that such an organization exists. In fact, members of that organization are among the highest elected officials of this country. However, before I tell you about this organization that is working to overthrow the government of this great country, let us look at some of the proof of conspiracy.

ON THE TRAIL

To study something, you have to at least know what the focus of your study is called. Unfortunately with the Eternal Conspiracy, it has been called many things by many people. This organization has been called "The Insiders", the "Great Conspiracy", the "Illuminati" and hundreds of other names. I believe that all of these names identify the same basic group of people. The Conspiracy seems to take a different name each time it raises its' ugly head. Then if it is defeated, it goes underground until next time it decides it is time to strike.

Mankind, after an unbelievable loss of life in putting down the threat posed by the Conspiracy, believing that the danger is past, the evil is dead, then becomes careless and the Conspiracy strikes again. Unfortunately, while millions have died on both sides of this "hidden" war the Conspiracy itself never seems to die.

But let us look at some descriptions of what we purpose to study. What is this Conspiracy? The following excerpts are from various writers who have either studied the secret societies or been prominent members in them.

"Beneath the broad tide of human history there flows the stealthy undercurrents of the secret societies, which frequently determine in the depths, the changes that take place upon the surface[51]."

". . .there is a power so organized, so subtle, so complete, so pervasive, that they had better not speak above their breath when they speak in condemnation of it.[52]"

"All secret societies and associations-. had two doctrines, one concealed and reserved for the Masters, .the other public[53]. ."

"I don't believe in great providential men, political celebrities owed their reputations, if not to chance, at least to circumstances which they themselves could not have foreseen[54]."

---

[51] Waite, Arthur Edward, THE REAL HISTORY OF THE ROSICRUCIANS, Steinerbooks, Blauvelt, N.Y. 1977.

[52] Sutton, Antony C., AMERICA'S SECRET ESTABLISHMENT, Liberty House Press, 2027 Iris, Billings, Montana 59102. 1986.

[53] Pike, Albert, MORALS AND DOGMA, The Supreme Council of the Southern Jurisdiction of the Scottish Rite. 1871.

[54] *Quotation credited to Otto Von Bismarck.*

"Not my talents and capacities made me great. But the fact that my mother was the Mistress of Soult, one of the "300", who all helped me[55]."

"I think there is an elite in this country and they are the ones who run an elitist government. They want a government by a handful of people because they don't believe the people themselves can run their lives . . .[56]"

Most researchers believe that all secret societies sprang from the same original secret society, an original secret society that had as its goal, world domination and control. Such a theory would be in keeping with one of the tenets of my theory as follows:

In keeping with my theory, outlined in chapter One, suppose that the original human rulers (The Priest Kings) appointed by the "Gods" (remember, I believe that the "Gods" of ancient history were simply a more advanced race that came to colonize and exploit the earth.) either lost their power and their lofty positions or were simply unable to maintain charismatic control when the "Gods" were forced to distance themselves from mankind. As a result, these "Servants of the Gods" who were ruling mankind were reduced to being religious leaders as they tried to keep control of men's minds once they lost control of men's bodies.

As civilization became more settled, so to speak, stronger, more charismatic leaders took the place of the Priest Kings as secular head or King. Since the Priest Kings could no longer directly rule as Kings, these religious leaders worked behind the scenes to take control of the governments by controlling the ruling King. There are many examples of this program being effective, ancient Egypt is a prime example.

Usually, this control was taken through the utilization of secret societies that included as members, many highly placed members of the government. The reward promised these government officials for betraying their King, or Pharaoh as it was in Egypt, was usually the promise of riches and power on earth and then, since they were usually told it was their god's will that this betrayal take place, guaranteed admittance to heaven or whatever their hereafter was called.

This program of control behind the scenes was first instituted in ancient Sumeria, the first recorded civilization. As time progressed, there were differences of opinion among the human members of this first secret society and various splinter groups were begun that in time, became competitors with the original conspiracy. Each splinter group was headed by a charismatic leader who purported to speak with the "Gods" and to know the true plan of the "Gods".

At one time, there are so many different secret societies that it is hard to tell one from another. For example, most people think that Adam Weishaupt's

---

[55] *Ibid*

[56] Quotation from speech given by President Ronald Regean.

Illuminati was the most evil organization that ever lived. However, most tend to overlook the fact that Adam Weishaupt's Illuminati did not openly exist for very many years before the Bavarian authorities suppressed it. However, it is alleged that Weishaupt received his training from another secret society, or secret order, if you will, the Jesuits. Additionally, it is entirely possible that his Order of Illuminated Ones, which was only formed in 1776, and allegedly suppressed in the 1780's, was a blind for the real Illuminated Ones, the Annunaki.

(Author's Note: There is a legend that and Adam Weishaupt looked remarkably alike and that after the suppression of his order in the 1780's, Weishaupt came to the United States killed George Washington and took his place. It is true that many of Washington's policies as President had a striking similarity with those of Weishaupt.)

If this is true, as many suspect, that Weishaupt's organization was a cover for the "real" Illuminated Ones, then it is these real Illuminati that directed the activities of the organization founded by Adam Weishaupt. These controllers do the dirty work and Weishaupt's dupes get the blame. It would not be the first time that this has happened.

THE REAL POWERS THAT BE

It is also amazing that most "normal" humans tend to overlook the real power of these secret orders. It seems that these secret orders are the real powers on this earth. Almost every nation has had to deal with the power of these orders. The French Revolution is a very clear example of what happens when these Secret Orders get the upper hand.

It is also very revealing that even some of the most famous names in world history believed in a behind the scenes secret order. Consider, if you will, the quotation from Bismarck earlier in this chapter, where he talked about French Marshall Soult being a member of the "300". This "300" was, and probably still is, a European organization whose membership is secret. This organization is allegedly the High Government of the Jewish Race, founded by Theodor Herzl, the founder of modern Zionism[57]. It is also interesting to note that there is much evidence that many of European Nobility is actually descended from Jewish stock though most of them try to deny it.

Consider the writings of Mr. Manly P. Hall, a famous Masonic writer. It was Mr. Hall who wrote:

"[they]. . .are the invisible powers behind the thrones of earth, and men are but marionettes, dancing while the invisible ones pull the strings. We see the dancer, but the master mind that does the work remains concealed by the cloak of

[57] Nicolov, Nicola M., THE WORLD CONSPIRACY, TOPS, 10170 S.W. Nimbus, Portland, OR 97223.

silence[58]."

In the same work Mr. Hall, incidentally also a 33rd degree Mason, wrote:

"In the remote past the gods walked with men and . . .they chose from among the sons of men the wisest and the truest".

With these specially ordained and illumined sons they left the keys of their great wisdom, which was the knowledge of good and evil.

". . .these illumined ones, founded what we know as the Ancient Mysteries[59]."

It would seem that these "Illumined Ones" are the real powers behind the thrones of the earth. So the question must be, how does one become one of these "Illumined Ones"? Mr. Hall also answers this in his book, *THE SECRET TEACHINGS OF ALL AGES.* In this work, he wrote:

"The arcana (or hidden knowledge) of the ancient Mysteries were never revealed to the profane (someone who is not one of the insiders) except through the media of symbols. Symbolism fulfilled the dual office of concealing the sacred truths from the uninitiated and revealing to those qualified to understand the symbols[60].

So consider what we have found. There is a body of knowledge that is known to only a few chosen Illumined Ones. Using this knowledge, the Illumined Ones control all of the thrones of the earth. It also appears that through the various secret societies, this information is passed to new Illumined Ones, carefully selected by those already possessing the information. Interesting concept; is this how the Annunaki, or the Ancient Gods, control human affairs?

So what are these Ancient Mysteries? I would give you a clue to what one of the supposedly most learned segments of our human society thinks of these Ancient Mysteries in pointing out that almost every established religion has tried to stamp out the secret societies and with the societies, the Ancient Mysteries. For example, it used to be forbidden for a Catholic to become a Mason. Why?

We appear to get the answer from the writings of Mr. Albert G. Mackey in

---

[58] *Hall, Manley P.,* What The Ancient Wisdom Expects Of Its Disciples, The Philosophical Research Society, Inc. L.A. 1982.

[59] *Ibid*

[60] Hall, Manley P., THE SECRET TEACHINGS OF ALL AGES, The Philosophical Research Society, Inc. L.A. 1977.

his two volume work, *ENCYCLOPEDIA OF FREEMASONRY*[61]. Mr. Mackey, also a 33rd degree Mason, was considered by many researchers to be the foremost and most accurate of the Masonic writers. He wrote:

"Each of the pagan gods. . .had, besides the public and open, a secret worship paid to him to which none were admitted but those who had been selected by preparatory ceremonies called Initiation. This secret worship was termed the Mysteries."

Also, in his *ENCYCLOPEDIA OF FREEMASONRY*, Mr. Mackey also wrote that Adam Weishaupt (alleged founder of the Illuminati) was a radical in politics and an infidel in religion, and that he organized the Illuminati, not more for the purpose of aggrandizing himself, than of overturning Christianity and the institutions of society[62].

Henri Martin, the famed French historian wrote in his *HISTOIRE DE FRANCE,* that "Weishaupt had made into an absolute theory the misanthropic gibes of Rousseau at the invention of property and society, and . . . he proposed as the end of Illuminism, the abolition of property, social authority and nationality. . ."

I would observe that the ideas of Weishaupt sound suspiciously like those of the Karl Marx and the Communist Party, coincidence?

So there we have it, the Ancient Mysteries was, and probably still is, a body of knowledge that was feared by organized religion. It is also that body of knowledge that allows the Illumined Ones to control the thrones of earth. Much that has been written about these Ancient Mysteries makes it seem that these Mysteries are actually knowledge of and a secret worship of the pagan gods.

To take this proposal a step further, my theory supposes that the so-called pagan gods were actually real, living, advanced beings that colonized this planet from elsewhere in the solar system. The alleged Ancient Mysteries is secret knowledge that is actually training and teachings from these advanced beings so that their protégés can control their fellow men.

THE TRUE ADEPT

According to Manly Hall, the true Adept revealed his identity to no one, unless that person was worthy of having that information. But it is believed that these Adepts had the knowledge to solve humanities problems. It is presupposed that what Mr. Hall calls a true Adept is actually an Illumined One.

Mr. Hall further wrote:

---

[61] Mackey, Albert G., FAN ENCYCLOPEDIA OF FREEMASONRY, The Masonic History Company, New York. 1873.

[62] Ibid

". . .no reasonable doubt can exist that the initiates of Greece, Egypt and other ancient countries possessed the correct solutions to those great cultural, intellectual, moral and social problems which in an unsolved state confront the humanity of the twentieth century[63]."

So it is entirely possible that you may know a true adept, but since he never reveals himself, you look at him as just one of the crowd. This means that there are among us individuals who have the answer to the problems that are plaguing mankind, but they refuse to reveal this information. However, ask yourself, what is a true adept? On the one hand the true adept can be someone who was trained in the teachings of the Annunaki or, it is quite possible, the true adept can actually be one of the Annunaki, whose true identity is concealed so that he, or she, can walk among us ordinary mortals.

I would point out that many U.F.O. abductees have talked about agents of the so-called "aliens" walking among us as they carry out their masters' bidding. The stories of the mysterious "Men in Black" are to be found in the history of almost every race on this planet and in records left by many early civilizations.

Many of those who come in contact with the unknown in so far as it deals with the enigma of the Unidentified Flying Objects (UFO) report visits from a trio of mysterious figures who invariably order them to remain silent about what they have seen. If, for some reason, the witness managed to obtain physical evidence, or photos, then after the visit by these mysterious figures the evidence is normally found to have vanished[64]. Are these figures representatives of alien forces, our own government or some other power on our earth? We do known and many never known the answer to this very important question.

WHAT'S IT ALL ABOUT?

Why do these secret societies and these adepts exist? What is their purpose in working behind the scenes? Why have they caused so much death and destruction in just the last three hundred years? To answer the questions, the works of several authors, who were allegedly members of this secret movement, must be consulted, as well as the recorded statements of some of the purported leaders of the movement.

According to all of these individuals and their written and spoken words, the true purpose toward which these secret orders have been moving is the creation of a NEW WORLD ORDER. A NEW WORLD ORDER which treats the common

---

[63] Hall, Manley P., *THE SECRET TEACHINGS OF ALL AGES.*, The Philosophical Research Society, Inc. 1977.

[64] Bender, Albert K., Flying Saucers and the Three Men, Paperback Library, New York. 1968.

man as cattle and puts the control of all resources in the hands of a few. A government by the Elite, or perhaps a long looked for return of the "Gods". Remember that every organized religion talks of the day when "God" returns to rule his creation. Let's look at what some of these New World Order members have had to say.

Associated Press Dispatch-July 26, 1968:

"New York Governor Nelson A. Rockefeller says as President he would work toward international creation of "a new world order'. . ."

The Declaration of Interdependence-January 30, 1976. (Signed by 32 Senators and 92 Representatives):

"Two centuries ago our forefathers brought forth a new nation; now we must join with others to bring forth a new world order."

The Seattle Post-Intelligence-April 18, 1975 (A quote by Henry Kissinger):

"Our nation is uniquely endowed to play a creative and decisive role in the new order which is taking form around us."

The Commencement Address at Texas A&M University-May 12, 1989 (From the speech given by President George Bush):

"Ultimately, our objective is to welcome the Soviet Union back into the world order. Perhaps the world order of the future will truly be a family of nations."

To recap at this point, we have some disturbing statements coming from our leaders. People who we have elected, or been appointed by those that we have elected, are actually proposing something that may not be in our best interest. We see Gov. Nelson Rockefeller, who later became vice-president under President Ford, vowing to work for a "new world order." Then we have large portion of the elected Congress signing a declaration proposing to work for a "new world order." Henry Kissinger is well known for his involvement with the Rockefeller faction, so his desire for a "new world order" is no surprise. However, it is all together a different thing to have our current President, George Bush, reference the new world order as an accomplished fact. It makes one wonder and fear for the safety of our country. It seems that we are surrounded by traitors. In later chapters, we will look closer at both Mr. Rockefeller and Mr. Kissinger.

But these statements really should not be any great surprise when everyone of the above referenced people, to include our current President are avowed members of the Council on Foreign Relation (CFR) a "public" secret society whose charter calls for the creation of a "one world government."

LOOKING BACK

However, the new world order adherents in our so-called freely elected government are nothing new. One important example comes from World War I. Our President at this time was Woodrow Wilson, a man who campaigned on a promise to keep us out of the war. In actuality he was looked at as a good, honest man who strongly believed in this country. The American people believed in him and put him into office. However, appearances can be very deceiving, especially in politics.

The truth was that Woodrow Wilson had been owned by the conspiracy since he had been Governor of New Jersey. When Senator Nelson Aldrich was pushing his plan for a central bank, Woodrow Wilson came out in strong support of it. During the financial panic of 1907, caused almost entirely by J.P. Morgan, Wilson had declared that "All of this trouble could be averted if we appointed a committee of six or seven public-spirited men like J.P. Morgan to handle the affairs of our country."

It was also Woodrow Wilson who was instrumental in overthrowing the monarchies of Europe after the First World War. His proposal was for the League of Nations to function as a one world government, with every country giving up control of it's' government to the new central government. Luckily this was defeated, a disappointment that seemed to stun President Wilson.

However, what few know is that immediately after the election, President Wilson's closest friend, closest Presidential advisor and a man who, by many, was called the President's "alter ego" Colonel Edward Mandell House [the Colonel was honorary], a man who had been employed by Rockefeller interests, began to work to force our entry into the war that Wilson had promised to keep this country out of. I would submit that the actions of Colonel House show that Woodrow Wilson planned all along to get this country into the "Great War". Without the President's knowledge and approval, it would have been impossible for Colonel House to manipulate people and events as history shows that he did.

How could a mere Presidential Advisor act with such independent power and authority? Even more importantly, why would this little known member of the Wilson Administration want us to get into the War? We will examine the background of this mysterious individual in a later chapter, but suffice it to say that his first loyalty was not to the United States, even though he was a close friend and an advisor to the President. To get an insight into the motivations of Colonel House, let's look at what Historian Walter Mills had to say about him.

"The Colonel's sole justification for preparing such a batch of blood for his countrymen was his hope of establishing a new world order of peace and security."

So the Colonel, based on his "hope for peace and security" was instrumental in getting us into a long, costly and bloody war. A European War that was actually a family argument between related monarchs. This was only one of series of Wars that had erupted between the ruling interrelated, dynasties of Europe since the Middle Ages. Had the U.S. not intervened, the war would have ended with the establishment of a new balance of power, but the stability of Europe would have remained intact and Communism would probably have died an early death or at best, been a minor player in world affairs.

World War I was a war that set the stage for World War II and the changing of our world forever. An unelected official having the kind of power that allows him to manipulate this country into a foreign war should be unthinkable. But in a later chapter you will see much more of Colonel House and his "surprising friends".

So in this chapter, we have begun to get an insight into the Conspiracy and some of the people who have been members. Remember, this Conspiracy is not a thing of the past to be studied dispassionately, but it is alive, well and living among us today. However, you have no real idea of what this Conspiracy is capable of today until you look at some of the things that its members have been responsible for in the past. The members of this Conspiracy are not radicals hiding in some back room and plotting the downfall of the nation against fantastic odds. On the contrary, the members of this Conspiracy occupy some of the most power positions in this land. The question is, who do they answer to, certainly not the American people.

Doubt me? Well read on.

CHAPTER FIVE

WE HAVE MET THE ENEMY AND HE IS US

Lies! Lies! It cannot be! The wars we wage are noble, and our battles are won by Justice for us, ere we lift the gage. We have not sold our loftiest heritage. The proud republic hath not stooped to cheat and scramble in the marketplace of war; Her forehead weareth yet its solemn star. . . . Was it for this our fathers kept the law? William Vaughn Moody

Many of you are of the great school of thought that says, history is dead and what happened then can't bother us now. Well, I propose to show you that you are wrong. I propose to prove to you that the Conspiracy of which I write is alive and well and living in America. I have made allegations that members of this hidden Conspiracy occupy positions within our government. Am I just rambling or can I back up what I say? You have to be the judge, but I would ask you to withhold making decisions until after you have completed this volume. Perhaps what I report is coincidence, perhaps simply bad judgment on the part of those who undertake these programs, or perhaps I am paranoid. However, remember the James Bond School of Thought:

Once is happenstance

Twice is coincidence, but

Three times is enemy action.

Based upon the actions of certain members of our State Department, I would say that we have found enemy action. However, I offer the evidence for you to be the judge.

THE FIRST STEP

As a first step in examining this hidden conspiracy, I am going to show you some of what is happening today. I am going to take you behind the scenes of some of the so-called State Department errors, and some of the so-called coups, that commentators have talked about since World War II. Once we are finished, see if you think that these were actual errors, after all.

The main idea to keep in mind is that each of the so-called errors was the handiwork of State Department officials that were primarily members of the Council on Foreign Relations (CFR) and were, for the most part, all trained in the Ivy League Schools of the northeast. Many of them enter and leave highly placed government positions, rotating back into education and other areas of influence. Later we will see why this last characteristic might be important.

A JUST WAR IS A GOOD WAR

We like to think that all our wars are just, that we fight for Truth, Justice and the American way. Since the late 1940's our enemy has been the "Evil Empire" of the Soviet Union. In the many "brushfire" wars and "police actions" thousands of American soldiers and untold millions of civilian "innocent bystanders" have died under the tank threads of the Russian Army, either directly or indirectly through Soviet controlled "freedom fighters". An Army that we, allegedly, proudly stand ready to combat, out numbered as we are, and to our ever lasting shame, an Army that we bought and paid for with American dollars and American technology.

I can hear you all right now. "IMPOSSIBLE!" you say. We would never help the Godless Communists. Ronald Regan called them the evil empire and we eventually defeated them through the strength of democracy. We are the last bastion of freedom in this old world. Right---and I have a bridge I want to sell you.

The actual truth is that we spend billions of dollars for defense every year against an enemy that we armed and trained. An enemy that we re-arm and retrain every year with better and better weapons and technology. Confused? Well you are not alone. Is it possible that the Soviet Army was created in order to give us an adversary that would so occupy our time and attention that we would miss the existence of another enemy that hates us both? I think that the facts will bear out this theory.

DEFENSELESS WE STAND

It may surprise you to know that in spite of all the nuclear missiles that this country is alleged to control, that we are virtually defenseless to a Russian attack.

That's right; I said that we are virtually defenseless to an attack by the Russians or anyone else for that matter.

Our nuclear arsenal is an offensive weapon, not defensive. Our arsenal is designed to destroy the enemy in his homeland, not defend our own homes. To defend our homes, we have to depend on the standing military, a military that our Congress is in the process of trying to reduce in size due to the "outbreak of peace." (However, as I wrote this in January 1991, we are calling up our reserves for our newest "moral war" in the Middle East, but more on this in a later chapter) and let us not forget the current war against the forces of terrorism that has stretched our forces to the breaking point. While at the same time, we are happily sending money in the name of foreign aid to our new friends in the Soviet Bloc that is being used to strengthen their own armies.

So what keeps the Russians from attacking this country? According to current military doctrine, their army is bigger and better armed than our own. Their armored vehicles are bigger and more powerful than our own. The Soviet air force and navy out number ours considerably. So what is our defense? According to our government, our best defense is their knowledge that if they destroy us, we destroy them, or the concept of Mutually Assured Destruction.

MUTUAL ASSURED DESTRUCTION

The concept of mutual assured destruction or MAD was designed, or the phrase was coined, back in the 1960's. At this time, if you will remember, it was expected that the Russians would attack just anytime and we all needed to be prepared to dig out of the rubble that would be left after their expected attack. Billions went into defense against an enemy who was almost a match for us militarily. An enemy that in 1945 had a shattered economic base, literally millions of casualties from World War II and no international military force to speak of.

On the other hand, we had the atomic bomb, the most powerful military in the world, a navy that could sweep any other country from the seas and an air force second to none. We had the power to literally destroy any country that we chose. In our magnanimous way, we set out the rebuild the world in our image. But something went wrong. Something went very badly wrong.

In less than twenty years or less than one generation, Russia went from a second rate power to one that has eclipsed us in military power. It has nuclear weapons to match or outclass our own, a military that is second to none, aircraft that can outclass our own and a navy that out numbers ours. How could this happen? Wouldn't the cost of such a military machine mean that the common people would starve, that the economy would be in a shambles?

At the same time that the Soviet Military Machine has been building, we have been disarming as fast as we can go. We have rifted, or fired, many of our finest, combat trained military officers, mothballed our mighty fleet and allowed what we didn't retire to become outdated and refused to replace our strategic air force with more sophisticated aircraft. We know that the Soviet Union out numbers us in Intercontinental Ballistic Missiles (ICBM) but we have no anti-ballistic missile system (ABM). The most unnerving part of this is that this lack of a competent ABM system is by agreement with the Soviet Union. In other words, we agreed to disarm ourselves[65]. According to the concept of mutually assured destruction, neither we nor the Soviets are supposed to have a defensive capability, only offensive. In other words, what would keep us from starting a war would be the certain knowledge that we would also be destroyed. Of course, such a concept was tailor-made for and by the liberal media that, for some unknown reason, has always viewed Russia as heaven on earth. Our own media has implied that we would be the ones to start the war, not the Soviets. Interesting concept.

WE HAVE THE BEST ENEMY THAT MONEY CAN BUY

As pointed out by Antony C. Sutton in his book, *The Best Enemy Money Can Buy*[66], the United States has been the greatest aid that the Soviet Union could ever have had in its military aims. Before all of you liberals start howling about my casting aspersions on the greatest man in history (some have even rated him a step above Jesus Christ) Michael Gorbachev, let me offer some examples of some of the acts of this great man:

In December, 1979, the Soviet Union invaded Afghanistan (It should be remembered that our President, Jimmy "Mr. Peanut" Carter "got tough with Moscow" in response to the invasion. He withheld our Olympic Team from the Moscow Olympics. Can you picture the hardship that this caused the Soviet leadership?). The initial Soviet military forces flew into Afghanistan on what were supposed to be civilian flights. Once on the ground at the main airport in Kabul, Soviet Special Operations troops quickly seized control of the city. The operation worked smoothly for these flights were filled with the cream of the Soviet Army, the Soviet Special Forces. However, the main forces comprising the mighty Soviet invasion force, especially the armored columns, came overland, by road.

The Soviet Army mounted a massive invasion of a country surrounded by some of the most impassable mountains in the world. How did the Soviets get their armored columns and especially their massive main battle tanks to such a backward, mountainous country? Why the Soviet Army traveled in comfort over a modern road system built courtesy of the United States Government.

This road building project was begun at the order of President Lyndon Baines Johnson as part of his "Great Society"[67] program. At a time when the United

---

[65] Bearden, T. E., FER-DE-LANCE., Tesla Book Co. Greenville, TX 75401. 1986.
[66] Sutton, Antony C.,THE BEST ENEMY MONEY CAN BUY, Liberty House Press. Billings. Montana. 1986.
[67] Ibid

States was in need of funds for numerous social programs for our own citizens, and when funds were needed to support our troops fighting in the midst of the Vietnam War these badly needed funds were spent to build a first class road in one of the most inaccessible parts of the world. At a time when thousands of our troops were being killed by weapons sent to North Vietnam from the Soviet Union, President Johnson sent U.S. Engineers to work with the Soviets to build, what amounted to, two super highways from the Soviet Union to Kabul. This project was designed to benefit only the Soviet Union. It had absolutely no benefits for the United States. So why did we undertake to build such a project that only benefited the Soviet Union and also pay the complete tab?

It is interesting to note that these two wide, modern highways had to be built in a country with few vehicles other than those belonging to the military. Due to the mountainous terrain, each of the highways had to have several heavily reinforced bridges constructed in order to complete the project. In a country where the heaviest privately owned vehicle might be an old pickup truck, these highways have bridges specifically designed to be capable of holding thirty (30) ton Soviet tanks. To build this road cost the American Taxpayers more than $640,000.00 per mile. What is the purpose of building such roads going to so desolate a place, except to accommodate military traffic? More importantly, why would the United States build such a road to benefit an alleged enemy?

A HIGHER REALITY

The following is an excerpt from a speech given by the Russian Revolutionary Vladimir Ilych (Ulyanov) Lenin.

"*The Capitalists of the world and their governments, in pursuit of conquest of the Soviet market, will close their eyes to the indicated higher reality and thus will turn into deaf mute blind men. They will extend credits, which will strengthen for us the Communist Party in their countries and giving us the materials and technology we lack, they will restore our military industry, indispensable for our future victorious attacks on our suppliers. In other words, they will labor for the preparation for their own suicide.*[68]"

This "Higher Reality" represents Lenin's belief that Communism is the final fate of the world and only the blind capitalists fail to realize this ultimate truth. He felt, apparently rightly, that capitalism as a system would be responsible for its own downfall. In a system where everything is for sale, he believed that the system would sell itself if the money was right.

The idea of higher reality has not been a secret; in fact the Soviets have told anyone who would listen about this unusual belief. The Communists have talked about it for years, only most Americans have never heard of it. The reason

---

[68] Finder, Joseph, RED CARPET, Holt, Rinehart & Winston. New York. 1984.

for this ignorance is quite simple; our own government covered this up. The very leaders responsible for seeing that our system survived, have been hiding the fact our government has been selling our enemies the very things that they need to defeat us and in order to allow them to purchase the items they need, we have been extending them the credit that they need to make the purchases. Of course, all of this assistance has been underwritten with US tax dollars.

I'M FROM THE GOVERNMENT, TRUST ME!

A prime example of this almost treasonous activity were some of the acts of the U.S. State Department under Secretary of State John Foster Dulles. Secretary of State Dulles appointed Dr. G. Bernard Noble as head of the Historical Office of the State Department. This office was, and is, responsible for keeping historical records regarding State Department functions and programs. However, it is alleged that under Dr. Noble, there was an official policy of distorting information and suppressing historical documents to cover up some of the more questionable programs undertaken by our own government. It should be noted that Dr. Noble was a Rhodes Scholar, a designation which as you shall see later, makes him suspect.

There were two other historians, Dr. Donald Dozer and Dr. Bryton Barron, who were also working in the State Department at this time. Both made the mistake of protesting this policy of information suppression and distortion being conducted by Dr. Noble. As is usually the case in government jobs, in spite of loudly touted programs to protect "whistle blowers", the powers that be decided that these two individuals were not "team players", so they were both terminated.

Dr. Barron later wrote a book on his experiences, called "Inside the State Department[69]. In this book, he made some very serious charges regarding what he termed high level wrong doing. This high level wrong doing would be called treason by some. However, in spite of the large body of evidence, their charges were never given any credence by the government.

Dr. Barron specifically charged that officials in our State Department were directly responsible for exporting military technology to the Soviet Union in contravention of existing US laws. Among the examples of illegally exported technology exported to the Soviet Union that he discussed in his book were:

1.) Advanced equipment designed specifically for manufacturing jet engines.

2.) Boring mills used in manufacturing tanks, artillery, aircraft and submarine atomic reactors.

---

[69] Barron, Bryton, INSIDE THE STATE DEPARTMENT, Comet Press, New York. 1956.

3.) Equipment used to balance shafts on engines for jets and guided missiles.

4.) Grinding machines essential in making engine parts, guided missiles and radar.

So as you can see, there is a solid body of evidence that not only does the United States State Department arm our enemies, but anyone who would alert the citizens of this nation to the betrayal and treason being carried out by the leaders of State Department is fired and discredited. All of this is done in the name of National Security, of course.

THE COVER-UP

In order to cover-up the fact many of the Russian scientific advances that have allowed the Soviet military to become an international threat to world peace are nothing more than an illegal "copying" of our own illegally exported technology. To cover up their illegal activities, our own State Department has created the myth of the Soviet "genius".

According to reports coming out of our State Department, the Soviet scientific community is making massive strides forward in developing modern technology. Yet, the State Department's own historical records show massive U.S. assistance to the Communist movement since the 1917 Revolution.

To show examples of the on-going continuing cover-up, consider the following:

- November 28, 1917, just after the Bolsheviks overthrew the Russian government, "Colonel" E.M. House, President Woodrow Wilson's alter ego and closest advisor wired the President and the Secretary of State the following cable from Paris[70].

"There has been cabled over and published here statements made by American papers to the effect that Russia should be treated as an enemy. It is exceedingly important that such criticisms should be suppressed."

As a result of this cable, the statements referred to that were critical of the new Soviet regime were stopped by the issuance of illegal government orders to the offending newspapers. It seems that "Colonel" House had a great deal of power within the Wilson administration. But we shall see a great deal more of "Colonel"

---

[70] Sutton, Antony C.,THE BEST ENEMY MONEY CAN BUY, Liberty House Press. Billings. Montana. 1986.

House as we progress through this sordid tale of betrayal and treason.

In 1968, the following statement was attributed to Nicholas de B. Katzenbach, (a C.F.R. member) then Assistant Secretary of State.

"*We should give no illusions. If we do not sell peaceful goods to the nations of Eastern Europe, others will. If we erect barriers to our trade with Eastern Europe, we will lose the trade and Eastern Europe will buy elsewhere. But we will not make any easier our task of stopping aggression in Vietnam nor in building security for the United States*[71].

On the surface, it appears that the administration was trying to protect trade and also make sure that potential enemies did not benefit in any military ways from US trade. However, at the very same time these statement was made by Assistant Secretary Katzenbach, the actual facts show that much of the technology used by the Soviets to build the military equipment that they exported to North Vietnam to be used against American military personnel during the Vietnam War came from the United States with the knowledge and support of the elected officials of this government.

It would seem that the State Department's idea of peaceful goods leaves something to be desired. To get a good idea of the "changing nature of peaceful goods", we need to go back to 1945 and the end of World War II.

After the end of World War II, the victorious Allies had to decide what to do with a defeated Germany. The U.S. Government set up a special commission to determine what should be done with the German automobile industry. This special committee concluded that any motor vehicle industry in any country is an important aspect of that country's war potential. The following were the findings of the committee:

1.) Any motor vehicle industry is a major factor in a country's war making capability.

2.) German automotive manufacturing should be prohibited because it was a war industry.

3.) Numerous military products can be made by the automobile industry. The committee attached a list containing over 300 items with strictly military applications[72].

---

[71] Ibid

[72] STUDY BY INTERAGENCY COMMITTEE ON THE TREATMENT OF THE GERMAN AUTOMOTIVE INDUSTRY FROM THE STANDPOINT OF NATIONAL SECURITY. (Washington D.C.: Foreign Economic Administration, July 14, 1945), Report T.I.D.C. No. 12.

HAVE A NICE GORBAZAM

Now re-read the above carefully. Look at number 2 above: German automotive manufacturing should be prohibited because it was a war industry. Now I ask you, if automotive manufacturing is a war industry for Germany, wouldn't logic dictate that automotive manufacturing would be a war industry for Soviet Russia as well? Surprisingly, in a similar study, some of the same committee members decided that in spite of their findings vis a vis Germany, automotive manufacturing would not be a war industry in the Soviet Union. Even more surprising, this decision was made with the members of this second committee being fully aware of the Soviet Union's official intention (Stated as early as 1927) to use foreign automobile technology for the building of military vehicles.

As if this official stated position wasn't enough, V.V. Ossinsky, one of the Soviet Army's top planners wrote several articles for Pravda in 1927 that specifically discussed the use of such automobile technology for military purposes. The entire current Soviet military-civilian manufacturing industry is made up of a few large plants designed, built by, and equipped with American technology. Current estimates reveal that about 90-95% of Soviet military vehicles are built in plants designed by American Engineers and built by American companies inside the Soviet Union. Among these American companies are such giants as:

Ford Motor Company

A.J. Brandt Company

Austin Company

General Electric

Swindell-Dressler

Budd

Hamilton Foundry[73]

Now I ask you, why the double standard? Why was it decided that Germany couldn't have an automotive manufacturing capability because it was a war industry, but the Soviet Union could? In the face of the determination that automobile manufacturing was a war industry, why did the U.S. Government give One Billion ($1,000,000,000.00) dollars (with no strings attached) to build the

---

[73] Sutton, Antony C., THE BEST ENEMY MONEY CAN BUY, Liberty House Press. Billings, Montana. 1986.

largest truck manufacturing plant in the world inside the Soviet Union?

This state of the art truck manufacturing plant covers 36 acres and this one facility has the capability to produce more military trucks than the entire U.S. output combined[74]. Could there be forces behind the scenes that we have no idea exist who desire that the Untied States have an enemy capable of matching, or even surpassing it, militarily? Could these forces be manipulating our government like a puppet on a string? Why do supposedly loyal American officials work diligently to support the military efforts of the Soviet Union?

The answers to all these questions will become evident as we progress. Suffice it say at this point that there is a substantial body of evidence that there is a secret society controlling our government and most of the Governments of the world. Doubt me? The proof will be shown as you progress.

TWENTY FIRST CENTURY WEAPONS

While we have been happily helping arm the Soviet Army, our scientific establishment has been helping modernize other areas of the Soviet Empire. In fact, some of the Soviet's most advanced work has been based on research done in the United States and passed onto Soviet officials.

One example has been work in the field of Scalar Electromagnetics[75]. This field is an extension of present electromagnetics to include the force known as gravitation. This field was originally developed by Nikola Tesla, who has been called one of the most brilliant individuals in history.

Through the use of scalar electromagnetics, electromagnetic field energy can be turned into gravitational field energy and vice versa. Using writing published in American literature, Soviet researchers have developed a method of using this electromagnetic field as a weapon; a weapon against which we have absolutely no defense.

Using this continuing research, the Soviets have launched the largest, most expensive weapons research program in history. More importantly, they have kept it hidden from prying eyes. These new weapons are now deployed and have been tested several times against a number of different targets. We have turned a blind eye to the entire program, even when one of their tests resulted in the deaths of Americans, on national television[76].

---

[74] Ibid

[75] Bearden, T. E., FER-DE-LANCE., Tesla Book Co. Greenville, TX 75401. 1986.

[76] Ibid

ENERGETICS[77]

The Soviets call this type of advanced weapons science energetics. We have believed that this term is only associated with conventional directed energy weapons such as the legendary particle beam weapon, lasers and such. All of which were based on American research and discoveries which were given to the Soviets.

As early as 1960, then Premier, Nikita Khrushchev, announced that the Soviets had a fantastic new weapon. On May 1, 1960, the U-2 spy plane of Francis Gary Powers was brought down by this new weapon. It is alleged that on April 10, 1963, one of the new Soviet weapons based on this research was used to destroy the U.S.S. Thresher, one of our atomic subs.

In Vietnam, it was kept very quiet by our government, but even some of our most advanced F-111's were brought down with some type of energy beam which caused the emergency indicator lamps on the panels in the cockpit to light up like Christmas trees. In fact, the Vietnam conflict was used as a testing ground for many Soviet developed weapon systems, all of which were based on exported American research.

So we must face the facts that our government has helped the communists create their movement, consolidate their power, conquer free countries all over the globe, build up their military and advance their scientific establishment. As we shall later see, moneyed interests in this country have also helped fund the communist movement. At the same time, we spend billions to defend ourselves from these same forces.

Now come the most important questions of all:

1. Why would government officials in our own government be willing to work for the downfall of our government?

Could the answer to this question be that perhaps these government officials owe their first loyalty to some organization other than the U.S. government?

2. Why would the most powerful capitalists in the world be willing to not only help the communists create their government (a government dedicated to destroying the capitalistic system) but also to fund said government when it proved incapable of even feeding its' own people?

Could it be that in some way those aforesaid capitalists actually have some control over the communist movement? Assuming that the most powerful capitalists in the world are not stupid, then they would only act out of self interest. Why would supporting the communists be in the best interests of such families as the Rockefellers, Warburgs and the Schiffs? Could they either know something that

---

[77] Ibid

we don't, or are they much more involved in the interworkings of the Soviet Union than they would want us to know? Could these powerful families be involved in the Conspiracy? Let us look further.

CHAPTER SIX

THE OCCULT PATH

The world is governed by very different personages from what is imagined by those who are not behind the scenes. Benjamin Disraeli

Most people, if they consider the issue at all, seem to believe that the word "Occult" has something to do with evil, satanic worship and the forces of darkness. As a result, many would-be researchers into the Occult world have been forced to end their studies due to the pressure from religious and other well meaning groups. The religious groups seem to feel that if someone wishes to study occult matters then that person must be inherently evil. Such an attitude is equivalent to "Ignore it and it will go away." In other words, if no one studies the occult, then there will be much less evil in the world. Unfortunately this is not the case, for I would submit that if one is not inherently evil, merely studying a subject will not make the student evil and all of the bible study in the world would not make a would-be Hitler a minister.

On the other hand, a materialist individual dismisses the occult as just so much hocus pocus. Obviously, a person who studies the occult is someone who deals with fantasy and as a direct result, is not someone who will be successful in this materialistic world. (Add to this that it is the materialistic individual who usually rises to positions of power and importance and it is easy to see how THE CONSPIRACY has lasted as long as it has.) Therefore, it comes as a great surprise to learn that some of the most famous people in history were very much involved in occult matters and steeped in occult knowledge. It is a further shock to the materialistic point of view that many major historical events in our history have hidden meanings that can only be interpreted through an understanding of occult lore.

Before we delve into the world of the strange and bizarre, I think that a general knowledge of certain topics is required. The first step in understanding occult lore is understanding what the word occult actually means. Our religious leaders, with the help of the CONSPIRACY, itself, have endeavored to equate occult with Satanic. Nothing could be further from the truth. The word occult simply means "hidden[78]". The occult path is quite simply, the hidden path. It is to this hidden path that we must go in order to find out for ourselves what is really happening in our world.

Why do men seek out the hidden path? Why do they dedicate lifetimes and fortunes to the effort of seeking out what is hidden, often with good reason, from men? What can be so attractive that men will brave the unknown and risk everything they have, to achieve it? Quite simply, it is POWER- whether it be over nature herself or other men, the goal of those who seek the hidden path is always POWER.

To begin to understand what is happening today in the underground conspiracy, it is necessary to seek out the roots of these secret societies that protect and disseminate the occult knowledge. For this reason, before we get down to talking about the present, it is important that we penetrate the mists of time and examine the beginnings of what may the first secret society-THE CULT OF ISIS.

THE CULT OF ISIS

Isis was one of the first goddess worshipped by men in the time of pre-history. She was allegedly THE GODDESS from which all other gods and goddess sprang. But at the same time, she always remained a virgin. There is much speculation that ISIS was the original Mother goddess worshiped by man prior to the other ancient religions beginning.

According to much research conducted over the last few years, The Cult of Isis was formed to pass on some advanced scientific learning that had to do with the creation of the human race. It is very possible, that in the occult teachings of the Cult of Isis is the very proof of my theory. For you see, Isis was allegedly one of the Annunaki who helped create our race. Most importantly, the answer to this question is within reach, for researchers have pinpointed what may have been the burial place of Isis, herself, (legend says that even the Gods could die under certain circumstances) in France[79].

Isis had a major effect on the human race. Her teachings even pervade most of our modern religions. Most are totally unbelieving when I point out that teachings of the ISIS CULT are to be found in the teachings of Christianity and

---

[78] Howard, Michael, THE OCCULT CONSPIRACY, Destiny Books, Rochester, Vermont. 1989.

[79] Wood, David, GENISIS, The First Book of Revelations, The Baton Press. Tunbridge Wells, Kent. 1985.

every other modern religion. Researchers far more versed in these matters than I point to several areas of the BIBLE that allegedly describe initiations ceremonies for new members of the ISIS CULT[80].

Perhaps in a later book I will delve into the Isis Cult, but at this time, I have another fish to fry, so to speak. Therefore, let us move onto the three "human" secret organizations that have had an impact on our society, 1.) The Prieure de Sion, 2.) The Order of the Rosy Cross and 3.) Freemasonry.

FREEMASONRY

Most secret societies have managed to, more or less, remain hidden from public view. Not so, Freemasonry. The Masonic Orders have been very much in the public eye, in almost every country where they exist. It has been much rumored that membership in the Masons can be a great assist in climbing up the ladder in the business world, a claim which the Masons, themselves, deny.

Many of the rank and file Membership of this order claim that the Masons is nothing for than a social organization like the Lions club. Allegedly, it is a group that works to improve the world. Of course, if this is the case, then why do the majority of judges, lawyers, businessmen and military officers maintain membership? The key to understanding the membership of very powerful people in this organization is that Masonry is one of the most important, powerful and influential organizations of modern time.

As Bernard Fay wrote in his book *REVOLUTION AND FREEMASONRY,* 1680-1800[81]:

"*The new faith in the future of humanity that spread in the eighteenth century was not simply an abstract fact or a mental force. It became a social force and a concrete fact through the agency of Freemasonry, which at once accepted it and advocated it; the great historical importance of modern Freemasonry results from this attitude that it took then. . . . Thus Freemasonry has become the most efficient social power of the civilized world. But it has been a hidden power, difficult to trace, to describe and to define. Consequently, most historians have avoided treating it seriously and giving it due credit.*"

Are Masonic Lodges simply social clubs as many claim, or are they actually something more? It is known that it was in the Masonic Lodges of France that the French Revolution actually began. In fact, according to legend, the Freemasonry Movement was merged, so to speak, with an even older secret order that had as its' goal world revolution.

---

[80] Ibid

[81] Fay, Bernard, REVOLUTION AND FREEMASONRY, 1680-1800, Boston: Little, Brown and Co. 1935.

It is important to note that the French Masons, many of whom were members of the nobility and thus very wealthy people with much to lose if the existing order were overthrown, were the core of the revolution. Why would these people act to overthrow the very system that gave them wealth and power?

Was the French Revolution merely a fluke or was it part of a master plan that could happen again?

Additionally, here are some other questions that you should ponder:

1.) Can Freemasonry be a source of power for members?

2.) Is Freemasonry a threat to the current world order?

3.) Is Freemasonry a force moving for the New World Order that the One World Government forces desires?

In the context of this present book, we will touch upon each of these questions, but you have to wait for a further book in the Occult Connection series for a thorough examination of these topics.

THE ORDER OF THE ROSY CROSS

The Order of the Rosy Cross rivals Freemasonry in age. According to legend, The Order of the Rosy Cross was created by Egyptian Pharaoh Thothmes III. This was the Pharaoh that built the most famous of the Egyptian Temples at Heliopolis, also called the City of the Sun, in the fifteenth century BCE. [The pillars that guarded the entrance of this famous Temple currently stand on the Thames Embankment in London and are called Cleopatra's Needles.[82]]

According to a pamphlet called Fama Fraternitatis, or A Discovery of the Fraternity of the Most Laudable Order of the Rosy Cross, published at Cassel in 1614, the Order of the Rosy Cross began with one Christian Rosenkreutz, born in 1378. According to this story, in 1384, Christian Rosenkreutz and one other left for Damascus, Syria to learn from the masters. His companion died and left Rosenkreutz, a mere youth of about 16 years of age to continue the journey. In the Far East, Rosenkreutz is alleged to have learned the Jewish Cabala from which he gathered the secrets that are passed down in the Order. Upon his return to Germany, Rosenkreutz gathered around him nine followers, or brothers as they are known, who constituted the first initiates of his new order. He was the head of this Order until his death in 1484.

According to the story, in 1604, the, then, inner circle of brothers

---

[82] Howard, Michael, THE OCCULT CONSPIRACY, Destiny Books, Rochester, Vermont. 1989.

discovered a heretofore hidden door within their stronghold upon which was written "Post 120 Annoys Patio". Upon opening the door, they discovered a vault which contained a brass tablet. Beneath the brass tablet was the one hundred twenty year old corpse of Christian Rosenkreutz, "whole and unconsumed". In other words, his body had not decayed in over one hundred and twenty years, similar to that of the children who witnessed the Fatima Miracle. Allegedly, much written material was found with the corpse which enlightened the Brotherhood on many matters. One of which was, allegedly, the coming new order in human affairs.

Many believe that Christian Rosenkreutz really lived and did all of the things that legend says that he did. Others believe that the story of this individual is a concoction used to try and give the order an older heritage than it deserves. What is truth, no one knows.

The Order of the Rosy Cross still exists today as an order of learning. Like the Mason's, some look at it with suspicion and some with envy.

THE PRIEURE DE SION

This Order is one of the most mysterious because even its very existence was hidden until recently. According to some researchers, the Prieure de Sion is a very ancient Order that was actually the inner circle of the Knights Templar, the monastic order of military monks who kept the Holy Land roads free for travelers. According to legend, this Order was a keeper of ancient knowledge and may have had possession or guarded the so called "Holy Grail[83]". Also according to legend, this Order also had the job of guarding the true descendants and heirs of the Christ.

Those who believe these stories of the Order believe that Christ did not die on the Cross, but rather a double took his place and was the one to actually die. It is said that the actual Christ was secretly smuggled out of the Holy Land to later die in Egypt. His earthly "wife", Mary Magdalene, and his children were smuggled out of Palestine by Joseph of Arimathema to southern France as he traveled to what is now Britain. There is evidence that the Merovingian Dynasty of France were blood descendants of Christ through his children who were allegedly smuggled out of Palestine. This Order had the very important job of guarding the blood line[84].

As an aside, it has been written that Jesus was a Rabbi and it is accepted that someone who was a Rabbi was married and normally had children. Could Christ have actually married? Most believe that Mary Magdalene was a prostitute that Christ saved, but newly discovered information shows that she was actually the head of a cult that worshipped the goddess.

Based in France, this Order exists today and still carries out its ancient task of guarding the pure blood line. According to documents found in Europe, some of

---

[83] Baigent, Michael, Richard Leigh and Henry Lincoln, HOLY BLOOD, HOLY GRAIL, Dell. New York. 1983.

[84] Baigent, Michael; Richard Leigh and Henry Lincoln, THE MESSIANIC LEGACY, Dell. New York. 1986.

the most famous figures of history were members of this Order. The names would shock you.

So now we have discussed four secret societies that all seem to have an unusually long history, 1) The Cult of Isis, 2) The Free Masons, 3) The Order of the Rosy Cross, and 4) The Prieure De Sion. Of these four which is the one that is today trying to subvert all of our freedoms? The answer will surprise you.

Most of those who have examined these types of secret Orders, such as the British Parliament, feel that the Masonic Order is the biggest threat to free government[85]. This conclusion has been arrived at in spite of the fact that, traditionally, the head of the British Masonic Order has been a senior member of the Royal Family.

Such a belief that the Masonic Order might be a threat to existing government is not without good cause, I might add. Historically it has been said that there was allegedly a connection between certain Masonic rituals and the Jack the Ripper Murders in the Whitechapel District of London in 1885. There was even a Sherlock Holmes story pointing out that the methods in which the Ripper's victims were mutilated had a great deal in common with the types of injuries suffered by the legendary Hiram Abiff, said to be the Architect of the Temple of Solomon in Masonic Lore.

However, there is also a great deal of evidence that points to an even more secret society from which all of these stem. This unknown secret society is alleged to have begun untold thousands of years ago and existed under the control of an unbroken chain of masters until the present day. Is this true, or simply the delirious ravings of the worst type of paranoid? Unfortunately in the study of secret organizations it is easy to mistake one of the "fronts" for the actual power behind the scenes. Such an error can result in the cutting off of only one head of the Hydra Monster, but still leave the creature living to strike again. Our job is to find the actual "main beast", so to speak. For only in finding and destroying this main beast can we be sure that we have ended the danger once and for all.

A HIDDEN CONNECTION

Before we go on, let's first see if there appear to be any connections between the various sects or movements that we have looked at thus far. If, as I suggest, there is a much more secret "master" order working through the various secret societies known to society, then there should be some evidence of even tenuous connections between the various groups.

In 1663, there was a Masonic Congress held at which time the first three

---

[85] Knight, Stephen, THE BROTHERHOOD, The Secret World of the Freemasons, Dorset Press. 1984.

degrees were created[86]. At this same Congress, a strong amount of Rosicrucian teaching was introduced into the craft. At this same time, a French Priest named Depuis wrote a book wherein he called for the Craft[87] to avenge the Knights Templar, the organization of religious warrior monks had earlier been suppressed by the Pope at the urging of Phillip the Fair, the King of France.

Depuis called for the Craft to depose the French King and the Stuart line of England since they were allied with the French Monarchy and most surprising, he also called for the overthrow of the Church, since the Pope had played a hand in the end of the Knights Templar. The evidence is almost conclusive that it was segments of the Masonic movement that originally funded and instigated the French Revolution. From this time forward, a strong faction of the Craft became anti-Stuart, anti-Church and anti-French. Coincidence?

However, when the revolt against the Stuart Monarch took place in England, an equally large portion of Masonry, called Jacobite Masonry, stayed loyal to the Stuart cause and many even followed the deposed Stuart King, James II into exile in France. It was also the Jacobite Masons who founded a Catholic lodge of Masonry in Paris. Though the lodge was Catholic in allegiance, it was also this lodge which eventually became the most militant against the Catholic Church and the French Monarchy[88]. As we will see later, it was Jacobite Masonry that gave rise to the famed Jacobin Clubs in Europe. It is also interesting to note that though it is thought that few Jews actually enter the Masonic order, the very name Jacobite was taken from two wealthy, influential Jewish men, both of whom were named Jacob.

In 1717, the Grand Masonic Lodge of England was chartered. This became a central authority, after a time, for the many Masonic lodges in England, part of the Continent and in parts of America. For a determination of what kind of people controlled the Grand Lodge, one must keep in mind that the Grand Lodge was known as an association of Freethinkers. For a better understanding of what constituted being a freethinker, no less a noted writer than Jonathan Swift characterized those called freethinkers as atheists, libertines, and despisers of religion.

It has also been pointed out that the ideology of Masonry, which was characterized by "an indifference to religion and a tendency towards cosmopolitanism and internationalism." This internationalism would supplant the Christian duty of patriotism and loyalty to the State by some kind of ineffective international humanitarianism[89].

---

[86] The original Masonic Order had only three degrees while Scottish Rite Masonry has, at least, 33 known degrees. Rumor has it that there are also a number of super degrees above the 33rd level.

[87] The phrase "The Craft" is another designation for the Masonic Order.

[88] Kelly, Rev. Clarence, Conspiracy Against God and Man. Kelly, Rev. Clarence. Western Islands, Belmont, Mass. 1974.

[89] Cahill, E., Freemasonry and the Anti-Christian Movement., M. H. Gill and Son, Ltd., Dublin. 1930.

Isn't the supplanting of patriotism and loyalty to the State exactly what the Conspiracy is attempting to have happen today, over two hundred years later? Another coincidence?

THE U.F.O. CONNECTION

I am sure at this point you are asking yourself how this discussion of secret societies ties in with UFOs and Ancient GODS, since these two topics were also discussed in the first volume of this series. The answer is quite simple. I believe that all three topics are interconnected. The problem is to wade through all of the disinformation and fantasy so that one can get a look at the true picture.

It is my belief that the true goals of all three groups: 1) UFO occupants, 2) Secret Society Members, and 3) The So-Called Ancient Gods were and are in control and have power over this Planet and the Human Race. In the literature, all three groups have called for a one world order where peace reigns forever, under their control of course. I, for one, am not in favor of such an event happening. I believe that man has a right to arrive at his destiny in his own way and in his own time. We don't need big brother pointing the way.

THE TOPIC

The intent of the entire series is to study the secret societies as far back into history as possible. However, such a study is impossible in a single volume. For this reason, I have chosen to deal with just one area at a time. In this particular volume, I have decided to deal with the most powerful secret societies that have had the most direct impact on our civilization. It may help you understand some of what is going on in the world today. It is all interconnected.

There are many who have theorized that all of the secret societies that inhabit the underground maze of alleged secret knowledge and strange beliefs had their births within the same "family". Even so famous a researcher as Kenneth Mackenzie, himself a Rosicrucian stated in his Masonic Cyclopaedia under the heading "Rosicrucians" that there was a very ancient society which stretched back into the dawn of time from which all of the major secret orders began.

It is my belief that this "very ancient society" has existed since the earliest days of civilization and is still alive and doing well today. I further propose that this "very ancient society" has never made itself known, but has instead acted through other, more public orders. I also believe that it is possible to prove that some of history's most famous, and infamous, have been members of this "very ancient society". In a later chapter, we will discuss some of the "famous" members of this hidden society. Were they working for public good, or working for goals more hidden? Don't rely on my opinion, but, instead, judge for yourself as we delve further into the unknown.

CHAPTER SEVEN

SETTING THE STAGE

There is a power somewhere so organized, so subtle, so watchful, so interlocked, so complete, so pervasive that they better not speak above their breath when they speak in condemnation of it. Woodrow Wilson.

Unfortunately, for the average American Citizen, we are a relatively trusting people. For most of us, paradise would be a refrigerator full of beer and twenty four hour a day football games. We out produce the rest of the world put together, have the highest level of technology the world has ever seen and a form of government that we are willing to die for. Most of us sleep soundly at night knowing that our elected officials are awake watching over us. We are smug in our knowledge that we are the greatest country on earth.

I believe that this is true, but I also know that we are living on borrowed time. My research has shown that our governmental mansion has a serious termite problem; termites that we put there and faceless people nuture. As we begin to examine who, what, when and how, I also want to look at some other beliefs of ours.

1.) Such is our view of the world events that we believe that the American way should be imposed on every other country. We "know" that if we find fault with our government, we can change it without bloodshed. After all, look at Watergate and what happened to Nixon. These two events are proof that our system works. Correct?

2.) Most Americans pay no attention to government and politics for we feel that our elected representatives know better than we how to do things and after all, we put them there, right?

3.) Americans have always fought on the side of truth and justice. Why look at our history, in the American Revolution we fought against unjust taxes and despotic government.

4.) Unlike most world governments, our government works for the best interests of the American People.

5.) Our elected officials work for the good of the American People.

6.) Our top officials are the most trust worthy people available.

7.) Capitalism is the sworn enemy of Communism, correct?

8.) The world freedom movement of today is proof, positive, that all people want to live free, correct?

If you believe all of the above statements, then I hope that this book will wake you up to the real world. This country has been manipulated, pushed, robbed and generally used since its beginning. The most unfortunate thing is that the culprits have usually been elected officials. The reason for this is that their first loyalty did not lie to this country, but instead to a secret organization that has been working for centuries to control the world and install their favored system of government on the people of the world.

To examine this idea, let's look first at the issues that led up to the American Revolution, circa 1776.

PRELIMINARIES

As I alluded to in the first volume of this series, almost every founding father of this new country was a member of a secret societies, but the involvement of secret orders in the forming of the United States is even more pervasive than most realize. Most of these secret societies were naturally European in character. However, what is not generally known is that many of these orders were political in nature. There is a great deal of evidence that many of the European wars were fought in order to advance the philosophy on one or another of these societies.

Another interesting fact about these secret societies is that their plans will span centuries in order to accomplish some goal. Additionally, they will shamelessly use individuals, usually members, but not always so, to accomplish their ends and then abandon these individuals to their own fates once they have accomplished what the Order requires.

In fact, if not for one of these Secret Orders, the Knights Templar, it is possible that Columbus would not have discovered America in 1492[90]. As I have previously mentioned, the Knights Templar were a monastic military order that was allegedly formed in the Holy Land around 1100 A.D. At one and the same time, there is a great deal known about this legendary band of warriors and little known about them. There is a lot of information known, but the question is how much of it is true? One thing that is true, however, is that this monastic order was actually the first banking order. Money could be deposited with one "Temple", or Templar group, in England and a document would be issued to the depositor confirming the amount of funds on deposit with the Templar Order. Then after completing the journey, the depositor could present the document to another "Temple" in France, for example and receive the deposited funds. This ancient concept is very similar to that used by Banks today.

THE CRUSHING OF THE KNIGHTS TEMPLAR

In the 13th century, around 1307 to be specific, the Knights of the Temple were persecuted by Philippe IV (also called Philippe the Fair) of France and the then reigning Pope, who was an actual puppet of Philippe. The Knights Templar had become too wealthy and powerful for their own good and raised the jealousy of the King of France who was in great need of fresh funding for his bankrupt treasury. Having taken refuge in the Templar Order located in Paris during one of the many revolts of the French people against his rule, Philippe had the chance to see, first hand, the vast wealth of the Order. Once the revolt was put down, Philippe began to work for the crushing of the Knights Templar.

On Friday 13, 1307, in accordance with a secret order issued by the Pope, Philippe caused all Knights Templar within his domains to be arrested and turned over to the Inquisition[91]. Even though it was alleged that the Knights had turned from worshiping God to worshiping an idol, the real reason that Philippe crushed the order was to get his greedy hands on the treasures of the Templars.

However, the best laid plans of mice and men often go astray. There is evidence to believe that the Knights knew what was planned for them. Witnesses later testified that the vast Templar fleet, with many of its knights and the entire treasury of the Order set sail shortly before the French raids began. The fleet, the knights on board and the treasure then vanished from the pages of history[92].

It is also known that many Knights of the Order, rather than surrender, escaped to other countries where they could hope for sanctuary from sister organizations. Many of these warriors, being considered the best trained fighters in the world, helped change history in their adoptive countries. For example, it was a

---

[90] Howard, Michael THE OCCULT CONSPIRACY, Destiny Books, Rochester, Vermont. 1989.

[91] Baigent, MIchael and Richard Leigh, THE TEMPLE AND THE LODGE., Arcade Publishing. New York. 1989.

[92] Ibid

force of Templars that helped Robert Bruce finally defeat the English forces in Scotland in 1314.

It was actually a very small mounted force of Templars that routed the English Army that day. Such was the many stories about the Templar's legendary military prowess that the mere appearance of a Templar unit on the battlefield was sufficient to send the English army running for safer areas. So decisive was the Templar involvement in the Scottish fight for freedom that many have said that it was as a direct result of the Templar involvement, that Scotland was a free kingdom for the next 289 years[93].

The Order of the Templars, as it was called, had members throughout the then known world. Under the orders of Jacques DeMolay, the last known leader of the Templar Order, many of the survivors of the destruction of the Knights Templar merely changed the names of their orders.

In Portugal, the Knights Templar took the name of the Knights of Christ . It is known, or at least strongly suspected, that Columbus' father-in-law was a member of this Order and it was with nautical charts inherited from this relative that Columbus undertook his famous voyage of discovery[94].

CHRISTOPHER COLUMBUS, INITIATE?

There have been many who have speculated that this was just the first of many occult (remember the word occult merely means hidden) influences which were involved in making America a super power. There have also been hints that Columbus's association with the Templars may have been much greater than just being the son-in-law of a member of the Knights of Christ . In fact, judging by his prominence after his voyages, it would be surprising if Columbus, himself, had not been a member of this or another of the many secret societies.

There have also been many historians who assert that Columbus was an illiterate man who was educated by a guild of weavers in Genoa. However, others have pointed out that the guilds were often used as cover by various secret societies who wanted to keep their identities hidden. Unfortunately, this view of Columbus, as an illiterate sailor, is not borne out by his writings of later years.

Much that we think that we know about Columbus is actually legend and rumor. History does not speculate much about Columbus' ties to the various secret societies. It is known that Columbus had affiliations with supporters of Dante, a former Grand Master of the Order of the Rosy Cross. The romantic story of Isabella of Spain selling her jewelry to finance Columbus's voyages may also be suspect since proof has been found that his voyages of discovery were actually sponsored

---

[93] Ibid

[94] Howard, Michael, THE OCCULT CONSPIRACY, Destiny Books, Rochester, Vermont. 1989.

by none other than the famous Leonardo da Vinci and Loranzo de Medici, both members of a number of the powerful secret societies of the day. These two very influential individuals also found Columbus other wealthy patrons among European Royalty[95].

It is also known that Columbus was very religious, always wearing a brown robe and girdle similar to that worn by Franciscan Monks, and he always believed that he had a special mission in life. There are many who maintain that Columbus also heard spirit voices while in trances and he is said to have believed that the new world was actually New Jerusalem.

As history reports, later in his life, Columbus was disgraced and returned to Spain in chains only to be once again restored to favor and allowed one last voyage. His dream of a spiritual Utopia on Earth was not to be, as soon after this last voyage he died, and it was said that his dreams seemed to die with him.

SIR FRANCIS BACON

Taking Columbus' place as the torch bearer for the unseen powers hiding in the shadows in regard to the recently discovered new world was Sir Francis Bacon (1561-1626). Sir Francis Bacon has been credited with being a genius by many historians. It is even suspected that he was the actual writer of the works of William Shakespeare. What is known is that during his early days as a lawyer, Bacon was initiated into a Secret Society known as the Order of the Helmet. The members of this group worshiped the Greek Goddess of wisdom, Athene (who may also be another name for ISIS). Additionally, Bacon was a student of Hermetic, Gnostic and Neo-Platonist philosophy as well as a student of the Jewish Cabbala[96].

Bacon was also one of those called a Utopian who believed that in some forgotten golden age man lived as one people in peace. He worked for the creation of a future society where all man would live subject to one law and would have no war. (This sounds suspiciously like the "New Order" that the secret societies today work to create.)

Bacon was far more practical than most of the Utopians, he created a blueprint for this perceived new order. In 1627, he wrote a novel called THE NEW ATLANTIS. In this novel, he wrote of an Invisible College along the lines of the Rosicrucian teachings. In fact, much of his novel had a distinct Rosicrucian bent. This novel actually was the impetus for the founding of the Royal Society by the Order of the Rosy Cross during the reign of Charles II[97].

There are many who believe that Bacon led what amounted to a double life. As alluded to earlier, many have long suspected that he was actually the author of the plays of William Shakespeare. Historically, there has been found no

---

[95] Ibid
[96] Ibid
[97] Ibid

documents that can be proved to have actually been written by Shakespeare. Also Bacon was highly placed in the Elizabethan Court and this court, as Bacon often remarked, was one where poetry and the theatre were scorned. So it was felt that he would naturally hide his authorship behind the name of another.

Others even feel that Bacon was the real author of the works of other contemporary writers of his day such as Edmund Spenser, Christopher Marlowe, and Robert Burton to name but a few. It is strange that none of the original manuscripts of the above named writers have ever been found. In fact, in the case of Shakespeare, none of his supposedly hand written originals have ever been found. For such a prolific writer, this would seem to be almost impossible.

Bacon himself often alluded to the fact that he would be known for who he really was long after his death. Could it be that this early genius gave us some of our most remembered plays? Could some of his original manuscripts still be in existence today? This is a very real possibility.

In 1911, following clues that he said he found in some of Bacon's known writings, Dr. Orville Ward Owen, an American Baconian from Detroit, headed an expedition to the mouth of the Wye River near Gloucester, England. He believed that he had discovered an underground hiding place, beneath the riverbed, prepared by Bacon to hold secrets not meant for release to the Elizabethan World. What he found, after much searching was a room sized vault made of stone and cement hidden beneath the riverbed. Unfortunately, it was empty.

However, several thousand miles away was a similar hiding place that some now credit to Bacon as another possible location for a cache of his works, the mysterious treasure of Oak Island. In 1920, much evidence was found that could well link the research of Francis Bacon in the preservation of books and the Oak Island Treasure. Bacon wrote of using Mercury to preserve books over long periods of time and many Elizabethan Era containers that had contained Mercury were found in a trash dump on the Island. Could one of the greatest minds of history, and a probable member of several secret societies have created the engineering marvel of Oak Island? Only when someone can manage to defeat the brilliance of the engineers who built the "Money Pit" will we know for sure[98].

How can we be sure of Bacon's secret society membership? The title pages of many of Bacon's works featured Masonic symbols and other symbols of various secret societies, a definite clue to his affiliations. It was through these works that Bacon became one of the most influential writers of his day, an influential individual who was intent on spreading his occult philosophy.

---

[98] O'Connor, D'Arcy, THE BIG DIG, Ballantine Books, New York. 1978, 1988.

ROYAL CHARTER

In 1606, King James I set up the Virginia Company which was granted the power to begin settlements in the province of Virginia. In 1607, Jamestown was founded as the first settlement in Virginia. It is interesting to note who the early members of the Virginia Company actually were. These were aristocrats who supported the Church of England and the Royalist cause. Among this number were:

Lord Southampton

Earl of Pembroke

Earl of Montgomery

Earl of Salisbury

Earl of Northampton

Sir Francis Bacon (1609) also Chancellor

This creating of the colonies was actually the first step towards the American Revolution. For even though Bacon allegedly owed his loyalties to King James, it is widely believed that he actually helped found the colonies in the New World in order that they would one day break from the motherland and form a democratic society. A democratic society that Bacon felt would be a power base from which certain hidden forces could arise to change the world to conform to his ideas of world order.

This use of political office to carry out personal plans is a classic example of a government official placing his secret society goals above his loyalty to his government. In a speech to parliament, Bacon referred to the founding of the colonies as the establishment of Solomon's House in America. A clear reference to Masonic symbolism[99], as Solomon's House is a reference to the Temple of Solomon.

It is interesting to note that several members of Bacon's family actually settled in the new world. They may have been the literal trail blazers for the Puritan Sect who came in 1620. Interestingly enough, there is evidence that the first Masonic Lodges in this Country were formed in 1620. From this date forward, Masonic influence was strong in the colonies. This influence would become so strong that only six (6) of the fifty-six (56) signers of the American Declaration of

---

[99] Howard, Michael, THE OCCULT CONSPIRACY, Destiny Books, Rochester, Vermont. 1989.

Independence were not Masons[100].

COLONIAL ECONOMIC FREEDOM

In the beginning, the American Colonies had economic freedom. The various Colonies issued their own script as well as allowed the money of various nations that traded with the Colonies to be used as mediums of exchange. This meant that the Colonial economy was not only sound, but also self-contained and growing at a far higher rate than that of the mother country. The English merchants also took the Colonial mediums of exchange as payment for goods shipped to Colonial ports.

This was a sound system, but it meant that the Colonies were able to stand on their own two feet financially without having to ask for handouts from the English Parliament. This was not viewed as a good thing by certain influential powers in England as it meant that certain groups were not able to exercise much control over the Colonies. After a series of secret meetings, it was decided by these influential powers that steps were to be taken to put a stop to this growing independence. However, these steps had to be taken very circumspectly for fear of a backlash. The first step was to get control of both the English Monarchy and the British money supply.

THE FIRST MOVE TOWARD REVOLUTION

In spite of growing troubles, most of the American Colonists were loyal to England and their King. Had the English government governed fairly and impartially, instead of allowing others behind the scenes to dictate policy for the Colonies, the United States would probably be a British satellite today. However, in 1694, William III was in desperate need of cash. A group of wealthy Englishmen, under the leadership of William Paterson formed the "Company of the Bank of England" and offered to loan King William one million, two hundred thousand pounds (about six million dollars) at eight per cent interest on the express condition that the Bank of England be empowered to issue notes to the full extent of its capital[101].

Paterson later wrote that "If the proprietors of the Bank can circulate their own fundation of twelve hundred thousand (1,200,000) pounds without having more than two or three hundred thousand pounds lying dead at one time with another, this Bank will be in effect as nine hundred thousand pounds or a million in fresh money brought into the nation."

In other words, what the King gave the Bank of England, a group of

---

[100] Ibid

[101] Griffin, Des, FOURTH REICH OF THE RICH, Emissary Publications. 1984.

private citizens, was the power to create money from nothing. In return for the loan of twelve hundred thousand pounds to the King, the Bank of England got the right to take 1,200,000 real pounds and turn it into 2,400,000 pounds with the stoke of a pen. One half of this amount would be in gold and one half in worthless script. Additionally, this group of private citizens had the right to collect interest on the funds loaned to the King. Not a bad deal, all things considered. The result of this action by the King was to give virtual control of the English economy to a private group. For the sum of 1,250,000 pounds, loaned to the King, fully secured and subject to a substantial amount of annual interest, the Company of the Bank of England had "bought" the country of England.

THE ENGLISH CENTRAL BANK

The Bank of England was actually nothing more than a privately owned, privately controlled central bank. The formation of this English central bank had been made possible as a result of certain activities of the Bank of Amsterdam. It was the Bank of Amsterdam that had financed Oliver Cromwell's attack on the English throne. The alleged reason for the Bank of Amsterdam's involvement was the so-called religious differences between the English and the Dutch. The resulting English civil war between the Royalists, who supported the King and Cromwell's forces resulted in the defeat and ultimate death by execution of King Charles.

Cromwell had long maintained that he was not a king, but merely the leader of his country. However, when he died suddenly in 1657, he left his "throne" to his son[102]. Unfortunately, Cromwell's son was unable to hold onto the tremendous power left him, and his father's secret backers were unable to help him, for in 1660, King Charles II regained the throne taken from his father by Oliver Cromwell. England was "free" again.

However, after King Charles II's death in 1685, new plots against the English throne began to take shape. These new plots culminated in 1889 with the final overthrow of Charles II's line when William of Orange was crowned King of England. William was able to come to power through the assistance of the same forces that put Cromwell on the throne and then ultimately removed his son. To repay his backers for their support, King William did four things:

1. Ordered the English treasury to borrow 1,250,000 pounds from the same International Bankers that had supported his move to become King of England.

2. Issued a Royal Charter for the creation of the Bank of England, and

---

[102] Cromwell's victory over the forces of the English King may well have an occult aspect which will be discussed later.

3. Permitted this same Bank of England to consolidate the National Debt, which didn't exist until the borrowing of this same 1,250,000 pounds, and to secure payments of interest and principal on the national debt through direct taxation of the people.

4. Prohibited private goldsmiths from storing gold and issuing receipts, which had been a practice for several hundred years, having begun with the Knights Templar. These gold receipts had been circulated like money. This prohibition resulted in the Bank having a monopoly on money in England[103].

WILLIAM PATERSON, BANKER.

In a study of the personalities around William of Orange the name of William Paterson is always prominently mentioned. Paterson and a group of wealthy Englishmen were the primary ones to profit from William of Orange coming to the throne. So One area that should be examined is who were William Paterson and his "group of wealthy Englishmen"? To whom did King William turn over control of the English money supply in return for being given a throne? It is to be supposed that King William had never heard the statement, "It matters not who sits on the throne, but he who controls the money actually rules".

Research has shown that William Paterson was a Scot., born in 1658 and who died in 1719. Is it a mere coincidence that the idea that he proposed to King William was the very same fractional reserve system that had been developed by the Knights Templar centuries before? Remember that members of the Knight Templar sought refuge among the Scots and later fought for Scottish National Sovereignty against the English. In fact, it was a Templar charge against the center of the English line that turned the tide for the Scottish forces in the last war between English and Scottish Royalty and resulted in Scotland remaining free for almost three hundred years.

Is it possible that Paterson was a descendant of one of the intermarriages between Templar and native Scot? The Templars were well versed in the Middle Eastern traditions of conquer your enemies by appearing to join them. From this point of view, an Englishman, or any other race for that matter, can sit on the throne, but if you control the purse strings, then you control the kingdom.

Where would the Scots have gotten the funds to form the Company of the Bank of England, when Scotland itself was so impoverished as a result of the English war to subjugate its northern neighbor? England was also in dire straits

[103] Mullins, Eustace, THE SECRETS OF THE FEDERAL RESERVE., Bankers Research Inst. 1991.

financially as a result of the various coups and financial reverses it had suffered over the years.

Remember that the entire Templar treasury disappeared along with the Templar fleet and many of the high officials of the Order when Philippe the Fair moved to suppress the Order. Did the Templar treasury reappear in the form of the Bank of England?

Another fact that history has been quiet about is that in a power struggle that took place the year after the Royal Charter for the Bank of England was issued, William Paterson was ousted and ceased to have any involvement in the Bank's operation. Who would be in a position to oust someone so prominent and who apparently had the ear of the King, himself?

According to what can be found, Paterson found himself unable to work with the stockholders of the bank. Many of these stockholders remain anonymous, but what is known is that there were approximately thirteen hundred and thirty, including the King and Queen of England, the Duke of Leeds, Duke of Devonshire, Earl of Pembroke and the Earl of Bradford.

It is not known whether or not the Rothschild family had any involvement in the formation of this central bank, but it was Baron Nathan Rothschild himself who is known to have said: "I care not what puppet is placed on the throne of England to rule the Empire on which the sun never sets. The man that controls Britain's money supply controls the British Empire, and I control the British money supply.[104]"

I would submit that unless the Rothschild Family had some sort of involvement in the formation of or backing by the powers behind the Bank of England, that what Baron Rothschild said would not be possible.

It is well known that the Rothschild power in France was unbelievable. In Baron Edmond de Rothschild, David Druck wrote that "James Rothschild's wealth reached 600 million marks. Only one man in France possessed more; that was the King, whose wealth was 800 million marks. The aggregate wealth of all the Bankers in France was 150 million less than that of James Rothschild. This naturally gave him untold powers, even to the extent of unseating governments whenever he chose to do so. It is well known, for example that he overthrew the Cabinet of Prime Minister Thiers[105]."

If history would have us believe that the patriarch of the family, Meyer Amschel Bauer Rothschild, did not begin to achieve financial prominence until around 1800, then how could James Rothschild have a fortune second only to the King of France in 1850? No matter how brilliant an individual may be in business, fifty years is a very short period of time in which to secure such a fortune. What were the other factors that led to such untold wealth?

---

[104] Ibid

[105] Druck, David, BARON EDMOND DE ROTHSCHILD, privately printed. N.Y. 1850. reprinted in THE SECRETS OF THE TEMPLE. Mullins, Eustace.

THE MONEY POWERS THAT BE

This situation with the creation of the Bank of England proved that money could actually be created from nothing. This method of creating money used by the Bank of England was actually the forerunner of our own "fractional reserve system" instituted by the Federal Reserve System[106]. The major problem seen by critics of this system was that this power to create money was held completely in private hands, not those of a government answerable to the people.

As with most bankers, the powers behind the Bank of England were concerned, not with the public good, but with their own profit. The philosophy of the Bank of England seemed to be "If profits were good during good times, then they should be even better during bad times." And as with all bankers, the Bank of England soon discovered that it had the power to create the "bad times".

Once they had control of the economy, this "Group of Wealthy Englishmen" soon had direct control of the King. It was through this control of the King, that the "powers behind the scenes" planned to regain financial control of the Colonies.

Thus in 1720, the English Government put out instructions to all Royal Governors to allow no more printing of colonial currency without a suspending clause. As a result, by 1738 the colonial currency had become so devalued as against English money that English merchants really didn't want to take it in exchange. At the same time, the colonies were undergoing unparalleled prosperity[107].

The main reason that the Bank of England wanted the Crown to stop the colonists from using their own money was that by not using English currency, the colonists didn't have to pay interest to the European Bankers for the privilege of using it. As far as the Bankers were concerned, this was a source of revenue that was slipping through their fingers. So what if it caused untold trouble for the colonies and the Royal Governors, money was money.

In 1751, the British Board of Trade, at the urging of the Bank of England, submitted a bill to Parliament to completely ban the use of Colonial Currency in New England. This law, which was quickly passed by Parliament, resulted in the Colonists being forced to borrow from the European Bankers in order to be able to conduct trade. In 1764, this ban regarding the use of Colonial Currency was extended to the rest of the Colonies[108].

Our history books talk a great deal about unfair taxation as being at the basis of the unrest that left to the Revolutionary War. Actually, the real reason for

---

[106] Greider, William, SECRETS OF THE TEMPLE., Touchstone Books. New York. 1987.

[107] Griffin, Des, THE FOURTH REICH OF THE RICH, Emissary Publications. 1984.

[108] Ibid

the war was the revoking of the power to create money that the colonies originally had been granted by the Crown. The true facts were that the money powers, the Bank of England and the powers behind this institution, had gained control over all of Britain and then tried to extend that power to this country.

THE PLAN

The plan of the Bank of England was clearly to try and drown the colonies in a mountain of debt. No less a figure than Benjamin Franklin stated that "The Plan of our adversaries is to render the Assemblies in America useless. . .It is in our interests to prevent this."

Exorbitant prices were placed on goods shipped to the colonies. The Bankers had forced an over production situation in England which made the actual cost of items shipped to the colonies extremely cheap. Then the colonists were forced to pay dearly for these same items once these items arrived in the new world. The result of this situation was massive profits for those on the "inside".

At the same time prices were being kept artificially high, the same law required that the colonists to pay for the products sent from England in "hard money", (i.e. specie or gold and silver coins). This requirement had the additional results of draining the colonies of hard money gained through trade with other countries. Slowly, the bankers planned to gain total control over the financial life of the colonies.

To further enslave the colonists, Parliament then passed a law forbidding trade by the colonies with other countries. All goods must be purchased from England. This forced the colonies to borrow from the Bankers and again this added to their profits.

In order to try and survive, the Colonies decided to band together. In 1774, the first Continental Congress was convened in order to try and come to a solution. In October, 1774, the Declaration of Resolution was issued. A boycott was organized of British goods. England then forbad trading between England and the colonies. A move that had the impact of effectively isolating the Colonies.

In spite of the fact that the Crown was slowly strangling the colonies, there had been no talk of breaking away from the mother country. The colonists were still loyal to their King. The impetus for the revolution actually came from England. On August 23, 1775, King George III, on advice from his aides and in answer to demands from the Bankers, issued a Proclamation of Rebellion. It was actually King George III who started the American Revolution. Each side continued to escalate the matter until July 4, 1776, when the Declaration of Independence was signed.

This seemed to be a revolution that no one intended. As far as the colonists were concerned, they were Englishmen, in spite of some grievances, the vast majority of the Colonists had absolutely no intention of splitting off from the mother country. It was the manipulations and exploitations by the Bankers that forced the split.

PERSISTENCE PAYS OFF

Unfortunately, there is a great deal of proof that in the early 1900's these same forces once again seized control of the finances of the former colonies. It was with the passage of the Federal Reserve Act that the United States turned its financial future and control over its money supply over to the same forces that had tried on at least two occasions to conquer it militarily. This transfer of power was done in plain sight with the assistance of the very people charged with safeguarding the nation, treason so terrible that no punishment would be sufficient to sufficiently punish the traitor. When you see the names of these traitors in later chapters, you will be shocked and amazed.

THE UNSEEN HAND

The major question that I have to ask at this point in time is, "Was the American Revolution planned by the secret societies in existence at that time?" There is much evidence that the International Bankers were organized at a very early stage as a force to be reckoned with. According to most writers and researchers on this topic, the foremost of the International Banking powers was the Rothschild Family who went from relative poverty to the heights of power in a very short period of time. In a later chapter, we shall look at this remarkable family more closely, but for now suffice it to say that it was the International Bankers that actually manipulated the American Colonies into splitting from the Motherland. It is part of history that both the colonies and the British Government borrowed from the same group of International Bankers in order to finance both sides of the Revolution. Therefore, it is logical to ask if this was all part of some plan.

MASONIC INVOLVEMENT

A careful study of the American Revolution also reveals that the influence of Freemasonry was pervasive. For example, St. Andrew's Lodge in Boston was involved in the so-called Boston Tea Party and John Hancock, the first Continental Congress President, was a member of this same Lodge.

Even the colonial rallying cry of liberty, equality, brotherhood, tolerance and the talk about the rights of man were actually taken directly out of Masonic teachings. This identical phrase was also the battle cry echoed by the French Revolutionists, and part of a plan devised by Meyer Amschel Bauer Rothschild to insure world domination by a select few. This plan of Rothschild's is discussed in a later chapter.

Even the philosophy of the day as it filtered its way to the common private of the line in both the American and British Armies was Masonic in content. Surprisingly enough, every major Army unit on both sides of the Revolution had a Masonic Lodge incorporated into it. (I was also surprised to find that this situation is still true today.) If ever a country was dominated with Masonic teachings, it was the fledgling United States[109]. There is another major point that history has conveniently overlooked. Even though history makes it look as if it was the outstanding military accomplishments of George Washington that made him the unanimous choice for Commanding General of the Continental Army, this is not true. If the truth be known, Washington had several opponents who competed with him for the top position. Their credentials were as good if not better than his. It was actually Masonic influence that resulted in George Washington being appointed Commander of the Continental Army and later President of the United States.

According to contemporary writers, most of the members of Washington's military staff were Masons and letters of introduction to Washington from prominent Masons could result in a commission as an officer much quicker than a Congressional Appointment. It was Masonic influence and assistance that resulted in professional soldiers such as Pulaski and Lafayette arriving to help train the new Army. It could almost be said that without the Masonic brotherhood, there would be no United States.

Interestingly enough, the British commanders were also Masonic members. This brotherhood among both armies resulted in some almost comic and many unbelievable happenings as brother Mason appealed to brother Mason in the heat of battle. Many "miraculous" happenings are the result of Masonic assistance.

INDIAN MASONS?

Though most think of such organizations as the Masons as being part of the European or Middle Eastern races, there is a large body of evidence that the beliefs of this venerable organization had even penetrated the Americans in the 17th and 18th centuries. The evidence shows that even the British Army's closest allies, the Mohawks were not immune to Masonic appeals. The Chief of the Mohawks, Joseph Bryant, was himself a Mason. At one point in the war, when several Continental soldiers had been captured and were about to be killed by the Mohawks, one of them (a Mason) appealed to Chief Joseph Bryant based upon his Masonic membership and was spared.

So up to this point, we have seen the influence of several different Secret Societies in the creation of this great country and in the events that led up to the Revolution. As we will examine in greater detail in a future book, each of these secret societies was at one time a part of an even older order. But for now you must

---

109 Baigent, Michael, and Richard Leigh, THE TEMPLE AND THE LODGE., Arcade Publishing. New York. 1989.

be content with the knowledge that this is true. Many could and have argued that the events described above just happened, that there was and is no conspiracy.

Naturally in this book, I do not have sufficient space to examine this time period in detail, however, in the next chapter, the unseen hand and the underground conspiracy become much more apparent.

THE LARGER PICTURE

However, at the same time that the British and European Bankers were trying to strangle the Colonies, there were many other things happening in the world. Historically, the late 1700's and early 1800's were a time of great activity by many secret societies.

The following are but a few happenings from this time period[110]:

1701- War of Spanish Succession begins. Iroquois Confederacy makes treaties with both the English and the French.

1702- Queen Anne's War begins in America.

1706- Benjamin Franklin Born.

1707- Buffon and Saint-Germain born.

1708- William Pitt Born.

1710- St. Germain (famous alchemist) allegedly born.

1712- Frederick II and Rousseau born.

1713- Queen Anne's War ends.

1714- War of Spanish Succession ends.

1717- Founding of Modern Freemasonry with the Grand Lodge of London.

1721- Masonry introduced to France.

1723- Anderson's Constitutions of the Freemasons published. Also publication of Ebrietatis Enconium and other anti-Masonic books published.

---

[110] Wilgus, Neal, THE ILLUMINOIDS, Sun Books, New Mexico. 1978.

1724- Publication of anti-Masonic "Grand Mysteries of the Freemasons Discovered".

1727- Benjamin Franklin founds "Leather Apron Society", a secret society similar to Masons.

1728- Masonry introduced to Spain.

1729- Catherine II born.

1730- Masonry introduced to America and India.

1731- Franklin initiated into Masonry. The Leather Apron Society became the Junto Club and later became the American Philosophical Society.

1732- George Washington born.
1733- War of Polish Succession began.

1734- Franklin elected Grand Master of Pennsylvania. Masonry introduced to the Netherlands.

1735- Masonry introduced into Portugal, Russia and Italy.

1736- Masonry introduced into Switzerland.

1737- Thomas Paine born. Masonry introduced into Germany.

1738- George III born. Masonry introduced into Turkey. Anti-Masonic Papal Edict issued. Apology for the Free and Accepted Masons published.

1739- Masonry introduced into Poland.

1740- Maria Teresa become Queen of Austria, Bohemia, and Hungary; Frederick II becomes King of Prussia, invades Austria; War of Austrian Succession begins.

1743- Cagliostro, Thomas Jefferson, Marat and Meyer Rothschild born. Masonry introduced to Australia and Denmark.

1744- King George's War begins in America.

1748- Adam Weishaupt born. King George's War ends, War of Austrian Succession ends.

1752- George Washington initiated into Masonry.

1754- Louis XVI born. French and Indian War begins. Adam Weishaupt begins training with Jesuits. Elect Cohens, forerunner of Illumines or Martinists founded by Martines de Pasqually of Paris.

1756- Seven Years War begins.

1757- Appearance of Skoptsi or Castrator Sect in Russia.

1760- George III become King of England.

1761- Chinese Emperor issues edict against Secret Societies.

1762- Illumines of France founded. Catherine II overthrows Peter III in Russia.

1763- Seven Years War ends. French and Indian War ends with French losing all American colonies.

1765- British Stamp Act imposed to help pay for French and Indian War debt. Sons of Liberty clubs formed to resist tax.

1766- Stamp Act repealed. Illuminati of Avignon founded by Pernety.

1767- Townshend Revenue Act, another British Tax on Colonies. Elect Cohens introduced to Lyons.

1768- Virginia legislature dissolved by Royal Governor for its opposition to Townshend Act. Weishaupt graduates from the University of Ingolstadt.

1769- Napoleon born.

1770- Boston massacre: British troops fire into a crowd. Townshend Act repealed except for tea tax.

1771- Amalgamation of all French lodges into the Amis Reunis. Russian Government discovers existence if the Skoptsi

1772- Grand Orient of France founded. First Colonial Committee of Correspondence founded in Boston by Samuel Adams. California, New Mexico and Texas become Interior Provinces of Spanish Colonies.

Cossack Rebellion in Russia. Tay Son Brothers start rebellion against Nguyen Family in Vietnam.

1773- Amschel Rothschild born. British Tea Tax on Colonies; Boston Tea Party. Weishaupt marries. Meyer Amschel Rothschild and others meet to plan a world revolution. Suppression of the Jesuits. Decline of the Ancient and Noble Order of the Bucks, early version of the Odd Fellows. Pugachov uprising in Russia begins.

1774- William Morgan and Solomon Rothschild born. Britain's "Intolerable Acts" designed to punish the colonies. First Continental Congress; Washington begins training troops. Louis XV dies, Louis XVI becomes King of France.

1775- Second Continental Congress authorizes naval warships, sets up secret committee to procure weapons, names Washington commander in chief of the American Army. George III proclaims America in open rebellion. Battles of Lexington, Bunker Hill, and Ticonderoga. Beginning of the "Guerse de Farines" in which the people instigated by the Prince of Conti and other Masons, invade Versailles begging for bread from Louis XVI.

1776- Illuminati founded by Adam Weishaupt. American Declaration of Independence adopted by Continental Congress.

1777- Nathan Rothschild born. Weishaupt joins Munich Lodge of Theordore of Good Council. Articles of Confederation adopted by Continental Congress.

1778- France recognizes American Independence. Conway Cabal plots to replace Washington.

1780- Weishaupt's wife dies. Cagliostro and Knigge Illuminated, Illuminati begins rapid growth.

1781- Cornwallis surrendered at Yorktown. John Hanson becomes first President of the United States in Congress Assembled.

1782- British Cabinet agrees to recognize American Independence, agreement signed in Paris. Hanson commissions great deal and finishes term. Elias Boudinot elected second President of Congress Assembled.

1783- Treaty signed between America and England; Washington disbands

Army and resigns. Hanson dies. Thomas Mifflin elected third President of Congress Assembled.

1784- Treaty with England ratified by Congress. Richard Henry Lee elected fourth President of congress Assembled.

1785- Weishaupt flees to Gotha; New Edict Outlaws Illuminati; Lanz struck by lighting and Illuminati papers found.

1786- Police raids uncover Illuminati papers in homes of Zwack and Bassus. Mirabeau illuminated by Mauvillon. Secret Congress held in Frankfurt where Louis XVI and Gustavus III of Sweden are condemned to die by Illuminati. Nathaniel Gorham elected fifth President of Congress Assembled.

1787- German Union formed by Bahrdt as a successor of the Illuminati. Washington elected president of the Continental Convention; new constitution adopted by the convention. Arthur St. Clair elected sixth President of Congress Assembled. Thomas Jefferson went to Paris to meet with a Brazilian rebel to discuss American aid to the revolution in Brazil.

1788- Byron, Fresnel and Carl Rothschild born. American Constitution is ratified by the states. Cyrus Griffin is elected seventh President of Congress Assembled.

1789- Washington elected President; first congress under the new Constitution. French Revolution begins, fall of the Bastille.

1790- Rebellion and massacre throughout France. Franklin dies.

1791- Louis XVI attempts to escape and is arrested. Thomas Paine writes Rights of Man in England. The anonymous work, Vie de Joseph Balsamo linking Illuminati and the French Revolution appears.

1792- James Rothschild born. Washington re-elected. War between France and Austria. Paris mobs attack the Kings Palace; Swiss Guard is massacred, Monarchy overthrown. Assassination of King Gustavus III of Sweden.

1793-1795- French Republic. Hundreds of thousands die.

1795- French Directory begins.

The last decades of the 18th century were filled with wars, rebellions, and mobs dealing out death and destruction to the established order. As a result of the many revolts that shattered the accepted boundaries of society, the old order was almost forced to its knees. Were the many uprisings that took place during this relatively short period of time only coincidence? Or perhaps the culmination of a phase of a long established and long running plan carried out by a secret order older than civilization.

As history has shown, this secret order is not infallible nor is it always victorious. It is simply patient, wealthy and willing to work and wait for ultimate victory. So let us now move ahead in our examination and look at some of the major players.

CHAPTER EIGHT

THE PLAYERS

In order to thoroughly study, and understand, what makes up the Eternal Conspiracy today, it is necessary to look at the major players. That is those major players that we are able to identify as most of them seem to cloak themselves in complete secrecy. The names of individuals may change, but the same family groups and organizations tend to pop up from year to year. Many of these individuals and groups are household names, but very few seem to actually know what they are up to.

If a secret order is determined to completely control a populace, there are certain areas of society that must be dominated:

1. Finance – Most countries today have a central bank that actually controls the flow of money. Those who run these banks are not elected officials, but rather "businessmen".

2. Religion – Religion has become big business and as such they seek to distance themselves from their own members.

3. Manufacturing – In almost every country, the largest customers are normally the governments and in the largest countries, such as the United States, which once had a largest manufacturing base in history, the movement offshore of these manufacturing entities continual to weak the economy.

4. The Media – The media had long been controlled by the financial elite.

5. Politics – The unfortunate fact is that in this day and age, only the financially elite can afford to run for office. Generally, someone seeks office not for the direct

payment received as an office holder, but for the much more lucrative opportunities that can now be obtained. Is it coincidental that every single president has left office a millionaire?

Part of what we are going to do in this and the volumes to follow is to study how the Eternal Conspiracy has been able to control society as a whole. They have been able to do this through various organizations designed to expedite control. One of the major groups involved in this Conspiracy, in fact this particular group was probably formed in order to further the Conspiracy, has been a uniquely European Institution called the Merchant Bankers that has allowed them to control world finance.

WHEN IS A BANK NOT A BANK?

Most people have the mistaken idea that they understand what a bank is and what is has the power to accomplish. However, one type of bank, called a Merchant Bank, is not a Bank as is understood by the majority of the American people. In the United States a Bank is a privately owned, governmentally regulated institution designed (allegedly) to serve the needs of its depositors. A Merchant Bank, on the other hand, is a privately owned institution that is not regulated by any agency and is usually used to manipulate investments on behalf of the owners and their clients.

The basis of the Rothschild Family power has been a chain of Merchant Banks located throughout the European countries. Through this chain of private financial institutions, they have been able to form an unbelievable network of cooperating banks. This cooperation among Bankers has enabled the Rothschilds to amass what is probably the largest fortune in the known world and one of the single largest holdings of any family in history.

As a result of this chain of cooperating banks and partial ownership (and usually total control) of various nations central banks, the Rothschilds have been able to dictate financial policy the world over. Naturally when you control the world's money supply, you also control manufacturing, national financial policy, and to a lesser extent, finance and the media.

POLITICAL PLAYERS

There are only a few internationally known political figures, but these few exercise an unbelievable amount of power. I am not talking about elected figures, but I am talking about the few international politicians, allegedly working for their own countries, but actually pursuing policies that do not directly achieve this goal. These few individuals are the ones that have changed the world's political spectrum. It is most interesting to discover that each of these International, all powerful figures owe their position in one shape form or fashion to the Rothschild Family.

But, less I steal my own thunder, instead of listening to me talk about these people, in generalities, read on and see the details of the backgrounds and histories of some of the world's most private and powerful forces.

CHAPTER NINE

THE POWER OF THE INTERNATIONAL BANKERS

This act (The Federal Reserve Act) establishes the most gigantic trust on earth. . . When the President signs this act the invisible government by the money powers, proven to exist by the Money Trust Investigation, will be legalized. Charles A. Lindbergh Sr.

It would have been impossible for any organization, public or private, much less a shadowy conspiracy to have made the inroads that the Eternal Conspiracy has made into modern society without an almost virtual control over the finances of the effected countries. The Conspiracy of which I write buys who and what it wants using money taken from the pockets of those over whom it would rule. This conspiracy offers more to its members than just the hope of future power. It also offers immediate rewards that can be beyond your wildest imagination.

As a prime example, it seems outlandish to think that a second rate, unknown politician, from an obscure town in the state of Georgia can become President of the United States. Or how believable is it that a "B" grade actor who hasn't made a major movie in some years can become Governor of one of our most powerful States and then President of the United States? These and many more unbelievable things are possible if the person being discussed has the right backing.

If you are unprincipled enough to desire to be part of the Conspiracy, then the conspiracy can and in most cases, does, make many of your dreams come true. But there is no free lunch; there is a price for this bounty. Just remember, you will always be owned by the conspiracy, just like someone who deals with the Mafia. You can never leave the Conspiracy, except through death.

To add to the confusion that exists whenever anyone tries to identify this shadowy organization, there is even some question as to who or what makes up the conspiracy. Many writers seem to feel that the International Merchant Bankers are the top level of the Conspiracy and everyone else works for them. This is most definitely not true.

The Conspiracy, by whatever name you wish to call it, has been in existence for many, many centuries. During this period of time, the Conspiracy bought, and operated through Kings, Princes and Popes. The International Merchant Bankers have only been an effective tool since the late 1600's. However, it is true that since that time, the International Merchant Bankers have been the major force that has brought most of the world under the control of the Conspiracy.

The Elite Insiders of the Conspiracy are individuals who are above suspicion. These are not the side walk agitators of 1917 Russia, nor the Karl Marxs' freezing in a garret while re-writing an obscure document furnished to him in order to allow Marx to appear to create what became known as the Communist Manifesto. No, these Insiders are the little known, super-rich, but totally anonymous manipulators from countries around the world. The Elite do not soil their hands with killing and oppression, but instead, they open their checkbooks and pay to have their enemies killed. But, in spite of their "clean hands" their guilt is certain, nonetheless.

In their drive for world domination, the Elite Insiders have used many tools. Some tools are useful for only a short time and then disposed of, such as a Richard Nixon, or a Jimmy Carter while other tools are useful for much longer, such as an Edmond Rothschild. But sooner or later, each tool has outlived its' usefulness and is discarded. Only the Elite, themselves, go on indefinitely.

THE ELITE

There are many in the world who point to the Jewish Race as being the cause of and power behind the Eternal Conspiracy. Allegedly this is the reason for the continual oppression that the Jewish people have undergone for centuries as those in the know try to stop the forces of the Conspiracy. Literally hundreds of books and articles have been written making the Jewish Race, as a whole appear to be involved in the conspiracy. However, as I pointed out earlier, this blame for the ills of society and the allegations made against the Jewish Race as a whole are simply not true. The Jewish people, as a whole, are no more responsible for the beginnings of the Eternal Conspiracy than is Santa Claus.

Granted that it is true that many members of the Elite of the Eternal Conspiracy are of the Jewish Race, but this is about as relevant as saying that because most of the founders of the National Association For The Advancement of Colored People (NAACP) were Jewish that this organization is a Jewish Organization. These are simply facts of life. However, the fact that so many Jews have been used as front members of the Conspiracy has been used as a screen to point those who would look away from the truth.

THE POWER CENTER

One cannot discuss the power of the Elite Insiders without the discussion coming around to the very small, but very mysterious enclave known as the City of London. Not the London, England that we are familiar with, but THE CITY, a one mile square enclave within the actual confines of the modern City of London. Within this one square mile area can be found the financial power of this planet consolidated in one location. Within the confines of the City of London, even the Queen of England must bend knee to the Mayor of the City. It is from this power center that the Elite Insiders control much of their empire.

For so small an area, the City wields a totally unbelievable amount of political and financial power. Many are certain that this is the seat of the secret world super government. It is also believed that from this seat of power, all political and financial actions are monitored by this colossal organization[111]

In 1874, Walter Bagehot, one of the best known Victorian Bankers, called the City of London "by far the greatest combination of economical power and economical delicacy that the world has ever seen." On the surface, the City (always capitalized) has lost some of its power, but it still controls much of the financial world[112].

There is more money made and lost in the City in a single year than the yuppies of Wall Street have ever dreamed of. It provides the so called "invisible earnings", estimated to be in excess of two hundred million pounds a year that helps Britain's balance of payments.

The City of London has a way of life that has gone unchanged for some five hundred years. The City has some very bizarre rules, but if you understand them and abide by them a fortune can be made. Some of these rules are hopelessly outdated, but if you try to change them, chaos would result. For example, the Bank of England is still guarded every night by a detachment of the Brigade of Guards, who each day in full dress uniform, march there to the sound of drums. This detachment of the Brigade of Guards has marched there each day since 1780, when a mob tried to storm the Bank. While there has not been any further trouble of that nature since 1780, but the Bank of England wants its Guards[113].

It is in the narrow twisting streets of the City of London where the operational arms of the conspiracy can be found, usually operating out of a peculiar firm known as a Merchant Bank. Not a true Bank in the terms that most of us think of in the United States, but a Bank in the European tradition. But make no mistake, these are very powerful institutions.

It was through the creation of the Merchant Banks and the various central

---

[111] Knuth, E.C., THE EMPIRE OF THE CITY, The Noontide Press, P.O. Box 1248, Torrance, CA 90505. 1983..

[112] Wechsberg, Joseph, THE MERCHANT BANKERS, Little Brown and Co. Boston, Toronto.1966.

[113] Ibid

banks of the many countries that the Conspiracy was able to utilize its' most potent weapons, an inflatable currency. This creation has been the means of enslaving us all.

Who, individually, actually started the original Conspiracy, eons ago, is a matter of conjecture. But whoever he, or she, was, they planned well. This Conspiracy has been so effective and so secret that even today, many do not believe it even exists, even though it has its' foot on the throat of us all. One master stroke was gaining control of the economy of the various major countries. For as we have observed before, if you control the money, especially an inflatable currency, you in the end, control the controllers. Therefore, one important tool that would be required for any group to aspire to total world domination would be the creation of or control of one of the major private banking houses of the world. Just such a creation was the world famous House of Rothschild.

THE HOUSE OF ROTHSCHILD

Naturally, no book on International Bankers, nor the Conspiracy for that matter, can be complete without discussing the most effective tool the Conspiracy has forged in centuries, the Rothschild Family. No Family has profited more from their involvement with the Conspiracy nor has any one family done more for the Conspiracy than this International Banking Family. From a minor cog in the infant wheel of international finance, in a few short years, the Rothschild family was a major force in the western financial world.

The Rothschild Family has been useful in several ways, as follows:

1.) Gave conspiracy researchers a visible target, i.e. International Merchant Bankers. Many have mistaken the tool for the user. In other words, many have come to believe that the International Bankers were the Conspiracy. This has been useful in taking the spotlight off of the real powers that actually pull the strings. As I observed before, the International bankers have done much to move the world toward a one world government, but their moves were all part of a grand design created by another.

2.) Since the Rothschilds are Jewish, (Meyer Amschel Bauer Rothschild was a Hassidic Jew. Hassidic Jews are among the most fanatical of the Jewish people and known for being very single minded in their approach to any issue. Rothschild (or Red Shield) believed that God has promised the Jews the ruler ship of the earth and he and his descendants worked tirelessly to accomplish this end) many have come to believe that the Conspiracy is a totally Jewish Plot. It is true that many of the visible power brokers are Jewish, but I think that this is more coincidence than design. For some reason, members of the Jewish race do tend to gravitate towards centers of financial power, have no qualms about manipulating matters to their advantage and are probably among the more ruthless of Bankers, but to describe the creation of such a vast century spanning Conspiracy as being totally Jewish in nature is to over look many of the facts. The religious affiliations of the Elite Insiders cover the gamut from Jewish to Catholic and everything in between. But it is useful as a distraction to have the world believe that the Conspiracy is purely a Jewish creation.

3.) Gave the Elite Insiders a willing, useful tool to almost virtually control the finances of the Western World.

However, make no mistake about it, the Rothschild Family, important as it is, is nothing more than hired help as far as the real Insiders are concerned. For without the help of the Elite Insiders, the Rothschild Family would probably not have the International Power that it does today.

The first reference to the Rothschild Family that can be found is dated 1585 and mentions Isaak Elchanan at the Red Shield (the word Rothschild actually means red shield). From this date until the early 1700's, the family trade was principally retailing. But in the early years of the 18th century, the family became money changers. Additionally, unlike many Jewish Families living in Frankfort-On-The-Main, they were not poor, but reasonably well off.[114]

In 1755, when Meyer Amschel Bauer (the name Rothschild was actually adopted by Meyer Amschel Bauer at a later date) was twelve, his father and mother died, leaving him an inheritance. So at an early age, he was thrown on his own to sink or swim.

Due to the chaotic conditions prevailing in Germany during these years, there were many opportunities available for someone who was smart and had a little money. Since Meyer Amschel Bauer had been employed by his father since age ten in money changing, he had a very good idea of the usefulness of money and also was able to spot the occasional rare and valuable coin that came into his hands. Additionally, since Germany was so divided into small countries, before anyone would depart on a trip of any length, they had to go to the money changer to have their coins changed into the currency of the country for which they were bound.

Meyer Amschel Bauer first went to work for the firm of Oppenheim at Hanover. During this time he made the acquaintance of a powerful military officer, General von Estorff. General Von Estorff was an coin collector, who paid the young man to find rare coins for his ever growing collection. Since the General was connected with the ruling house of Hesse, young Bauer saw a chance to use this new connection to his advantage and he used it very well indeed.

---

[114] Corti, Count Egon Caesar , THE RISE OF THE HOUSE OF ROTHSCHILD, Western Islands, L.A. CA.1972.

Later, Bauer's contacts with the General and his knowledge of coin collecting resulted in Meyer being brought into contact with Prince William of Hesse, son of Frederick II of Hesse, grandson of King George III of England and son-in-law of King Frederick V of Denmark who was also married to a daughter of King George III of England.

In 1769, Meyer Amschel Bauer used his contacts with the Prince to petition for a title, a title in those days being very useful. The petition was granted and so on September 21, 1769, to the name Rothschild was attached the title, "Crown Agent to the Principality of Hesse-Hanau." The title stood him in good stead, opening several doors that would have been closed to him otherwise due to his ethnic origin.

Prince William, Bauer's benefactor had married before Bauer did, but found that he had little liking for his bride. Bauer, on the other hand took a bride he deeply cared for and founded a family that eclipsed the power of many titled heads of Europe. Incidentally, Prince William founded several lines, all illegitimate. The Haynau, Heimrod, and Hessenstein lines are all descended from Prince William.

Prince William was known for his very broad religious views, associated much with Masons and practiced complete religious tolerance within his domain. Additionally, he was a very smart business man. Following in the footsteps of his father, Prince William sold his own Regiment of soldiers to England in 1776. At this particular time, England was desperate for new military troops to use in trying to hold her empire together, for this reason, a sizeable portion of the British forces in the field were mercenaries hired from other European countries. As a result of his sharp business dealings with the British Government, Crown Prince William cleared a profit of 3,500,000 marks from his "selling" of his soldiers.

These funds were managed for the Prince by the Amsterdam financial house, Van der Notten. Often England would pay in Bills of Exchange, which had to be discounted. This task was handled for the Prince by another Jewish agent, Veidel David[115]. When the bills of exchange were converted into cash, the funds were then turned over to Van der Notten. At this time, Meyer Amschel Bauer Rothschild was a very small fish indeed in an ever growing ocean.

In 1785, the Prince's father, Frederick II, died leaving the Prince a fortune of an unheard of amount and the throne of Hesse-Cassel. The Prince continued to conduct international business, but used tried and true agents, unfortunately for him, not Rothschild. It was not until 1790, that Rothschild's father-in-law brought him together with a Crown Treasury official named Buderus.

Buderus had become the Prince's favored treasury official when he found a way to increase the Prince's income from one of the Prince's dairies. As a sign of the Prince's favor, Buderus was entrusted with the accounts of the Prince's private purse. Being aware that his favored status would last so long as he could please the

---

[115] Ibid

Prince, it was Buderus who was responsible for the creation of the Salt Tax, which greatly increased the Prince's revenues. Naturally, after the introduction by his father-in-law, Rothschild sought out Buderus and made a great friend of him. It was this friend, Buderus, who finally convinced the Prince to entrust Rothschild with the handling of some of his bigger accounts. In fact some accounts state that Rothschild and the Prince became such good friends that they were inseparable, with the Prince even taking Rothschild to Masonic meetings where his advice was eagerly sought after by the members. According to these same stories, Rothschild was a de facto member of the Masonic movement even though his religion and the Masonic rules forbade him from becoming an actual member.

It was the French Revolution that actually began the real rise to public prominence of the Rothschild Family. As a result of the confusion caused by the execution of the King of France, and Napoleon's later rise to power, the political climate in Europe drastically changed. The old established ways of doing business had to change to keep up with the changing political conditions.

While these momentous events helped the cause of the Frankfort Bankers, it was the conquering of Holland by the French in 1795 that caused the greatest of good fortune for the enterprising Merchant Bankers of Frankfort. The very powerful Amsterdam Bourse, which had handled much of the European financial transactions for all of the titled families of Europe up until that time, almost totally collapsed as a result of the invasion by the French. With few avenues open to the wealthy, this collapse of the established order brought the bulk of the business to Frankfort and the Bankers of this city. Foremost among them to receive some of this new business was the good friend to Prince William, Meyer Amschel Bauer Rothschild[116].

Rothschild had raised a large family, which now stood him in good stead. Instead of being forced to hire strangers into his business who could later become competitors, Rothschild put his children, and their spouses, to work in his Merchant Bank. As a result, the inter-workings of the Rothschild Bank always stayed confidential.

Prince William, seeing a tremendous opportunity available to him after withdrawing from the war against the French, became a banker to most of the European World. In the negotiating of the numerous loans that funded the continuing wars that swept Europe, Jewish middlemen were normally used to ensure the safety of the principals. Soon the Rothschilds were acting as the liaisons between many of the rulers of the day. Their influence was spreading, as was their fortunes. Between 1795 and 1800, Rothschild's assessed wealth went from 2,000 gulden to over a million gulden. This is quite an increase for a man who had begun his career as a humble Jewish merchant.

In 1798, Meyer Amschel Bauer Rothschild's youngest son, Nathan, decided to move to London and open a branch of the family Bank. He took with

---

[116] Ibid

him approximately twenty thousand pounds (or a quarter of a million gulden) as the initial funding for this first branch of the House of Rothschild. During the Napoleonic Period of France, the Paris office of the House of Rothschild was opened. The financial empire, as well as the influence of the Rothschild Family was growing.

ROTHSCHILD COMES OF AGE

According to what we have seen so far, it would be difficult in the 1790's for Rothschild to have wielded the amount of power that would have been required for him to have been a major force in the events that led up to the French Revolution, since he was only worth a million gulden in 1800. However, what we have seen thus far is not the entire story. What we have seen thus far was the "public" story of the rise of the House of Rothschild.

According to William Guy Carr, in his book, Pawns In The Game[117], at the same time that Rothschild was beginning his public climb to fame and fortune, there appears to have been a private series of activities that did more to extend Rothschild's power that all of his banking efforts put together. In fact, it would appear that Rothschild's entry into service as a member of the Eternal Conspiracy seems to have happened prior to 1773. For it was in that year that Rothschild, supposedly a mere Merchant Banker trying to establish his business in other countries, called for a meeting to be held in his home town of Frankfort. Attending that meeting were twelve of the wealthiest and most influential men in Europe.

Now picture this if you will, a young Jewish man, Rothschild was only thirty years of age when he organized this meeting, calls for twelve of the top men in Europe to make the long and difficult journey to Frankfort to meet him and wonder of wonders, they actually come. How can this young man wield this type of power in a period when Jews were considered third or fourth class citizens and barely tolerated at best? I would submit that some unseen power was already sponsoring him prior to this time, a power that these twelve knew of, respected highly and perhaps feared.

ROTHSCHILD'S PROPOSAL

At this meeting, Rothschild proposed that these twelve wealthy and influential men join with him in pooling their resources in order that they might finance and control the World Revolutionary Movement. He further purposed that they use the World Revolutionary Movement to win ultimate control of the wealth, natural resources and manpower of the entire world. Though the entire idea sounded ludicrous, when offered the world, these twelve powerful men agreed to

---

[117] Carr, William Guy, PAWNS IN THE GAME, Privately Printed. 1956.

join with Rothschild and even more amazing, grant him total control over the pooled resources. This agreement reached, Rothschild proceeded to lay out his plan.

Rothschild proposed that the program be backed by all of the power that their combined resources and political connections could buy. Through the manipulation of this same wealth, it would be possible to create such adverse economic conditions that the population of the target country could be reduced to a starvation level. Then the conspiracy could send in paid propagandists to rouse the people against the established order and incite revolution. Potential enemies could be attacked with "invented infamies" that would bring them into disrepute.

This is the identical program that was used to incite the French people to turn against their rulers. I would submit that, in fact, the first "test" of Rothschild's program was the French Revolution.

Further parts of Rothschild's program were laid out in a manuscript that he presented to the assembled members of his "conspiracy". The major points raised in this manuscript were as follows[118]:

1. LAW was FORCE in disguise.

2. Political freedom was only an idea not a fact. In order for the conspiracy to usurp political power all that was necessary was to preach "Liberalism" so that the voters would yield some of their power and prerogatives which the conspiracy would gather into their hands.

3. The Power of Gold had usurped the power of Liberal rulers and it really didn't matter whether the conquerors of a nation were internal revolutionists or external invaders because the winner would have to come to the conspiracy for financial help.

4. The use of any and all means to reach their final goal of world domination was justified on the grounds that a ruler who governed by the moral code was not a skilled politician because he left himself vulnerable and in an unstable position.

5. The right of the conspiracy lies in force.

6. The power of the conspiracy must remain invisible until the very moment when it has gained such strength that no cunning or force can undermine it.

---

[118] Mullins, Eustace, THE SECRETS OF THE FEDERAL RESERVE., Bankers Research Institute. 1991.

Other points raised by this manuscript to which Rothschild referred included:

1. The use of liquor, drugs, moral corruption and vice to systematically corrupt the youth of the world.

2. The right to seize property by any means and without hesitation, if by doing so they secured submission and sovereignty.

3. That the conspiracy had been the first to put the phrase Liberty, Equality and Fraternity into the mouths of the masses. (This three part phrase had been a Masonic teaching for hundreds of years. Additionally, it was the battle cry of those who brought about the French Revolution.)

4. A new aristocracy would be created which would be based on wealth and wealth would be controlled by the Conspiracy.

5. Future wars would be directed so that both sides had to borrow from the Conspiracy and thus get further into debt.

6. All outlets of information, i.e. the media, would be controlled by the conspiracy.

7. Panics and financial depression would be controlled and would to eventually result in a new world order and a One World Government.

The next two hundred years saw the House of Rothschild make its' greatest profits during times of wars and financial upheavals. In other words, this plan has been religiously followed[119].

HOW TO PRESERVE THE FAMILY FORTUNE

When Meyer Amschel Bauer Rothschild died, he left a most unusual will, which, with the exception of a few key clauses, has remained secret to this day. His will was very specific in it's' instructions to his heirs and the punishment for any one who failed to follow these instructions was said to be severe. A few of the rules laid down in his will that have leaked to the public were as follows:

---

[119] Knuth, E.C., EMPIRE OF THE CITY, Noontide Press. P.O. Box 1248, Torrance, CA. 90505. 1983.

1. The eldest brother shall be the head and manager of the Rothschild wealth in its entirety. The rule of seniority does not exclude the rule of ability, but the latter can be applied only after a vote from the whole family.

2. All marriage of family were to be made within the family, among cousins, so that the wealth may not be divided or lost to outsiders.

3. The wealth shall remain undivided.

4. Meyer's will shall not be shown to anyone outside the family.

5. The Orthodox Jewish faith shall be kept by each and every member of the family.

6. All public inventories should be avoided and no inheritance suits should be filed among family members. Anyone who does not follow this rule shall be deprived of his inheritance.

7. The entire wealth, which is to remain undivided, shall be owned jointly by the family and managed only by the men. The women members of the family, as well as the husbands of the Rothschild's sisters do not have the right to participate in the firm's management.

By this will, Meyer Amschel Rothschild intended to and did create a financial dynasty that now holds the world by the throat.

THE PROBLEMS WITH KINGS

As Meyer Amschel Rothschild had discovered, there were fortunes to be made financing Kings. However, the lenders do face certain problems, such as what kind of collateral does a country give for a loan? What if the King has the Banker killed rather than pay off the loan?

According to economics Professor Stuart Crane, there are two means used to collateralize loans to governments. Just as a business gives up some control over its policies in return for loans, so governments have given up some political control in return for the billions upon billions of dollars that International Bankers have loaned over the years. Probably the most influential individuals in international politics are the International Bankers[120] However, the ultimate advantage that an International Banker has is that if a country gets out of line, then the Banker can finance the enemies of that uncooperative country. This was a game that the

---

[120] Allen, Gary and Larry Abraham, NONE DARE CALL IT CONSPIRACY, Double A Publications, Suite 403, 18000 Highway South, Seattle, Washington 98188.

Rothschild Family learned well how to play and one of the major points outlined by Rothschild in his meeting with the twelve conspirators referred to above. Meyer Amschel Rothschild eventually had five sons and positioned them to best serve the conspiracy. One ran the Frankfort Bank and the other four ran Banks in London, Paris, Vienna and Naples[121].

According to several authorities in the field of economics, at the end of each war of the nineteenth century, there was a new structuring of the "balance of power" around the House of Rothschild in England, France and Austria. Each power block was used as a threat to keep the others in line and ensure that loans were repaid. Many of these wars of the nineteenth century were actually manipulated in order to "punish" countries or rulers who did not toe the Rothschild political line. While the Rothschild Family was obviously not the originators of this procedure of using the threat of war as a collection method, they did refine it to an art form. Over the centuries since the Rothschilds have become a power in the Conspiracy, millions have died so that the Rothschilds could be sure of making a profit.

---

[121] Ibid

CHAPTER TEN

OTHER MAJOR PLAYERS

Of course, the Rothschild Family was not the only family that the conspiracy worked with or through. Though the conspiracy does not want any competition, it will not, knowingly, create a monopoly for one of its' hired minions. After all, the conspiracy doesn't want any internal power struggles.

Of almost equal statute to the Rothschild Family is the Hambro Family. In fact, the Hambros Bank Ltd. is the world's largest Merchant Bank[122]. Naturally, the site of this major bank is in the famous City of London.

Hambros Bank Ltd. prides itself on being consciously unorthodox. It will cater for anything that involves money. The risks are unimportant, in fact, some of their greatest profits have been made from reverses to the British Empire. So how did this Bank get this attitude, indirectly from the United States?

CARL JOACHIM HAMBRO

Carl Joachim Hambro came to the United States in 1830, intending to work as a commercial apprentice. While here, he learned a new method of milling flour by the use of steam. This knowledge he promptly turned into money in Sweden. This began a tradition of investment in the U.S. market.

Like the Rothschilds, the Hambros made much of their fortune out of war and misery. It would seem that while the Rothschild's were at the center of the European dealing, the Hambro's dealt with those that were not deemed important

---

[122] Wechsberg, Joseph, THE MERCHANT BANKERS, Little Brown and Co. Boston, Toronto.1966.

enough for the Rothschild's to support. It was as a result of funding the war that his native Denmark was having that Carl Hambro became Danish Baron Carl Hambro. In spite of this, Hambros Bank, Ltd. was still in the shadow of Rothschilds. However, the Hambro's were powerful enough to be called the "King Makers[123]."

It was with the help of Carl Joachim Hambro that Italy was unified and the Italian Royal Family was placed on its throne under King Victor Emmanuel. Without the financial support of the House of Hambro, the unification would have been impossible.

The revolutionaries in Italy were all working to forge a new country out of the several smaller warring states on the peninsula. However, as a simple fact of life, without funds, no new country can be born. The faction trying to unite the country sent representatives to England to ask for the help of the Rothschild Family. They were refused. Then they turned to Carl Hambros.

With the help of the Hambros Bank, Ltd. a bond issue was floated and funds were raised to allow the fight to be carried on to its conclusion. So it was that King Victor Emmanuel was eternally indebted to Carl Hambro.

Two years later, Carl Hambro again "stage managed" the placing of a second ruler on a throne. This time, the Country in question was Greece. In 1862, a revolution had deposed King Otto, son of King Ludwig of Bavaria.

The Greek people wanted Prince Alfred, second son of Queen Victoria as their new King. However, under an agreement, Great Britain, France and Russia had agreed that no member of their Royal Families would sit on the Greek Throne. Therefore, it was forbidden that Prince Alfred become King Alfred. Into the breach stepped Carl Hambro.

A Dane by birth, Carl Hambro used his influence and connections to suggest that the Greek emissaries look at Prince Wilhelm of Denmark. It just so happened that Prince Wilhelm "happened" to be visiting London at the same time the Emissaries were there. It was also strictly coincidence that Prince Wilhelm and Baron Hambro happened to attend the same church service that the Emissaries did and that they were able to get a good look at him. From this coincidence, Prince Wilhelm was offered the throne of Greece[124].

Though the evidence that Carl Hambro was involved in the conspiracy is circumstantial at best, it is a fact that Carl's oldest son, Everard, who became the sole owner of Hambros Bank, Ltd. after Carl's death in 1877, was a close friend of John Pierpont Morgan, a major Conspiracy member in the United States[125].

---

[123] Ibid

[124] Ibid

[125] Ibid

THE BARINGS.

Much less known than the Rothschild Merchant Banks, but probably as powerful is Baring Brothers & Co. Limited. At Two hundred and Two years old, it is the City of London's oldest Merchant Bank. The English Barings were founded in 1717 by a German, Johann Baring, who moved to Exeter in that year. Johann (later changed to John) Baring died in 1748 leaving four sons. It is these sons who developed the name Baring into a synonym for wealth and power.

Historically, the merchant bankers of London are the true descendants of the merchant traders of Venice. The wealth and power developed by these trading families was maintained by intermarriages between the merchant families and other wealthy families. In this way, truly unbelievable fortunes were created and maintained.

The Barings were the greatest international Bankers on the European scene long before the Rothschilds were even thought of as Bankers[126]. In fact, as recently as 1903, a German diplomat reported to the Foreign Office in Berlin that "anybody who wants to place a loan in London on a grand scale must apply to the Barings." In other words, the Barings were some of the major powers on the European scene until recently, and are probably still forces to be reckoned with in the financial world.

It has been said that the Bank of England is the "mother bank" of the international conspiracy. If this is true, then the Barings are still powerful forces, for no other Merchant Bank in London has sent as many directors to the Bank of England. These directors have been:

Alexander Baring-1805

Humphrey St. John Mildmay

Thomas Baring

Edward Charles Baring (First Baron Revelstoke)

John Baring (Second Baron Revelstoke)

Sir Edward Peacock

George Rowland Stanley Baring (Third Earl of Cromer) appointed as Governor of the Bank of England in 1961.

The Baring family has five separate peerages, (Ashburn, Northbrook,

---

[126] Ibid

Revelstoke, Cromer and Howick) and has been a major power both in the City and in Government for centuries. Using this power, the Barings have financed both sides of wars and have even been able to supply Britain's allies by sending shipments through the enemy's lines with impunity. The Barings even sent supplies to the American Colonies through the British blockade.

It was banking families such as the Barings, and they were, in fact, foremost among them all, that worked to make Britain a great mercantile power. It was, in turn, this mercantile power that allowed the founding of the British Empire.

Up until the American Civil War, the Barings were deeply involved in financial transactions in the United States. Almost all investment in the United States from England was handled by Barings as an intermediary.

It was the Barings that taught the United States Government the mechanism of influence and control that has been developed to an art in this Country.

In 1783, Francis Baring, the younger son of John Baring the founder of the English Barings, and partner in John and Francis Baring & Company in London (the firm that later became the Merchant Bank) opened a business in Philadelphia and became associated with the local business powers called the Philadelphia Group. Among the members of this group were Robert Morris, Thomas Willing, William Bingham and Robert Gilmore.

William Bingham was reportedly the richest man in America and it was he, who in 1793 offered Francis one and a quarter million acres in Maine at a cost of two shillings per acre. In 1795, Francis sent his son, Alexander to look the matter over and two years later, Alexander returned home with the land purchased, a new wife, Anne Bingham, William's daughter and a nine hundred thousand dollar dowry. It was also in 1795 that Barings became an international banker for the United States Government.

In 1798, the Barings assisted the United States in the undeclared war against France by purchasing armaments and shipping them to the United States. Then in 1802 when the Louisiana Purchase took place, it was the Barings that financed the transaction. The most interesting thing about this transaction was that at the time that Barings began to finance the deal, Britain was at war with France. Barings asked the British Government for permission to complete the transaction since it would give France much needed capital with which to conduct its war against Britain. However, in spite of the sheer lunacy of the request, which would aid Britain's enemy, Britain gave the deal the go ahead.

All in all, the Barings were the premier financiers until 1818 when they were the powers behind the sale of French Bonds. Shortly before this, France had been in grave need of raising capital in order to pay restitutions to the British arising out of the Napoleonic Wars. However, there was simply no money left in France. What France did have, however, was credit.

The French contacted Barings and worked out the deal for selling French

Bonds. During two issues of bonds the deal made millions for all concerned. However, just prior to the third issue, the Rothschilds asked to have a piece of the pie. Barings was willing, but Hope & Co. of Amsterdam, the world's oldest merchant bank, and a partner in the bond deal, was not willing to let the upstart Rothschilds into the transaction.

In revenge, the Rothschilds used French money they were handling on other transactions for the European Powers to buy up the French Bonds forcing the price to rise. Naturally some of the leading statesmen of the day purchased the bonds. Then without notice, Rothschild's dumped their bonds on the market, forcing the price to drop like a rock. The future of the bonds was destroyed and hundreds of investors lost their investments. But the worst was that the Merchant Bank of Baring Brothers lost its place among the premier Merchant Banking Houses. They were eclipsed, from this time forth, by the House of Rothschild.

So began the dominance of the Rothschild Family that has lasted to this day. Has this dominance been beneficial to the world in general, or detrimental? One result of this dominance is that today, the House of Rothschild controls the majority of the central banks of the world. This gives definite credibility to the information in the last chapter regarding the secret meeting of the twelve wealthy men with Rothschild in 1773. It would seem that the House of Rothschild may be the only ruling house left in the world.

Still doubt me, well read on and decide for yourself.

CHAPTER ELEVEN

THE ROCKEFELLER DYNASTY

"Competition is a sin." John D. Rockefeller Sr.

There is much that is uncertain about the Rockefeller family. The line seemed to come from obscurity almost overnight. No one is even sure what their ethnic origins might be. According to one story, they are descended from French Protestants. Another story points to their having a German origin; while still another theory, which seems to have much merit, is that the Rockefellers are actually Jewish in origin[127]. However, in checking some of the research found in THE ROCKEFELLER FILE, referenced above, I went to Dr. Malcolm Stern's work entitled AMERICANS OF JEWISH DESCENT and found that indeed, the evidence supports the idea that the Rockefeller Clan is probably of Jewish origin.

Whatever may have been their origin, this family has come, in this last part of the twentieth century, to be one of the dominate forces in world politics. Who are these financial rulers? When and how did they amass their wealth?

WILLIAM ROCKEFELLER

Grandfather of the current generation of the Rockefeller family was William Rockefeller. Nicknamed "Doc", this Rockefeller was a traveling medicine man who sold bottles of petroleum, at $25.00 per pint, as a cure for warts, snake bite, cancer and numerous other ills. In other words, he was a traveling con man. It was this traveling con man that gave birth to the men who came to control America.

---

[127] Allen, Gary, THE ROCKEFELLER FILE., '76 Press, Seal Beach, CA.1976.

JOHN D. ROCKEFELLER SR.

John D. Rockefeller Sr. was probably the most intelligent of William's children. He also went on to become one of the most hated men in America due to his totally ruthless business moves. Though he, like so many others, professed to be a deeply religious man, he proceeded to make a mockery of everything that he professed to believe in by destroying anyone and anything that stood in his way as he moved to the top of the financial world.

It was in 1859 that John D. Rockefeller Sr. first became involved in the infant oil business. While still in his late teens, he had been a broker in Titusville, Pennsylvania, when his partners asked him to go look at the new oil business. After his study, he decided that while the search for oil could make the lucky finder a lot of money, the refining of the crude oil was what he considered the most profitable end of the business. It was at this time that he decided to start the company that became known as Standard Oil.

Standard Oil eventually became the original basis of the Rockefeller vast fortune. To Rockefeller, the only efficient way to run a business was by having a monopoly. However, at the time he started Standard Oil, there were numerous small competitors in the marketplace. This was soon changed as Rockefeller's Standard Oil began to dominate the market through the use of coercion, bribery, kickbacks and other underhanded schemes.

Rumor also has it that when negotiations failed, John D. Rockefeller was not above a little violence when needed. Using these techniques, coupled with what appeared to be unlimited wealth (from an unknown source) Rockefeller built an empire that spanned the globe.

According to Ferdinand Lundberg in his book The Rich and the Super-Rich, "Rockefeller was of a deeply conspiratorial, scheming nature, always planning many years ahead." The characteristics described here are those that are mentioned when discussing the members of the conspiracy. Additionally, this is the same advance planning always shown by the Conspiracy. Additionally, there are many rumors that the Rothschild Banks financed the original operation of Standard Oil. In other words, we have now come full circle and found the hand of the all powerful Rothschild clan once again. Could the Rothschild Banks have been the source of Rockefeller's seemingly unlimited source of funds?

Most people think of oil when the name Rockefeller is mentioned, however, today this commodity is now just a small cog in the Rockefeller machine. Let us look at the development of and some of the enterprises that the Rockefeller Empire encompasses.

* As an example of the wealth of Standard Oil (a.k.a. Standard Oil Trust, Standard Oil of New Jersey, Esso and Exxon) according to the February 18, 1974 of Time Magazine, this company declared annual profits of $2.4

Billion Dollars, the largest annual profits ever earned up to that time by any industrial company. Current figures for this company are seemingly hard to get for recent years.

* As of 1974, according to Fortune Magazine, if Exxon were shorn of is' foreign holdings it would still be the 9th largest industry in the United States.

* Individually and through family trusts, the Rockefellers have effective working control over Mobil, Standard of Indiana, Standard of California and many other allegedly competing oil companies.

The Rockefeller family controls First National City Bank (Citicorp) and Chase Manhattan Bank (created by the merging of Rockefeller owned Chase Bank and the Kuhn, Loeb controlled Manhattan Bank).

As of 1971 Chase claimed $36 Billion in assets, but this only included assets directly owned by Chase, not the business conducted through affiliated banks.

Chase (as of 1974) had 28 foreign branches wholly owned by it and over 50,000 corresponding banks.

Chase is the only bank that has a full time envoy at the United Nations. The Chairman of chase has also met with heads of state and conducted international diplomacy on the same par as a head of state. A lot of power for a "simple" businessman.

* Chemical Bank of New York is yet another Rockefeller controlled institution. It is controlled by the Harkness Family, but Edward Harkness was one of John D. Rockefeller's closest associates.

* The Rockefeller Group of Banks is, as of 1974, heavily interlocked with the board of directors of Metropolitan Life, Equitable Life and New York Life. Control of these insurance companies gives the Rockefeller Group access to billions and billions of investment dollars through the assets of these three giant insurance companies.

* According to various sources (as of 1975), the following companies are owned (either through individual holdings of stock by the family or the family trusts), or controlled (through control of the major banks or "friendly boards) by the Rockefeller Group:

Exxon

Mobil Oil

Standard of CA

Standard of California

International Harvester

Inland Steel

Marathon Oil

Quaker Oats

Wheeling-Pittsburgh Steel

Freeport Sulphur

International Basic Economy Corporation

United Airlines

Northwest Airlines

Long Island Lighting

Atlantic Richfield Oil

National Airlines

IBM

Mobil

Texaco

IT&T

Westinghouse

Boeing

International Paper

Minnesota Mining & Manufacturing

Sperry Rand

Xerox

National Cash Register

National Steel

American Home Products

Pfizer

Avon

Merck

Penn Central

TWA

Eastern

Delta

Braniff

Allied

Anaconda Copper

DuPont

Monsanto

Olin Mathison

Borden

National Distillers

Shell

Gulf

Union Oil

Dow

Celanese

Pittsburgh Plate Glass

Cities Service

Stauffer Chemical

Continental Oil

Union Carbide

American Cyanamid

American Motors

Bendix

Chrysler

C.I.T. Financial

S.S. Kresge

R.H. Macy

Consider that the above list is just those interests that are known about to the average reader of financial journals. What is not known about is the staggering amount of political power that the head of this financial dynasty can command. The fall of the all powerful Nikita Khrushchev took place immediately after a Rockefeller "vacation" to Soviet Russia, at a time when international tensions were at an all time high. A coincidence?

CHAPTER TWELVE

THE GAMES BANKERS PLAY

"The tragedy of war is that it uses man's best to do man's worst." Ralph Waldo Emerson

In the last chapters, we have seen how the financial control of the world has become consolidated in the hands of a few International Powers Brokers, called Merchant Bankers. Each of these Power Brokers is linked to the others by both personal and business ties. Many of these families have followed the example set by Mayer Amschel Rothschild and carried out programs of intermarriage so that their power and their fortunes would not be "diluted" by marriages with outsiders.

So what has been the actual power of these particular International Bankers and how have they used this massive power? Would you believe that a few men have been responsible for the changing of the social structure of their time and eventually affected the lives of every living American? The very idea boggles the mind of the average man on the street. How can the activities of mere bankers change the social structure of the entire world? However, an astute reader of history can find the hidden hand of the International Bankers involved in several key situations in history.

There are many researchers who feel that the Eternal Conspiracy has taken control of various countries and used these countries for the carrying out of the wishes of the hidden powers. This is called the Conspiracy Theory of History by the liberal establishment and is ridiculed at every opportunity. However, again, an unbiased reading of history will tell enough that the astute reader can detect the manipulations of entire countries by forces that seem to be random in nature, but actually are highly sophisticated in their actions and effective in their programs.

The most obvious meddling with the social structure of the western world came during the late 1700's, when Agents of Meyer Amschel Rothschild instigated the French Revolution[128]. Now there have been allegations against the Rothschilds for almost two hundred years, but no one has produced any concrete proof. In order to get a clear picture of the situation as it was during the time of Meyer Amschel Rothschild and to see some of the proof of his involvement, let's examine the events that led up to the French Revolution.

THE FRENCH REVOLUTION

King Louis XVI, in spite of what our "unbiased" history books tell us about this man, was a good king. Upon assuming the throne, of his own initiative, he began to institute many reforms designed to bring France out of the dark into the sun. He willingly instituted many changes that both benefited his people and stripped the nobles of hereditary powers. The revolt that began in 1789 was started, not by the French people, but by outside agitators financed by those who would maintain the status quo. The original leaders were, perhaps not surprisingly all members of the Royal faction who were jockeying for the power they felt would be theirs if the liberal King Louis were to be deposed. The feeling was that Louis XVI was too radical, for the changes that the King proposed would have severely limited the power not only of the nobles but that of the King, himself[129].

The unrest began as early as 1778, when the Grand Orient Masonic Lodges of France, under the leadership of the Illuminati and Adam Weishaupt, began to plot and plan for the revolution. The reader must remember that Weishaupt's goal was first the overthrow of the French Monarchy then the Roman Catholic Church. His first move in this direction had been the infiltration of the Masonic Lodges of France.

Weishaupt had long been rumored to be funded by Rothschild and it did seem that his moves were well financed. As far as anyone could figure out at the time, the plan seemed to be for the revolution to sweep away the monarchy and bring on a general state of war in Europe with Rothschild financing all sides.

Of course, Rothschild, assuming that he was really the mastermind behind the Revolution, was not pinning all his hopes on the Masonic Lodges. His agents organized and funded several other political factions, such as the Royalist-anti reformists; the pro Duke of Orleans faction; the Girondins, the Jacobins (named for Jacob Joseph and Jacob Isaacs, friends of Rothschild. The Jacobin Clubs were organized in France, England, Germany Italy and many other countries) the

---

[128] Webster, Nesta H., THE FRENCH REVOLUTION, publisher unknown.

[129] Nicolov, Nicola M., THE WORLD CONSPIRACY, TOPS, 10170 S.W. Nimbus, Portland, OR 97223. 1990..

Montagnards, the Dantonists, the Sans Culottes and others[130].

So involved in the politics of the various European Powers were the members of the Jacobin Clubs that the term Jacobin became a name for the "Old" Masonic Order and the backers of the "Pretender" to the British Throne. In fact it was funds raised by the French Jacobins that paid for the ill fated invasion of Scotland by "Bonnie Prince Charlie".

What is the most bizarre of the entire matter was that at the very same time agitators were inciting the people against the King over his alleged failure to institute various political reforms; the King was trying to institute the very reforms that the revolutionists wanted. Therefore, the French Revolution was totally unnecessary and actually resulted in making conditions for the French people much wore than they already were. There was absolutely no need for millions of innocent people to die in order to "free" the people from the King. However, only under the chaotic conditions of civil war can millions of deaths be justified and an entire country looted by those motivated solely by profit.

Naturally, besides conspirators, in order to have a successful revolution, money is required. Those behind the French Revolution had a large amount of ready cash, enough to import foreign thugs and killers and keep them on a retainer until it was time for them to go into action. These funds allegedly came from the Rothschild Banks, funneled through the Illuminati[131]. Many have doubted the involvement of the Rothschilds in the atrocity known as the French Revolution. However, there is fairly substantial proof available that in fact the Rothschilds were, if not actively behind the conspirators, at least helped with their funding.

A WITNESS

According to several sources, the Famed Magician, Cagliostro, was enrolled in Germany in the late 1700's as a member of the Illuminati. In fact for several years, he acted as a recruiter and a messenger for the leadership of the Order. He was directly responsible for recruiting some of the most influential personages in Europe into the organization.

However, the powers that controlled Europe were not asleep. Cagliostro's travels were watched with a very careful eye by several of the more astute European Leaders, among them the Pope. In 1790, Cagliostro was interrogated by the Holy See in Rome regarding his membership.

According to his testimony, during his initiation into the Illuminati, Cagliostro was allowed to examine papers that stated the aims of the Illuminati was to overthrow the existing thrones and altars and that the first throne to be attacked would be that of France. The second prong of the attack on society would be against the Church of Rome, itself.

---

[130] Ibid

[131] Ibid

Knowing that such activities take a great deal of money, The Church was quite interested in what Cagliostro knew of the Order's funding. It seemed that he did know something about the funding of this monstrous conspiracy. During the time of his indoctrination, Cagliostro found out, from his Initiators, that the secret society possessed a large sum of money dispersed in banks in Amsterdam, Rotterdam, London, Genoa and Venice[132]. Cagliostro maintained that some of the documents he read mentioned that the Rothschilds' had charge of the Order's funds.

It is also a fact that at this period of time, only the Rothschild Family had the organization and network necessary to handle such a large mass of funds for such a clandestine operation. This allegation by Cagliostro is especially important if you remember the secret meeting referred to in Chapter Nine where Rothschild and the twelve co-conspirators pledged to use their resources in order to fund the World Revolutionary Movement[133].

THE ROLE OF SECRET SOCIETIES

There have been many stories regarding the involvement of many different secret societies in the French Revolution. I am sure that all of us have heard the story of the man who jumped onto the Guillotine when King Louis XV's head fell into the basket, dipped his finger into the Royal Blood and yelled to the crowd "Jacques DeMolay, thou art avenged."

Assuming the story to be true, the gentleman was of course referring to the suppression and destruction of the Knights Templar by the French throne. Jacques DeMolay had been the last known Grand Master of the Knights Templar. Philippe the Fair, King of France had coveted the treasures of the Templars and, with the agreement of the Pope, he moved to arrest the Knights and seize their treasures. However, the best laid plans of mice and men are sometimes doomed to failure.

To everyone's amazement, the entire treasure of the Templars was missing and most of the Knights were gone. There were always rumors that the Knights of the Temple had merely gone underground rather than disbanding. It is known that the Templar's vast naval fleet and most of the treasure of the Temple vanished from France and have never been seen since[134]. It may well be true that the Templars' acting from behind whatever front they had created for themselves, had a hand in the overthrow of the Royal line.

What is known is that the International Merchant Bankers, especially the Rothschilds, had a hand in the funding of the Revolution. The Rothschilds were, in

---

[132] Webster, Nesta H., WORLD REVOLUTION, Constable & Co. LTD., London. 1921.

[133] Carr, William Guy, PAWNS IN THE GAME, Privately Printed. 1956.

[134] Baigent, Michael and Richard Leigh, THE TEMPLE AND THE LODGE., Arcade Publishing. N.Y. 1989.

a way, heirs of the Templars. The Knights Templar had pioneered the banking trade, actually issuing a form of bank draft that could be obtained at one "Temple" and cashed at another. Allegedly, they were the first of the International Bankers. The Rothschilds were actually following in the tracks of the Knights Templar. Could there possibly have been a more solid connection?

There is some evidence that the Templars had been planning some sort of way of becoming a major force in Europe. Much of their power as well as their reason for existence had vanished when the Holy Land had been retaken by the Moslems. If Rothschild's mysterious backers were descendants of the Templars and the Templar fortune was put at his disposal, then this would explain how Rothschild could become so powerful so fast.

A REVOLT OF THE COMMON PEOPLE

History records and teaches us that the French Revolution was one of the few times in history when the government was so despotic that the common man took to the streets to change things for the better. However, as we have seen above, this was just not so. True the masses did rise up in revolt, but at foreign instigation.

Rather than besmirch the names of agents of the conspiracy, and not wanting to place their own necks at risk, those who write of this period try and place the blame for such things as the Reign of Terror on the frustration of the oppressed masses. However, the actual truth is that the majority of the more bloodthirsty of the "common people" were actually little better than cut throats and killers of the lowest social class. Their targets for "Madame Guillotine" was anyone who they had a grudge against, no matter how insignificant. The true "victims" of this revolt, besides the nobility, was the middle class, the backbone of French Society.

So thoroughly was the middle class decimated that most skilled trades in France were hard to fill. Many services were almost non-existent until new people could be trained. Some victims were chosen for death simply because someone thought that they were obviously "high born" and turned them in as enemies of the Revolution.

What most students of history have missed is that this alleged movement of the people was shrewdly manipulated by an inner circle made up of some of the very elements that the revolution was supposedly aimed at overthrowing, members of the Nobility. In fact, records have shown that one of the prime movers behind the uprising was Louis Philippe, the Duke of Orleans, cousin to the King[135]. The Duke recruited Mirabeau, a talented speaker, and spent a fortune recruiting agents to incite the masses. In fact, it was the Duke of Orleans' agents that actually caused the food shortages in Paris that was one of the main causes of the revolt against Louis

---

[135] Nicolov, Nicola M., THE WORLD CONSPIRACY, TOPS, 10170 S.W. Nimbus, Portland, OR 97223. 1990..

XVI.

At this point, I would again remind the reader that one of the main points in Rothschild's proposal for World Domination was that the financial resources of the conspiracy would be used to manipulate the economy of the target country so that shortages would occur that would anger the masses against their leaders. Eventually, the anger of the population would become so out of control that they would rise up and depose their leaders. This is exactly what happened in the French Revolution.

Once the French government had fallen and the King was imprisoned, it was a small clique of rebel leaders that actually made all of the decisions. In spite of the French slogan of "Liberty Fraternity and Equality" the masses were still being led around by their noses by those in power. The newly elected National Assembly was merely a rubber stamp for the actually group of men that seized power during the confusion. This small group of power brokers ruled with the same unfettered power as the King had enjoyed, that is, until the inner circle had a falling out among themselves over the best course of action to take to solidify power. To no one's surprise, members of the leadership began to die as well, almost as if their hidden masters no longer had any use for them. Remember my early remark about tools disposed of when no longer needed?

There has been much written, both pro and con, regarding the involvement of the Masonic Orders in the instigation of the Revolution. I would think that it is hard to miss the involvement of the more common secret societies such as the Masonic Orders in the Revolution since the very slogan of the Revolutionaries, "Liberty, Equality, and Fraternity[136] " was lifted directly from Masonic teachings. However, some people see only what they want to see.

It is most interesting to note that even Robespierre, one of the most powerful and radical men in Revolutionary France, claimed before the Assembly on June 26, 1794 (in his last speech) that:

"*I don't trust all of these foreigners whose faces are covered with patriotic masks and who try to appear better Republicans than we are. These agents of foreign powers must be destroyed.*[137]"

Unfortunately, Robespierre never went as far as naming these agents of foreign powers or even the identity of the foreign powers. Perhaps he never had time to name names, because for his daring at pointing the finger at his true masters, Robespierre, himself, was sent to die in the public square. Like many others who had achieved the heights of power with the assistance of the

---

[136] Webster, Nesta H., THE FRENCH REVOLUTION, publisher unknown.

[137] *Nicolov, Nicola M., THE WORLD CONSPIRACY, TOPS, 10170 S.W. Nimbus, Portland, OR 97223. 1990..*

Conspiracy, he had dared to think himself too powerful to be removed and he tried to use his power to attack those who had placed him in power. He was wrong.

THE SUN NEVER SETS ON THE BRITISH EMPIRE

There has been a great deal of information circulated regarding the Conspiracy that allegedly has its' headquarters in the City controlling the British Government. There are numerous writings that tell of the power and control wielded by the rulers of this one mile square enclave. If these stories are true, then it would seem that there would be some evidence that British foreign policy would seem to openly favor the International Bankers. Amazingly enough, if the allegations are seriously considered it appears that there is such evidence proving that a Conspiracy exists.

It would seem that since the rise to power of the Rothschild Clan in controlling the finances of Britain, that every major war has seen the total destruction of the "enemy". This has led to the "reconstruction" of the defeated country's economy by loans from the International Bankers and resulted in the creations of new power blocks that have resulted in ever larger profits for the Eternal Conspiracy.

The first, and the most overwhelming evidence of British Government assistance to and domination by the International Bankers, and the major rise in Rothschild fortunes, is found during the Napoleonic Wars. The payrolls for the British troops serving on the Continent were difficult to get to their destination until it was decided that the House of Rothschild should handle the payments through their French Offices. By the end of the war, the House of Rothschild had firm control of British finances and was the official banker of the British Government.

The most interesting part of this entire scenario is that there is much evidence that Napoleon received much of his support and funding for his wars from the French Branch of the House of Rothschild. After the death of his father, Napoleon, then a Major in the Artillery, was in dire financial straits. According to history, Talleyrand introduced the young Napoleon to Amschel Rothschild who was looking for a protégé.

Rothschild desired a leader who would carry out his wishes and assist in his plans to weaken the Catholic Church and keep Europe in a constant state of War. Accordingly, he ordered his banks to finance and protect the young man. Napoleon used this protection and funding until he reached such a pinnacle that he declared himself Emperor.

Napoleon apparently thought that he was invincible and this well appeared to be true. No power on the planet was able to stand before Napoleon's armies. It was only when Napoleon turned on his Masters, by trying to put the welfare of his subjects first, that he was brought down into ruin by the very man who had raised him to power. It only cost millions of lives and millions of dollars to do the job.

Britain dedicated over two decades to trying to bring down Napoleon.

Even so, in spite of the fact that the rest of Europe was united against him, Napoleon would probably not have been defeated at Waterloo had he not become ill and Marshall Soult been placed in command of the French forces. Later Napoleon, himself, wrote that he felt that he had been poisoned in order to keep him from leading his troops. Marshall Soult was a relative, a cousin, I believe, of the Rothschild Family.

BRITISH MILITARY FORCE

As an example of the continuing pro-war stance of the British Government, let us first examine the modern cyclical wars that were conducted by Britain and her allies during the period from 1793 to 1918, then we will look at the wars conducted by the "Allies", as the post imperialist period has become to be known. Most of the cyclical wars were entered into in order to preserve or control the shifting balance of power; however, some were actually wars of imperialistic expansion. The listing of these modern cyclical wars is below[138]. Those cyclical wars that are considered of major historical importance are so indicated. Also indicated are those that were actually wars of imperialistic expansion.

Cyclical Wars

1. Napoleonic War - 1793-1815
England, Prussia, Sweden, Russia and Austria
vs.
France

2. Turkish War - 1827-1829
England, France and Russia
vs.
Turkey and Egypt

3. Crimean War - 1853-1856
England, France, Turkey and Sardinia
vs.
Russia

4. American Civil War - 1861-1865 (Considered pivotal)
England, France, Spain and the Confederate States of America
vs.

[138] Knuth, E.C., THE EMPIRE OF THE CITY, The Noontide Press. P.O. Box 1248, Torrance, CA 90505. 1983.

Russia and the United States

5. Franco-Prussian - 1870-1871 (Considered pivotal)
France, England and Austria-Hungary
vs.
Germany, Russia and Italy

6. Russian-Turkish - 1877-1878
Turkey, England, France and Austro-Hungary
vs
Russia and Germany

7. Egyptian War - 1882-1885 (Imperialistic Expansion)
England, France and Austro-Hungary
vs
Egypt, Turkey and Russia

8. Spanish American - 1898-1899
United States and England
vs
Spain and Germany

9. Sudan War - 1898-1899 (Imperialistic Expansion)
England
vs
Sudanese-Egyptian Nationalists
10. Boer War - 1899-1902 (Imperialistic Expansion)
England
vs
Orange Free State and South African Rep.

11. Partition of Siam - 1899-1909 (Imperialistic Expansion)
England and France
vs
Siamese Nationalists

12. Russian-Japanese - 1904-1905 (Pivotal)
Japan and England
vs
Russia and Germany

13. Morocco Conflict - 1904-1906 (Imperialistic Expansion)
"The Allies" and Italy

vs
Germany and Austro-Hungary

14. Persian Conflict - 1907-1912 (Imperialistic Expansion)
England and France
vs
Russia and Germany

15. Morocco "Affair" - 1911 (Pivotal)
England and France
vs
Germany

16. Tripoli War - 1911-1912 (Pivotal)
Italian reward or material quid for quo
vs
Turkey

17. 1st Balkan War - 1912-1913 (Pivotal)
Greece, Serbia, Bulgaria and Montenegro
vs
Turkey

18. 2nd Balkan War - 1913 (Pivotal)
Rumania, Greece and Serbia
vs
Bulgaria

19. World War I - 1914-1918
"The Allies" and Italy, Rumania, Greece, Serbia, Montenegro and others.
vs
Germany, Austro-Hungary, Turkey and Bulgaria.

These wars were for the most part, entirely unnecessary until one looks at what took place in order for these wars to happen. The British Government was forced to borrow vast sums of money from the International bankers in order to pay for the troops to fight these wars. At the same time, the "enemies of Britian" were borrowing from these same International Bankers in order to pay for their side of these same wars. This resulted in vast fortunes being made for the Bankers while thousands of British troops died on the battlefield. This little detail was overlooked by the Bankers as they rejoiced over the accomplishment of another of the points in Rothschild's plan for world domination.

CHAPTER THIRTEEN

THE PLAN CONTINUES

In the first book in this series[139] I discussed the evidence that the Conspiracy may be using a type of germ warfare as part of its programs in order to reduce the population of this world. Additionally, there is evidence that this germ warfare program may be being conducted against certain racial or sexually oriented groups. I discussed the research of Dr. William Campbell Douglass and others in laying out a scenario that would substantiate my theory.

As you might recall, Dr. Douglass stated that AIDS had been created at Fort Detrick, Maryland and then used to contaminate the small pox vaccination program of the World Health Organization that was conducted in Africa. I was amazed with the number of responses that I received to this particular chapter in the earlier book. This caused me to delve further into the question of whether or not there was a solid basis to the theory that AIDS and other diseases may have been intentionally created by scientists.

There have been advanced two alleged reasons for such a deadly program being carried out. The first was that it was part of a germ warfare attack on the free world by the Communist nations. As proof of this allegation, researchers pointed to the fact that many loyal Communist Scientists were involved in the research at Fort Detrick, Maryland, the alleged starting point for the AIDS virus. The other scenario and the one to which I attach credence is that AIDS and other deadly viruses have been created at the orders of the Conspiracy and are being used to selectively eliminate segments of society that do not fit in with the master plan devised by the hidden Masters.

My scenario would explain why these germ warfare programs are so

---

[139] Hudnall, Ken, THE OCCULT CONNECTION: UFOs, Secret Societies and Ancient Gods, Omega. Press, El Paso, Texas 79912. 1996.

widespread. For example, the continent of Africa has untold riches in mineral deposits, but the unstable political situation and the warlike local inhabitants make it impossible to openly mine these riches. However, if for some reason all or most of the local inhabitants of the target regions died or were forced to move away or were too ill to oppose a take over, then these riches could be mined in peace and quiet. The owners of these mining operations would become wealthy over night. I would suggest that this is a major incentive for anyone with the resources to do so to create a virus to decimate the populations of undeveloped countries.

MAGIC

In our modern world, technology has reached a point where we can actually work what our ancestors would call magic. Unfortunately, so much of this super technology has been subverted to serve the purpose of those who would dominate and enslave us. A case in point is the almost pathological fear that most third world countries have regarding our main intelligence organization, the world famous, or is it infamous, Central Intelligence Agency (C.I.A.).

Most of us, if we give it any thought at all, shrug off the rumors regarding C.I.A. atrocities. After all, we are the good guys, how can we be doing the things that have alienated a good third of the world.

THE CENTRAL INTELLIGENCE AGENCY (C.I.A.)

The Central Intelligence Agency was created from the Office of Strategic Services (OSS) of World War II fame. It had been decided that in the post World War II world that America needed a good intelligence service. Originally, its' mandate was to gather information from foreign countries and turn this information over to experts to study. Unfortunately, when powerful people are allowed to work in darkness and secrecy, they tend to procure additional power.

As a very real example of what uncontrolled power can do when coupled with immoral medical experiments, it is known that in the 1950's, Allan Dulles, then Director of the CIA., and a member of the Council on Foreign Relations (CFR) and a Rockefeller crony, backed a program involving strange, experimental medical procedures and mind control. In and of itself, he probably had the authority to authorize such a program, but he went one step beyond, he authorized a program to be developed that could control people against their will. In other words, he was looking for a way to enslave the minds of others.

This unauthorized program was carried out in Canada in order to try and limit leaks and bothersome exposure to potential media problems. In these Canadian experiments, the CIA backed the work of Dr. Donald Ewen Cameron, a world famous psychiatrist who developed a technique he called depatterning, or destroying one's personality through electro-shock, drugs and surgery[140].

As a perfect example of what can happen when immoral men are given unlimited power, Dr. Cameron, with CIA knowledge and support, trained some of the most infamous "torturers" known in the world today. It was one of these "medical men" trained by Dr. Cameron that worked on the C.I.A.'s own William Buckley, station chief in Beirut, Lebanon who was kidnapped and broken by terrorists[141].

It is acts such as these that have caused rumors to run rampant throughout the world that the CIA is behind almost every evil from acid rain in the Far East to the famine in Ethiopia. It would be laughable if it were not for the fact that it has turned out that our CIA has, in fact been behind much evil in the third world countries. As if this weren't bad enough, there are even stories leaked to the media that our own CIA may be responsible for one of the most deadly diseases of our time, AIDS.

Is this rumor true? Is a branch of our own government in the business of wiping out entire segments of the human race? There are many who believe that the CIA may have created the AIDS virus to wipe out the gay population or perhaps to depopulate the continent of Africa. Of course, the CIA has been a Third World whipping boy for years.

It was to prove or disprove this theory that started me on my research into the question of whether or not the CIA, or any other U.S. Government Agency, for that matter, might have created the AIDS virus. I wouldn't have been surprised to discover that the answer to the question was in the affirmative, but the preliminary results of my research shows that while it probably wasn't the CIA., as an organization, that is, that created AIDS, there is a great deal of data that does make it look like this deadly disease was created in the laboratory and was not a natural occurrence.

During the course of my research, I came across an unbelievable number of articles, newsletters and books that dealt with some of the little known information regarding the origins of the AIDS virus. Most of these documents contained information that tended to discredit the official position as espoused by the Center for Disease Control (CDC).

To make matters even worse, I found some information that made it appear that there might even be a conspiracy to keep the American Public misinformed. According to a Dr. Robert G. Grant, "there is a conspiracy of silence although at times it seems more to resemble a campaign of disinformation with clear political overtones[142]. This is certainly a very strange approach to so deadly a disease. Why would government organization charged with combating AIDS put out disinformation about that disease that would tend to confuse the population and

---

140 Thomas, Gordon, JOURNEY INTO MADNESS., Bantam Books. N.Y. 1989.

141 Ibid

142 Grant, Dr. Robert G, "Emergency Disease Alert--AIDS," American Christian Voice, Box 37053, Washington, D.C.

disrupt programs designed to stop the disease?

One of the most fascinating of the newsletters that I found was a copy of a newsletter called *THE BULLETIN OF THE COMMITTEE TO RESTORE THE CONSTITUTION*[143] that is dated March, 1988. In this news letter is a reprint of an article by Dr. William Campbell Douglass M.D. entitled "WHO MURDERED AFRICA". This was not intended to be a rhetorical question for according to Dr. Douglass, the WHO stands for the World Health Organization, an agency of the United Nations.

This article, discussed below, originally appeared in the September, 1987 issue of *THE CUTTING EDGE*[144] Dr. William Campbell Douglass, publisher. This magazine is a continuing update on the AIDS epidemic. This article was also the basis for a chapter of my earlier book.

THE WORLD HEALTH ORGANIZATION

For those who are not aware of the existence of the World Health Organization, it is a creation of the United Nations. Allegedly, the World Health Organization was originally intended to combat diseases on a world wide basis; unfortunately, it has become, according to many, merely a propaganda tool for Eastern Bloc Countries. However, now it is necessary to ask, is the World Health Organization (WHO) responsible for the spread of the AIDS virus? Dr. William Douglass makes it quite clear that, as a result of his research, he believes that the World Health Organization has been responsible for millions of deaths in Africa. These deaths were not caused directly, of course, but, instead were done through the use of the AIDS virus.

Such an accusation is bad enough, but to make matter even worse, he goes on to say, we have all had our lives endangered by this disease. In other words, he throws out the concept of the "dangerous classifications" and takes the position that we are all in danger from this killer disease.

As Dr. Douglass correctly points out, AIDS is a virus, and like all types of virus, by its' very nature, it can be passed on to others. This would seem to make it appear that the CDC's position that AIDS can only be passed by "close" sexual contact or sharing a dirty needle.

As Dr. Douglass also so correctly points out, a common cold is a virus, just like AIDS is a virus. We have all, at one time or another had a common cold. We have all caught colds and not known how we caught them. We have also all been around a friend who has a virus and later come down with the virus ourselves.

---

[143] Roberts, Archibald E. LT COL., AUS, ret. Director, P.O. Box 986, Ft. Collins, CO 80522. (303) 484-2575.

[144] THE CUTTING EDGE, Douglass, Dr. William Campbell M.D., 2470 Windy Hill Rd., Suite 440, Marietta, GA 30067.

Consider the implications of what would have happened if the common cold was as deadly as AIDS.

SEX

In the area of sex, there has been much talk regarding the passing of AIDS and other virus' through "unsafe sex". In fact even as I write this, there is news that a famous Basketball Star has discovered that he has been exposed to AIDS. He apparently was infected through having sex with someone who was infected. So this makes one ask what is considered as "safe sex".

In regard to this question, the CDC as well as other "responsible agencies" has taken the position that using a condom will lessen the chances of getting AIDS from sex. However, according to the research of Gene Antonio in his book, The AIDS COVER-UP, women who use condoms have a 400% greater risk factor of contracting this deadly disease and women using birth control pills have a 350% greater risk factor[145]. According the Dr. J. Nicholas Gordon, M.D. only abstinence before marriage and mutually monogamous sex afterwards are the best methods of preventing sexually transmitted AIDS[146] However, when Dan Quayle, Vice-President of the United States made this same comment, he was ridiculed by the press.

THE ORIGINS OF AIDS

There has been much wild speculation regarding the origin or the AIDS virus, but Dr. Douglass very analytically looks at the suspects that have been named as the main carriers of aids, the homosexuals, the green monkey and the Haitians, to name a few. These so called carriers, he insists were only pawns in what he describes as a viricidal attack on the non-Communist world. For Dr. Douglass, like so many others, seems to see AIDS as a form of biological warfare, as it may well be. However, as has been seen recently, the target of these attacks is not just the non-Communist world, but rather the Human Race in general.

Dr. Douglass states that if you believe the government propaganda that AIDS is hard to catch, i.e. can only be caught through close sexual contact and sharing infected needles, then you are going to die even sooner than the rest of us.

To demonstrate what he is saying regarding the risk involved with virus', Dr. Douglass points to yellow fever, which is also a virus in order to show that no direct contact whatsoever is necessary to catch some virus' from infected people. This virus can be caught from the bite of a certain type of mosquito. Malaria is a parasite also carried also by mosquitoes, a parasite that in the last century was quite

---

[145] Antonio, Gene, The AIDS Cover-up, Ignatius Press, San Francisco, 1987.
[146] Gordon, J. Nicholas, M.D., Director of Student Health Services, Ga. Tech., Atlanta, GA. "Information About AIDS."

deadly to infected humans.

ANOTHER CARRIER

The malaria parasite is many times larger than the AIDS virus (like comparing a pinhead to a moose head) yet the mosquito easily carries this relatively large organism to man. It is only recently, after several Physicians raised the question, that our government has had to admit that AIDS can be passed by at least one type of mosquitoes, the Asian tiger mosquito, to be specific. This particular type of mosquito has been recently introduced into the U.S. and is found predominately in the Southeast section of our country (i.e. Georgia, Florida and Alabama).

To show the dangers of this mosquito carrier, one has to only look to the Florida town of Belle Glade to see what can happen when the Asian Tiger Mosquito has free rein to pass the disease. The Tropical Disease Center, located in Florida has studied the disease spread in this town and concluded that the Asian tiger mosquito was the most important vector in the spread of the disease in this tiny town. The percentage of AIDS cases in that town is astronomical in comparison with the rest of the country.

Dr. Douglass also points to the example of the tuberculosis germ which can live outside the body and be passed to uninfected people who handled the effects of those already infected. The infection process is possible due to the fact that the tuberculosis germ can survive for a time outside the body and still be deadly. Infection of new victims is possible as long as the germ is alive. Well, new studies show that AIDS virus can survive for a period of from ten to fifteen days outside the human body. This would mean that sheets stained with the body fluids of AIDS patients can actually infect new victims for ten to fifteen days, in the same manner as the tuberculosis germ.

Viruses grow in both animals and humans. Fortunately, for us, most animal viruses do not affect humans. However, there are a few major, and deadly, exceptions such as yellow fever, smallpox and plague. Other animal viruses effect just the infected animal and are not passed to other animals or to man, such as bovine leukemia found in cattle and another virus found in sheep called sheep visna virus. Both of these viruses cause a very lethal form of cancer.

It is also to these viruses that we have to look for the beginnings of the AIDS virus, for the AIDS virus is a very unusual type of virus. To understand what the AIDS disease is, you actually have to look at the animal world and viruses that in their natural state do not and cannot be passed to humans. Specifically you have to look at the two animal diseases mentioned above, one that effects cows called the bovine leukemia virus (BLV) and the other being a disease that occurs in sheep called sheep visna virus.

These two diseases have something in common; they are both "retro viruses", meaning that these viruses' can change the genetic composition of the cells that they invade. Sounds a little bit like AIDS doesn't it?

Dr. Douglass found evidence that the World Health Organization asked for the creation of an AIDs like virus in it's' publications[147]. Specifically he points to such statements as "An attempt should be made to see if viruses can in fact exert selective effects on immune functions. The possibility should be looked into that the immune response to the virus itself may be impaired if the infecting virus damages, more or less selectively, the cell responding to the virus."

It is interesting to note that it is sheer insanity to think that anyone would possibly want to develop such as disease for, as Dr. Douglass correctly points out, if you destroy the immune system, you destroy man. It is at this point that both this author and Dr. Douglass asked the same question "Is it even remotely possible that the World Health Organization would want to develop a virus that would wipe out the human race?"

Of course, it is possible to find a rational explanation for the original research in this area. It would appear that scientists were looking for a way to suppress the immune system in specific areas for use in organ transplants. One of the main causes of death in organ transplant recipients is rejection of the new organ by the body. A method of reducing the immune response would save thousands of lives. However, what was developed was a virus that seems to completely destroy the immune system.

I know what some of you are thinking at this point. You are remembering all of the great scientists, as well as the various medical groups who have publicly stated that AIDS was caused by the African green monkey biting a native, who in turn passed the disease on to others.

There is only one fatal flaw in this theory, there has been no proof that AIDS occurs naturally in any animal. This being the case, then how did the Green Monkey get the disease, assuming, of course, that he ever had it in the first place?

(Authors Note: Since this was first written, I have discovered that the Green Monkey has had an AIDS type virus for as long as man has known about the Green Monkey, however, the Green Monkey is not harmed by the virus. Nor is there any evidence whatsoever that can show that the Green Monkey passed this virus to man.)

It should also be noted that AIDS seemed to spring up almost simultaneously in the United States, Haiti, Brazil and Central Africa. This virus sprang up almost simultaneously even though it can have from a five to twenty year incubation period. Therefore, in order to spring up simultaneously in several areas of the world, it had to have started independently in those same areas of the world. Dr. Douglass points out that it is not even genetically possible for the bite of the Green Monkey to pass the disease to man. So much for that "official" theory.

---

[147] Allison, et al. Bull, WHO 1972, 47:257-63 and Amos, et. al. Federal Procedures. 1972, 31:1087

Dr. Douglass quotes the research work of a Dr. Theodore Strecker, who is alleged to have found proof that the National Cancer Institute in collaboration with the World Health Organization actually made the AIDS virus in their labs at Fort Detrick, Maryland (now part of the National Cancer Institute). He further states that AIDS was created by combining two retro viruses, bovine leukemia and sheep visna virus. Then the combination was injected into human tissue cultures and allowed to mutate. This procedure created the very first human retro virus, one that has shown itself to be almost one hundred percent deadly.

(*Authors Note: There seems to be some confusion on the point of Dr. Theodore Strecker. There are actually two people, brothers, named Strecker. Dr. Robert Strecker, a medical doctor practicing in Los Angeles, CA. and Theodore Strecker, an attorney practicing in St. Louis, MO. Theodore Strecker was heavily involved in disseminating the AIDS research conducted by his brother and other researchers.*

One evening Theodore Strecker was found dead, with a .22 caliber hole in the back of his head. The death was classified a suicide. Rumor has it that research material in his possession was missing when the body was discovered.)

Now let's get to the good part, or the bad part depending on your point of view. According to Dr. Douglass, and confirmed in other research I have conducted, the U.S. Government invited doctors from around the world, to include many from the Communist Bloc to participate in the anti-cancer research going on at Ft. Detrick. This was part of Richard Nixon's war on Cancer. This program was also confirmed by Carlton Gajdusek, Chief of the National Institute of Health's Laboratory of Central Nervous System Studies and also the Laboratory of Slow, Latent and Temperate Virus Infections[148].

Mr. Gajdusek is quoted in an article in the March, 1986 issue of Omni magazine (page 106) as saying, in response to a question as to whether or not Ft. Detrick was a biological warfare center, that:

"No, emphatically no! There is no defensive or offensive warfare microbiology done at Ft. Detrick today. It is the national cancer research facility of the NIH. In this facility (referring to the research facilities at Ft. Detrick) I have a building where more good and loyal communist scientists from the USSR and mainland China work-- with full passkeys to all the laboratories-- than there are Americans. With night working U.S. citizens and foreign Communist investigators here, obviously there is no "secret" bacterial warfare going on. Even the Army's Infectious Disease Unit (a euphemistic name for the Army's Germ Warfare Unit) is loaded with foreign workers not always friendly nationals. It is a valid basic research unit on worldwide problems of infectious diseases in which no classified

---

[148] Omni Magazine, March issue, 1986. page 106.

or secret activities unfold."

(Author's Question: Isn't this kind of like hiring the burglar to guard your valuables?).

In the 1972 issue of a document called the Federal Proceedings of the United States, representatives of the World Health Organization said:

"In the relation to the immune response a number of useful experimental approaches can be visualized". This same spokesman went on to say that a good way to test this disease would be to put it into a vaccination program, then wait for the results. It was felt that very good statistical data would come out of the study of "sibship", or injecting brothers and sisters at the same time and seeing who dies first. (Author's Comment: Kind of chokes you up, knowing that you might be a part of a WHO Study, doesn't it.)

Dr. Douglass contends, as do many others, that the World Health Organization's smallpox vaccination program conducted in Uganda and other central African states, Haiti, Brazil and Japan in 1972 was used to test this new killer virus. The epidemiology result from these countries confirms that this had to be the manner in which the disease spread.

Are you prepared to dismiss these finding as the opinion of simply one Physician? Well, let's look further. In the January 11, 1986 issue of Lancet[149], Dr. R.J. Biggars stated that "The AIDS agent . . .could not have originated de novo." Now we have a serious medical journal questioning the "Green Monkey Theory". A good start toward proving my point, but is it possible that Dr. Douglass is simply paranoid and seeing a pattern where it does not exist?

In Easy Reader, Jon Rappaport wrote about an interview he conducted with Robert Matthews, technical correspondent of the London Times[150]. In this interview, Mr. Matthews, told Mr. Rappaport that the World Health Organization, itself, had suspected that its smallpox immunization program might have some connection with the rapid outbreak and spreading of the AIDS virus. As a result, an outside consultant was hired to perform an independent study and the study confirmed the connection. The WHO quickly buried the report[151].

It is quite possible that the World Health Organization was totally innocent and its facilities were used by renegade physicians who were actually members of the Conspiracy. Unfortunately, when it appears to have discovered that it was used by a person or persons unknown, the World Health Organization acted in a manner designed to assist the true culprits in escaping. It covered up what had happened.

---

[149] Lancet, January 11, 1986

[150] Rappoport, Jon, "News Blackout on Pox Vaccine Link to AIDS Protecting WHO? Easy Reader, June 4, 1987, p. 12.

[151] Ibid

Unfortunately, for the human race, this was not, and is not, the only cover-up going on. The United States medical community has had a cover-up of its own going on. This was in regard to an even more blatant attempt to "infect" the American people. As we will see in the next chapter, we may all have a "time bomb" ticking away in our veins.

CHAPTER FOURTEEN

A TRAGIC MEDICAL COVER-UP OF THE GREATEST THREAT TO THE HUMAN RACE

"Despite cases in which smallpox vaccination plainly failed to protect the population, and despite the rampant side-effects of the methods, the proponents of vaccination continued their attempts to justify the methods by claims that the disease had declined in Europe as a whole during the period of its compulsory use. If the decline could be correlated with the use of the vaccination, then all else could be set aside, and the advantage between its current low incidence could be shown to outweigh the periodic failures of the method, and to favor the continued use of vaccination. However, the credit for the decline in the incidence of smallpox could not be given to vaccination. The fact it that its incidence declined in all parts of Europe whether or not vaccination was employed."
Leon Chaitow, **Vaccination and Immunization.**

Is it true, was the black death of the twentieth century, called AIDS, created by scientists and intentionally spread around the world? Is it even remotely possible that immunization programs designed to eradicate ancient diseases that have plagued mankind have also spread an even more dangerous killer?

Dr. Eva Lee Snead, M.D. of San Antonio, Texas has also determined that there is a connection between the AIDS virus and governmental sponsored immunization programs. To begin her research, Dr. Snead started with several questions on her mind:

1. How did AIDS start?

2. If AIDS doubles every 14 months (this was the rate at the time of her article) that would total only several thousand cases since 1977 (the first reported official AIDS case). How did the number of cases come too numbered in the millions?

3. Why does AIDS affect primarily those in their late 30's? With the incubation period being anywhere form 20 to 30 years (this data may or may not be still valid), what happened 20 to 30 years ago that could have infected them?

Dr. Snead looked at the fact that the polio vaccine immunization program was begun about thirty years ago and administered to millions of people. This particular immunization program was directed at children, many of whom are now in their late thirties. Is this significant since the average age of the population that seems to be effected the most strongly by AIDS is in their late thirties?[152]

A COVER-UP?

It is most interesting to note that Dr. Snead obtained much of her information from the Food and Drug Administration (FDA) through the Freedom of Information Act. The data she received went back thirty years, and showed that the FDA had known about the contamination of the vaccines for several years but had taken no action to deal with the issue. It is very unnerving to be made aware that at the same time the Government, and most physicians, were crowing about the benefits of having your children vaccinated (if you are old enough to remember, vaccinations were made mandatory for public school attendance) that the medical community was aware that there were severe and potentially deadly problems with the vaccination program.

In fact, in 1960, even before the start of the high profile polio inoculation program, the World Health Organization (WHO) issued a bulletin informing the medical community that undesirable viruses were being found in the very vaccines that were being used to inoculate American school children. In 1963, "Science Digest", the Journal of the New York Academy of Sciences reported that humans are susceptible to simian tumor virus. "Science Digest" also reported the "near disaster" of the polio immunization program[153]. So why was no one outside of the medical community and the FDA told about this monstrous screw-up?

---

[152] Snead, Eva Lee, M.D., "AIDS--Immunization Related Syndrome," Health Freedom News, Monrovia, CA., Jult, 1987.

[153] "Near Disaster with the Salk Vaccine." Science Digest, Dec. 1963.

POLIO

Just like the World Health Organization's smallpox immunization program, the American polio immunization program was also exported to Africa, Haiti, Brazil and many other third world countries. Is this a pattern? Are potentially deadly programs developed in the advanced countries and then "tried out" in the third world countries?

Even if this is the case, it would seem that there are occasionally errors made in the program. Interestingly enough, in 1977, the Atlantic Monthly reported that millions of Americans had been contaminated with a disease called SV-40[154] [155]. No big deal, right? At least it wasn't AIDS.

Perhaps, however, researchers discovered some very unusual things about Simian Virus-40 (SV40). First, it is passed the same way as AIDS. The clinical findings in regard to SV-40 are identical to AIDS. So we have the Polio vaccination program contaminated with a virus that produces something identical to AIDS which also has the identical clinical symptoms. We could call SV-40 the swine flu, but it will still kill.

I remember that little ditty I heard in the Army: If it walks like a duck and quacks like a duck and looks like a duck, chances are it's a duck.

If a disease is passed like AIDS, has symptoms like AIDS and the clinical findings are identical to AIDS, then no matter what we call it, isn't it possible it's AIDS? For those of you, who have not heard of SV-40 before, read on.

SIMIAN VIRUS 40 AND THE POLIO VACCINE

AIDS is called HIV, (incidentally, there are now HIV 1 and HIV 2). However, another virus, some thirty years old caused almost the same clinical findings as AIDS, this was a virus called SIMIAN VIRUS 40 (SV-40), also suspected as being called by the African Green Monkey. This particular virus also causes birth defects, leukemia and many other forms of malignancy[156]. Additionally, the following symptoms of SV-40 and AIDS are similar:

a. Interference of T-Cell Formation: The SV-40 cell cultures inhibit proliferation of T-cells and can be caused by direct inoculation or by contact with

---

[154] Bennett, William and Joel, Gurin, "Science That Frightens Scientists," Atlantic Monthly, Feb. 1977.

[155] Excerpt from a Letter from Lynn M. Draft, White House Policy Staff, to Dick Gregory, April 11, 1977. Quoting: "It is true that the SV40 virus was discovered in the early 1960's. It is also true that the virus was found in certain viral vaccines prepared from virus pools grown in monkey kidney cell cultures. However, the virus had not been recognized as a contaminant prior to that time, although millions of people have received the vaccine during the 1950's" ". . .contamination of the vaccine was unintentional due to lack of knowledge."

[156] Ibid

individuals who harbor the virus[157].

b. Development of Malignancies: SV-40 caused a large percentage of lab animals to develop malignancies[158].

c. Body Wasting: SV-40 causes a decrease in protein production, also a decrease of albumen, a sign of severe body wasting[159].

d. Increased Birth Defects, Tumors, Leukemias: Results of the study indicated a high frequency of leukemia and human mongolism[160].

Dr. Snead made an attempt to research SIMIAN VIRUS 40 in the medical literature and found that all reference to it stopped in 1964, as if it had never existed. However, she did discover some literature that discussed the fact that this virus may have contaminated the polio vaccine[161].

SV-40 is also a very unique virus in another way. It is a virus, and like AIDS, a virus is defined as any particle, natural or man-made, which can enter a cell and cause this cell to make copies of itself. Only the living cell has this reproduction power. SV-40 has the ability to carry information in a piggyback fashion into a cell. Research shows that this may be the part that SV-40 plays in the AIDS virus. It was felt by some researchers that SV-40 may predispose to secondary viral infection by destroying the immune system. It is interesting to note that SV-40 was present, yet passed undetected, in the early stages of development of the Salk and Sabine polio vaccines[162].

A BINARY VIRUS?

As a result of the discovery of SV-40 a new theory has arisen. Is it possible that AIDS is a binary virus? In other words, is it possible that AIDS is actually two viruses that work together to create the killer strain? By this I mean is it possible that HIV by itself is not deadly? There are many whose blood show exposure to AIDS (this is shown by the fact that the blood shows the development of AIDS anti-bodies) but who do not have what we have come to call AIDS itself. What I am purposing is that someone who already has been exposed to HIV is not really

---

[157] *Todaro, G.H., and Green, H., Virology, pages, 752-754, 1968.*

[158] *Snider, Arthur J., "Near Disaster with the SALK Vaccine," Science Digest, pages 40-41, Dec. 1963.*

[159] *Henry Ford Hospital Medical Journal, Vol. 15, summer 1963.*

[160] *"Proceedings of the National Academy of Sciences," p. 1170, July 1962*

[161] Horwath, B.L. & Fornosi, F. Acta Microbiologica Hungary, Vol. 11, pages 271-275.

[162] Ibid

dieing. However, when this person is also exposed to SV-40, or some other activating mechanism, then the two combine to produce a truly deadly virus.

If this is correct, then as a result of the 1960's polio vaccination program, most Americans who have reached their 30's have been exposed to SV-40. If one of those people is exposed to someone with HIV, then they will die. However, until that time, they walk around with that time bomb ticking away. Remember, SV-40 cannot be detected with most medical tests; however, HIV can be detected. So when one of those with AIDS has tests, only the HIV show up, not the SV-40. In this manner, the binary nature of the virus is kept hidden.

Naturally, those of you with medical training are going to object to a non-medically trained individual such as myself advancing a theory in such an area. However, I would submit that at this time there is no proof that HIV is deadly or even gives rise to AIDS. As my proof, I will point to data given in AIDS INC., the work by Jon Rappaport I have quoted from several times. According to Mr. Rappaport, depending on what study you read, HIV has been isolated in only 50-80% of those with full blown AIDS. This means that in 20-30% of those with full blown AIDS, HIV has not been present.

According to Koch's postulates, from every person with a given disease, remove the same germ in every case. Then inject this germ into animals and in every case, this should produce all of the symptoms of the original disease. Therefore, in every case of AIDS, extract the HIV "germ" and inject it into an animal. If your theory is correct, the animal should develop AIDS.

Unfortunately, this has not worked. As pointed out earlier, in 20-30% of the cases studied, the HIV virus has not even been present. Additionally, in a medical study conducted in the U.S. 100 chimps were injected with high concentrations of HIV. Two of the chimps immediately developed infected lymph glands. However, in thirty weeks the condition returned to normal. In the other ninety eight chimps, there were no AIDS symptoms at all. It has been over four years since some of these chimps were injected.

MORE PROOF

Additional proof of the connection between immunization programs and AIDS came from no less a source than the United States Army. A 19 year old recruit, in perfect health, after his in-processing small pox vaccination, developed AIDS and in a very short time died. This incident brought the matter to the attention of Walter Reed Army Hospital. However, in typical fashion, officials tried to hide the truth behind a wall of lies and suppositions.

Even though there was no proof that the recruit had ever been previously exposed to AIDS, it was decided that perhaps the vaccination program merely activated dormant AIDS. The Walter Reed Medical Team even submitted a paper to the New England Journal of Medicine reporting their discovery of the connection between vaccination programs and the possible stimulation of dormant

AIDS disease.

Even the front page story of the London Times for May 11, 1987[163] confirmed the fact that the AIDS virus was spread through the World Health Organization's smallpox vaccination program of 1972. Quoted as their source for the story, which was written by Pearce Wright, Science Editor for the London Times, was an unnamed (he wished to keep his identity secret for fear of his job and his life) advisor to the World Health Organization, as well as, the Walter Reed Army Medical Center in Washington D.C.

However, in this story, the London times, conforming to party line, took the position that the small pox vaccination merely triggered dormant AIDS, instead of being the route of original infection. Of course, there is no medical evidence that there is such a thing as "dormant" AIDS, but it would seem to prove my theory that AIDS is a binary virus, where the vaccination might furnish the "activating" element to complete the required binary virus.

LOOK AT THE NUMBERS

If you get caught, lie, seems to be the position taken by the World Health Organization. However, if the reader isn't convinced yet regarding the culpability of the World Health Organization, let's look at the infection figures for the countries involved in the original small pox vaccination program.

The seven African countries with the most reported cases of AIDS are also the seven countries with the most people given the smallpox vaccine in the World Health Organization's vaccination program. Those seven countries are,

Zaire, with 36,878,000 people vaccinated;

Zambia, with 19,060,000;
Tanzania, with 14,972,000;

Uganda, with 11,616,000;

Malawi, with 8,118,000;

Rwanda, with 3,382,000; and

Burundi, with 3,274,000 people vaccinated.

Incidentally, Brazil, the only South American country covered by the

---

[163] London Times, Front Page Story, "Small Pox Vaccine Triggered Aids Virus", by Pearce Wright, Science Editor.

vaccination program, also has the highest incidence of AIDS in South America.

According to Dr. Douglass, AIDS didn't exist in the U.S. before 1978. He feels that it was actually here but not triggered until later. It is known that the first officially diagnosed case of AIDS was reported in 1973. The patient was a Northern European female medical doctor who was working for a medical mission in Africa. Allegedly the first case of AIDS in this country was brought by a homosexual male flight attendant on an international flight from Africa. However, Dr. Douglass maintains that it was another factor that triggered the AIDS virus in this country in 1978. He feels that this triggering mechanism was another government program. In his writings, Dr. Douglass submitted his theory that the disease was introduced or triggered in this country through the Hepatitis B vaccine program.

To prove his theory, Dr. Douglass points to a Doctor W. Schmugner, a Russian born and trained physician who came to this country in 1969. This Russian Doctor, in only a short time after his arrival in this country, became head of the New York City Blood Bank shortly before 1978. According to Dr. Douglass, for Dr. Schmugner to climb so high in the medical community so fast took behind the scenes assistance. This proposal brings us back to the Conspiracy.

According to Dr. Douglass it was allegedly Dr. Schmugner who set up the rules for the hepatitis vaccine studies. His guidelines called for it to be tested only on homosexual males between the ages of 20 and 40 who were not monogamous. Therefore, newspaper advertisements were taken out in the five cities where the testing was to be conducted. These advertisements called for homosexual male volunteers between the required ages.

In 1981, the Center for Disease Control (CDC) reported that four (4%) percent of those receiving the hepatitis vaccine were AIDS infected. In 1984, the CDC reported that sixty (60%) percent of those who received those vaccinations were now AIDS infected. Since 1984, the CDC has refused to give out anymore statistics on the program[164]. Rumor has it that the incidence of infection among those who took part in the vaccination study is now close to 100%.

Two things should be noted, the first is that Dr. Schmugner is now dead, therefore, we can't question him as to his motivation or his associations. The second is that the Hepatitis B vaccine tests were conducted in New York City, Los Angeles, San Francisco, Chicago and Miami, all cities with a large homosexual population and a growing AIDS population.

Because of the numerous genetic combinations possible with this virus (according to Dr. Douglass the number is 9,000 to the fourth power), there can never be a vaccine. After all, how can you develop a drug vaccine for a disease that simply changes its' molecular design to combat the vaccine? There are certain drug treatments that do seem to alleviate some of the worst effects of the AIDS virus; unfortunately, most of these drug treatments have side effects that are as bad or

---

[164] Data released by the Center for Disease Control..

worse than the disease itself.

However, according the T. E. Bearden in his book AIDS--Biological Warfare, there is a cure, but medical science is refusing to accept it[165]. This cure does not depend on drugs of any type which of course offends the drug companies. This cure depends on electromagnetism.

[I highly recommend that those of you interested in following up on this topic read a book called AIDS- Biological Warfare, by Lt. Col. (RET) T. E. Bearden, Tesla Book Company, P.O. Box 1649, Greenville, Texas 75401, 1988.]

I would not want to leave you with the idea that the World Health Organization set out to wipe out the human race. However, the evidence is fairly clear that it was the smallpox vaccination program that may have started or spread this dreaded disease. The why, we may never know and at this point, it really doesn't matter. What does matter is how do we stop the further spread of this killer disease?

It is possible that we may have created a monster in the name of research. Did a virus created from monkey cells in the 1960's, called SV-40 become introduced into the cultures from which the polio vaccine was created? This vaccine was given to almost every American as part of the program to eradicate polio in the early 1960s. (I had this one myself.) It would appear that while we may have been able to eradicate the polio virus, we inadvertently crated an even more dangerous threat. Or could this, currently, dormant, disease, have been intentionally infected into the population so that if need be, an activating agent could be injected to kill rebellious portions of the population. If so, what do we do now?

BIOLOGICAL WARFARE

Before we leave this chapter, I think it only fair that we take one last look at the area of Biological Warfare (CBR or CBW). Is it possible that what we call AIDS is the result of chemical or biological attacks on certain groups of the population? Such an attack would make it easier for invaders to overwhelm sick or dying defenders. It could of course be justified in that many lives would be saved and the war shortened if the enemy simply died in their beds. For these and many other reasons more and more military leaders are authorizing the use of such weapons against their enemies. After all, enough plague germs to decimate a continent could be carried in test tube and created in a laboratory the size of an average kitchen without any special equipment.

As for who would use such weapons, according to a 1975 Fort Belvoir, VA publication entitled Decontamination of Water Containing Chemical Warfare Agents, ". . .it is theoretically possible to develop so-called ethnic chemical

---

[165] AIDS: BIOLOGICAL WARFARE. Bearden, T.E., Tesla Book Company, P.O. Box 1649, Greenville, Texas 75401, 1988

weapons, which would be designed to exploit naturally occurring differences in vulnerability among specific population groups. Thus, such a weapon would be capable of incapacitating or killing a selected enemy population to a significantly greater extent than the population of friendly forces."

Reported in a study called *A HIGHER FORM OF KILLING*, the comments of a Dr. Leonard MacArthur before a 1969 House Appropriations Committee are interesting. In a discussion of budget funds for defense for 1970, Dr. MacArthur made the following statements:

"*Within the next 5 to 10 years, it would probably be possible to make a new infective microorganism which would differ in certain important respects from any known disease-causing organisms. Most important of these is that it might be refractory to the immunological and therapeutic processes upon which we depend to maintain our relative freedom from infectious disease.*"

SARS

It would seem that in the last years of the 20th century and first of the new century, a number of heretofore new diseases have suddenly appeared on the scene. As if the threat of AIDs is not enough, now we have one that is called, for lack of a better name, SARS. The appearance is that some individual or group of individuals is experimenting to find a truly killer disease with which to decimate the human race.

SARS is a mystery virus that causes severe acute respiratory syndrome in those infected. It has given a new dimension to the current national emergency that cases of what I believe will be identified as SARS have broken out in refugees from New York City in the aftermath of the terrorist attacks of September 11, 2001.

The World Health Organization has announced that experiments in monkeys have confirmed the identity of the virus that causes severe acute respiratory syndrome as being the mysterious SARS. This is truly an important step toward developing new drugs to combat the disease. Tests are under way in pigs and poultry to see how susceptible those animals are to SARS.

SARS, which made its first appearance in China, has sickened 13,293 people in 28 countries and killed 1,161. Scientists have determined it is caused by a new member of the corona virus family, so named because a crown shape is seen when the viruses are inspected under a microscope. Researchers had been almost certain the new form of corona virus first isolated from sick patients March 21, 2003 by the University of Hong Kong was the cause of SARS, but they could not say for sure until they had satisfied what is known as Koch's postulates – the four scientific tests that verify whether a virus causes a certain disease.

The first test requires that the virus be found in all the sick people, but not in healthy people. The second isolates the virus from a sick patient and shows that it multiplies in a lab dish. The third step uses the virus from the Petri dish to make a lab animal sick with the same disease as that seen in humans. The final step requires isolating the SARS virus from the sick lab animal and showing it can grow in a Petri dish.

A team led by Dr. Albert Osterhaus, the director of virology at Erasmus Medical Centre in Rotterdam, Netherlands, carried out the final two verifying steps. Further research confirmed that Koch's postulates have been fulfilled, so we can now say for certain that the new corona virus is the cause of SARS.

Early in the hunt for the cause of SARS, scientists found a virus belonging to the paramyxovirus family in some patients. It was later determined that this was the human metapneumovirus, which is known to cause respiratory problems in children, the elderly and people with weak immune systems. A few days later, scientists in Hong Kong found the new corona virus, providing a new track for researchers to pursue.

This discovery prompted a theory that perhaps both viruses play a role, with one causing the disease and the other making it worse. Osterhaus said they infected two groups of monkeys with either the corona virus or with the human metapneumovirus. In a third group, the monkeys were infected first with corona virus, then with the metapneumovirus.

The animals infected with the corona virus alone developed the full-blown disease. They developed clinical symptoms and the lesions that are identical to those that have been seen in people who have died from SARS. The animals infected with human metapneumovirus developed only very mild symptoms and definitely not the typical SARS pattern.

The third group did not develop a more serious version of SARS. Therefore, the conclusion was that the corona virus alone is capable of causing the typical symptoms. Symptoms of SARS include fever, shortness of breath, coughing, chills and body aches. The findings were announced in the middle of a daylong meeting at the WHO's Geneva headquarters of scientists from laboratories around the world working together to find the cause of SARS and tests to diagnose it.

WHO said the scientists agreed to name the new virus simply SARS virus, despite earlier proposals that it should bear the name of Dr. Carlo Urbani, the WHO doctor who first alerted the world to the existence of SARS in Hanoi, Vietnam, and who died from the disease on March 29.

It must be stressed that although the SARS virus is part of the same family of viruses that cause the common cold, it is quite different from the common cold virus. Genetic studies have indicated that the SARS virus shares some similarities with the mouse hepatitis virus and the avian infectious bronchitis virus, which come from a different branch of the corona virus family. It is reasonable to imagine that the SARS virus came from animals, although its genetic code does not give any clear leads as to exactly where it came from. The genetic makeup is not very close to any of the known animal or human corona viruses, they say. The virus has probably existed for a long time in animals in the southern Chinese province of Guangdong, where SARS was first detected.

WHO experts in China have reported they discovered unreported SARS cases in Beijing military hospitals but had been barred from giving details. Another WHO official estimated there had been 100 to 200 cases in Beijing since March, 2003; the official total being 37.

Is it possible that, if AIDS was created by a person or persons unknown, that it was a precursor to SARS, a newer, more deadly form of infection that killed quicker than AIDS and was harder to identify? A sick, dying population is very easy to conquer.

A NEW DANGER

In addition to new, deadly diseases appearing out of no where, there are also new dangers coming from the animal kingdom. There is a new danger making its way across this country. The cause of this danger is an ant, but an ant unlike anything we have ever seen before. This ant inflicts a very dangerous venom that, thus far no one has shown any immunity for. This creature is not indigenous to this country, but actually comes from Australia. How it arrived in this country is not yet known, but it seems to have made its way to Louisiana and is now moving outward.

Though it sounds crazy, this killer ant could blind people with its venom and has done so in its march across Australia. The yellow crazy ant, aka Anoplolepis gracilipes, is not really known outside of Australia, but it has been blamed for the death of 20 million red crabs on Christmas Island since 1989, and a swag of other native birds, animals and plants. Experts in the field that study such creatures, have described it as one of the world's worst species of ant, it does not bite or sting - instead it sprays acid into the eyes of animals, and potentially humans.

The ant sprays formic acid as a means of subduing its prey - if people get the acid on their hands and then rub their eyes, they are basically putting acid in your eyes. If left untreated, the victim can go blind. Sight is the primary means by which we are able to dominate the animal kingdom.

It is what we see out in the natural world with lizards, with birds, smaller mammals and with the crabs that were mentioned. The poor animals that come in contact with these ants, once sprayed with this formic acid, don't die directly from the ants. They die of starvation because they are blind and thus cannot hunt their normal food.

Hundreds of millions of the ants have invaded north-east Arnhem Land in the Northern Territory of Australia, and could easily spread further in a huge environmental and economic threat to Northern Australia. They are widespread throughout the tropics of the world, so they will definitely go right through northern Australia if left unchecked. However, those that have been transplanted here to the United States seem to have shown no discomfort as they move into cooler climates."

It is not a matter of how long it would take for these killer ants to overrun this country. It is simply a matter of when it will happen. Several Australian Organizations, such as the CSIRO, along with the Dhimurru Land Management Aboriginal Corp and the Northern Land Council are developing a three-year plan to wipe out the population of these ants currently infesting Australia. The population is currently now confined to a 90km radius around the mining town of Nhulunbuy, on the northeastern tip of the territory. The real fear regarding the little yellow crazy ant is that their depredations will destroy the culture, land, the way of life in that area.

It is currently believed the ants may have been introduced accidentally by military personnel during World War II. It is all speculation, of course, but the largest infestation is very near to where there was an American military base back in World War II, and judging by rate of spread estimates, the introduction of these creatures can actually date it back to that time as well, around the 1940s."

Many seem surprised by the name of crazy ant, but it was observed that massive swarms of the 1cm long creatures, just look crazy, hence the name. If some animal or human disturb a nest, just turn over a rock or something like that, you basically come upon tens of thousands of these deadly little ants that are just running around erratically. Hence the name crazy ants, it just looks like a really crazy mess.

A "NEW" MYSTERY FLU

There has been a mysterious, flu like illness that has stricken scores of hospital workers in Southeast Asia. This illness has stumped a battery of tests for known bacteria and viruses. It has now been confirmed that it represents a new human disease of unknown origin.

Approximately 2 weeks after the terrorist attack on New York City, the Center for Disease Control (CDC) was tracking at least 14 cases of a mysterious disease that bore a striking resemblance to the SARS illness in the United States, including that of an unidentified patient, who at the time, had recently arrived from travel to Asia, who turned up in a Los Angeles County emergency room with a high fever and difficulty breathing. Now, medical authorities are tracking over 200 similar cases confined in various regional areas all over the east coast of the Untied States.

A check of the records of all of those infected with this mysterious ailment show that each one comes down with a particularly dangerous case of pneumonia -- fluid filling their lungs -- and many of those sickened in Southeast Asia have had to be placed on ventilators. World Health Organization epidemiologists quickly gave the disease a name -- SARS, or severe acute respiratory syndrome -- and have confirmed thirty-four deaths and 1,167 cases worldwide.

Under prodding by the United Nations' health agency, China has disclosed an outbreak of 1,305 cases from November through February that appear similar to SARS, but which contained symptoms that have not been traditionally connected with this disease. There were fifty-five deaths in China, but none of the cases were ever included in the official World Health Organization count.

Prevention Director, Dr. Julie Gerberding, of the Center for Disease Control (CDC) originally announced that 10 of the 14 initial suspected cases in the United States were "almost certainly not" SARS. In fact, it was almost impossible to determine the cause of those cases. However, suspicions at the time felt that "it would not be surprising" to find the illness soon in the United States.

Cases of this SARS like disease have been confirmed in Canada, where two members of a Toronto family have died after returning from China. One member of that family subsequently visited Atlanta. Cases are also suspected in Switzerland, Germany and the United Kingdom. At the time of her announcement, Dr. Gerberding said she was confident that laboratories in the United States or in eight other nations testing for the disease would pinpoint its cause. But the disease detectives are now fairly sure it is a bug they haven't encountered before.

The epidemic that is slowly spreading in the United States at this point is behaving like that of a viral illness spread by "close contact" with infected patients in the home or hospital. Like SARS, it appears to be highly contagious but unlike SARS, that requires contact with droplets of infected body fluids through cough or sneezing, this new disease appears to be spread through the air. In other words, SARS may well have been a precursor, a test, if you will, of this deadly new disease.

Consequently, doctors and nurses who observe common infection control practices -- isolating patients and using face shields, gowns and gloves -- should keep the microbe from spreading, if the disease in question is SARS, but if it is Disease X, these common control practices will have little if any impact on the spread of the disease.

Nearly all the cases worldwide of SARS have involved travelers from China and Southeast Asia, or the health care workers in hospitals that have treated them. The first case outside of the Chinese outbreak was that of an American businessman who was admitted to a Hanoi hospital after travel in China. He was transferred to a Hong Kong hospital, where he died a few days later. Meanwhile, 42 Vietnamese workers from the Hanoi hospital where this patient was treated, and one child of a worker, came down with the disease. Two Vietnamese patients died."

If this SARS was a test as part of the development of this new disease, then it is clear that as the disease has shown its virulence, and scientists have been able to isolate and work on antidotes for this strain of the disease, whoever has developed it mutates the disease slightly. This would mean that somewhere in the world is a very complete lab staffed by some very brilliant microbiologists who are working diligently to produce a mutated virus that has a 100% lethal effect!"

Subsequently, 195 cases of a similar type of disease in the Hong Kong region have been reported within a seven day period, including at least 80 Hong Kong hospital workers. This outbreak appears to be part of the original SARS outbreak. Additionally, suspected cases of Disease X have since been reported in Singapore, Thailand, the Philippines and Indonesia. A Singapore doctor, who visited a medical conference in New York, was hospitalized after he became ill on a flight from New York to Frankfurt.

"In San Francisco, the three flights that arrive daily nonstop from Hong Kong are being greeted by a Centers for Disease Control and Prevention quarantine officer, who warns passengers to be alert for the symptoms of SARS and now Disease X. The passengers are being instructed if they become ill, to tell doctors that they've been to Asia. The incubation period of the illness is believed to be less than seven days.

The peculiar outbreaks stemming out from the disaster in New York City all appear to be Disease X and it is spreading rapidly. There is speculation that this disease can be spread by something as simple as a garden sprayer which can be easily hidden in something as innocuous as a briefcase. Investigation has shown that similar outbreaks have been seen at 83 hospitals covering an area from New Jersey to Tennessee. The new disease is spreading rapidly.

"These Hospitals that have positively reported cases have admitted more patients with probable cases of the new unknown disease in the last two weeks — over 6,280 — than in the rest of the world combined, including Mainland China. There have been accusations from doctors in Mainland China, however, that the authorities there have been undercounting cases of SARS and other new diseases, all of which involve severe acute respiratory syndrome."

In addition to SARS and this mystery flu, there have been recent outbreaks of West Nile disease as well as a deadly bird flu that has jumped the species barrier. Clearly there is a biological war ongoing with the human race as a whole being the target.

THE CHINESE FACTOR

Several of the new diseases that threaten mankind seem to being coming from China, as if this huge, rather unsophisticated country is being used as a testing ground for these diseases.

China has been fighting the disease with quarantines for months, while Vietnam swiftly quarantined its outbreak at the French Hospital in Hanoi, Canada, Taiwan and Singapore have quarantined thousands of people in their homes in the last week for coming anywhere near SARS patients or for visiting a hospital where such patients were treated."

The major problem with this reaction is that mixed in with SARS cases are those of the deadly new disease that has now been identified by the CDC. Singapore, a country with a reputation for stringent public policy, announced that

that it would install closed-circuit televisions outside the doors of quarantined residents to make sure they stay home. Their national plan is for Security officials to call residents at random intervals each day and ask them to show themselves in front of the camera outside; any resident who is away from home and unable to do so will be required to wear an electronic tag that will automatically notify the authorities if the wearer leaves home.

However, in spite of these swift and rigidly enforced quarantines, Hong Kong officials have been skeptical that quarantines are truly effective. The Hong King response to the spreading SARS epidemic shows their mindset. Hong Kong ordered only people sharing households with SARS patients to stay home for 10 days, and to report daily to clinics for medical evaluations.

However, other countries are more suspicious of possible contagion. Malaysia has barred most citizens of Hong Kong and China from visiting while Singapore imposed a quarantine on lower-income workers arriving from SARS-affected countries, Hong Kong's top health officials held a news conference to announce what they initially described as some of the toughest quarantine rules anywhere in the world. This new disease, if it spreads anything like SARS, could result in every country walling itself off from its neighbors. Could this be a type of divide and conquer?

In a recent statement issued by the Hong Kong authorities, Dr. Margaret Chan, Hong Kong's health director, acknowledged that the new rules would still only affect a few hundred people who lived in the same households as people who have been admitted to hospitals with SARS in the last 10 days. She gave no rationale for the rules, but it seems that there are two primary reasons for taking this approach. First, it seems clear that the Hong Kong authorities really don't believe that this outbreak is as serious as other countries believe.

Dr. Yeoh Eng-kiong, Hong Kong's secretary of health, welfare and food, said that just as quarantining people with HIV, which causes AIDS, might discourage people from seeking treatment, broad restrictions on people with SARS and their families might also lead to infected people avoiding hospitals. City officials have also been leery of seeming to tread on people's civil liberties. Dr. Yeoh has publicly stated that an isolation order would restrict people's freedom, and that is not something people in Hong Kong are used to. Yet calls for tighter restrictions have been growing there, even from politicians like Emily Lau, the leader of one of the largest pro-democracy political parties here and a member of the Legislative Council."

Under the Hong Kong scenario the main restrictions on human rights will be that the police will make unannounced visits to the homes of these family members to make sure that they do not go out, and health workers will visit the quarantined families at their homes instead of asking them to go to clinics. The debate here over how far to go in restricting the movements of people who might be infected has echoes of similar debates over quarantines that have lasted for many years in the United States, including questions over whether to restrict the movements of patients with tuberculosis and the AIDS virus.

Ms. Lau frequently leads marches and demonstrations in favor of greater civil liberties but now she has a new cause: She wants the government to round up all close family members of SARS patients and quarantine them in remote camps in the territory's northern hills. She believes that it is important to protect the whole community, and that she hopes these people will understand. What has been so surprising is that in spite of the traditional Hong Kong freedoms all seven political parties in Hong Kong have endorsed the same position."

Dr. Yeoh said that household members could move into the camps if they wished, but would not be compelled to do so. The government used the so-called holiday camps for the internment over the last 10 days of 240 people from a housing complex where nearly 300 other people fell sick, but it was announced that the 240 people could go home if they wished.

The government in Hong Kong and many governments overseas are setting 10 days as the interval for quarantines because most infected people fall ill during that time. But a friend of mind in the Hong Kong Public Health Service told me that several Hong Kong doctors have reported a few cases involving people who fell sick as long as 16 days after exposure to the virus. Now they have been treating this outbreak as SARS, but from what according to what you have discussed that was said in the briefing this morning, they may be dealing with a mutated strain and not realize it.

The reluctance to quarantine large numbers of people also reflects the growing view among many doctors there that quarantine would not work. While the medical authorities have taken one approach, the legal authorities have been less than enthusiastic about supporting the suggestions of the medical authorities. Dr. Anthony Hedley, a professor and former chairman of the department of community medicine at Hong Kong University said at a governmental meeting that "you have to have very good reasons for depriving people of their liberty, and I don't think it would be easy to put together a good case medically for putting another 1,000 people in quarantine.

Chinese officials have said that the disease, whether it is SARS or this mysterious Disease X, is still spreading on the mainland, although they insisted that it was not spreading as fast as it had been earlier. Vietnam and Singapore acknowledged that each had a cluster of new cases that appeared to have escaped the quarantine.

Canada appears to have slowed the outbreak, but has still been reporting a few new cases each day and even the United States has added SARS to the list of diseases for which people can be quarantined in the United States. Unfortunately, the mechanics of such a quarantine has not been established to provide guidelines for instituting such a quarantine. Dr. Anthony Fauci, director of the National Institute of Allergy and Infectious Disease, said on the ABC program "Good Morning America" that he did not anticipate an immediate need to impose such a quarantine, however.

One of the problems is that SARS and now this mysterious Disease X, is easily misdiagnosed as influenza or some other ailment. This problem was brought home for Hong Kong doctors when a top Hospital Authority administrator there, Dr. Fung Hong, was hospitalized in late March with the suspicion that he had SARS. The disease was then misdiagnosed and he was later released. He was then readmitted when he developed pneumonia. Doctors then determined that his malady turned out to have been SARS after all, though some of the symptoms were not typical of SARS.

Dr. Yeoh has said that some people could contract the virus that causes SARS and spread it to others without exhibiting the full list of symptoms that the World Health Organization has warned doctors look for, notably a high fever. The problem is that most medical diagnosis is based upon determining the characteristics of a disease. However, as noted by Dr. Malik Peiris, the microbiologist leading SARS investigators at Hong Kong University, such disease characteristics can undermine the effectiveness of quarantine by making it hard to identify everyone who has the disease. He also said that it becomes difficult if there are a significant number of asymptomatic infections."

Dr. Leung Ka-lau, the president of the Public Doctors Association in Hong Kong reported that with 2,998 cases there over a single month, and it was found that over 2,000 of these cases had been covered up by reporting authorities, and more than 1,000 more cases showing up over the past winter in cities just across the border in mainland China. The result of the new cases and failure to report them to the authorities resulted in their being too many people to quarantine now who might have been in contact with SARS patients. It is becoming very obvious that this rapidly spreading disease could rival the ravages caused by the Black Plague.

To make matters worse, according to the World Health Organization, a few so-called super shedders can become extremely infectious and spread the disease to many people — Singapore has already traced 91 cases there to one infected woman. That raises the additional tricky question of whether to quarantine large numbers of people with no apparent illnesses in the hope of restricting the movements of a few super shedders."

A shedder is a term that has been applied to anyone who has the tendency to leave infected people in their wake, almost shedding the disease if you will. An example would be Typhoid Mary, who was alleged to have spread that disease just by being in the same room as a non-infected person."

Dr. Howard Markel, a professor of the history of medicine at the University of Michigan has made it clear that medical science has no way to identify a super shedder. Therefore, until medical science knows more about who is a super shedder, you're probably going to overstep in terms of how many people you quarantine."

Knowing the tendency of the average citizen to react with violence toward anything threatening, when word of this gets out there will be mass chaos in the streets. It is widely believed that once word spreads, that these super shredders will be tracked down and lynched. There is already fear of AIDS, this SARS and other emerging diseases, and now this mysterious new disease that is apparently being spread by bio-terrorists. Out of fear of infection those that do not die of the disease itself will be slaughtered by their own neighbors. There will be sheer panic that anyone with so much as a sniffle could be infected with this mysterious disease. An allergy could be the same as a death sentence. This could tear the United States apart!"

A SUSPICION

There is no doubt that there are a large number of secret societies and little known orders that given us many of our leaders. Each one believes that it passes down secret knowledge that it is not good for the general masses to know. Many of these secret orders work for the establishment of a one world government at the expense of the governments that they supposedly serve. Is it possible that these well known individuals that we have elected to lead us actually owe their loyalty to some other group or higher order? There is a great deal of information to support this premise.

It is also certainly evident that there has been a lot of behind the scenes work done in order to design new diseases that strike at the very heart of the human race's very existence, bypassing natural barriers. There also appears to have been a program put in place to intentionally destroy much of the population of Africa, sort of an international social-engineering program.

All of this certainly supports the theory that there is a hidden race operating from the shadows with the ultimate goal of either eliminating or controlling the Human Race. Having reviewed some of the more obvious efforts to destroy the Human Race, it is time to see if there is any clear and convincing evidence that such a hidden race actually exists.

PART II

THE EVIDENCE

FOR THE EXISTENCE

OF A

HIDDEN RACE

CHAPTER FIFTEEN

LIGHTING THE SHADOWS

The evidence to support the premise that there is a very effective and efficient plan to destroy or at least significantly reduce the numbers of the Human Race reported in Part one of this book was relatively easy to find. If, as I suspect, the Gods are planning to return to rule the Human Race as their ancestors did in the time before recorded history, they must first reduce the technologically advanced Human Race to the level of a subservient race. This can be done through war, pestilence and other forms of sudden attack.

The information supporting the existence of a Hidden Race that lives in the shadows and influences events in the real world is much more difficult to obtain and when it is found, the establishment normally ridicules both the information and the one that puts it forward.

BLUEPOINT FOR INVASION

There has been a lot of speculation about aliens from outer space and the possibility of invasion. Even at this late date, the questions regarding aliens from outer space and unidentified flying objects have not been answered. Or at least, the powers that be have not admitted publicly whether or not UFOs are actually space craft. However, in spite all of the mystery; it is interesting to note that there is a complete outline of an invasion of our planet to be found in no less an authority than the Holy Bible.

One of the most dramatic Biblical verses that protects invasion from outer space is found in Matthew 24:30-31 and reads as follows:

"And then shall appear the sign of the Son of man in heaven, and then shall all the tribes of the earth mourn, and they shall see the Son of man coming in the

clouds of heaven with power and great glory. And he shall send his angels with a great sound of a trumpet and they shall gather together his elect from the four winds, from one end of heaven to the other."

The Bible further states that this invasion will take place during the lifetime of those that witness the founding of a reborn Israel, which took place in 1948[166]. So this prediction leads us to believe that we have yet to face a full scale alien invasion in the very near future. But more important than this, are these invaders written about in one of the Holiest books on the planet already among us? The evidence points to the fact that they are already here and have been here for eons. In fact there is a great deal of evidence that the arrival of an advanced race actually predates out own.

PROOF OF EARLY CONTACT

If an earlier race once existed on this planet and even now hides in the shadows, then their must be some proof. Let us look first at evidence that early humans had some contact with a more advanced race. Before you, the reader, decides that the very idea is silly, at least take the time to look at the evidence.

The early Egyptians called themselves the first initiators and the first civilized people on this planet. However, is this true? I think not, as there clearly was at least one advanced race in contact with early man that instilled the concept of earthly gods and a healthy fear of these early gods in the minds of early man.

As an example of the impact of this early contact, the word "angel" was considered so dangerous to utter that it was banished from Jewish rites, and at the Laodicean Council Christian Church forbade referring to angels by name[167]. If angels were only man's personification of the word of God, then why was so much fear attached even to uttering the very name of these mysterious creatures? It would seem to me that this fear came from negative contacts of early man with creatures who, for lack of any better term, were called Angels. Were these Angels members of this early, more advanced race that once oppressed the Human Race?

There was a very open fear of the gods found in the reconstructed histories of the Phoenician and Assyro-Babylonian history. This fear revolved around even the mentioning of the name of the Planet Venus. Evidence shows that 5,000 years ago, the Planet Venus suddenly appeared in our solar system. How could a planet just suddenly appear? Many researchers believe that it is from this newly arrived planet that the advanced visitors early man referred to as gods came to this planet

---

[166] Gladden, Lee and Vivianne Cervantes Gladden, Heirs of the Gods, Rawson, Wade Publishers, Inc., New York. 1878.

[167] Charroux, Robert, Masters of the World, Berkley Publishing Company, New York. 1967.

came[168].

In Asia Minor, the six main gods, Baal, Astarte, Ishtar, Marduk, Bel and Ashur were identified with the planet Venus. Additionally, the three main early races of the Americas, the northern plains, Peru (Incas) and Mexico (Aztecs), worshipped gods that were identified with Venus, the Morning Star, Orejona, Vircocha, Quetzalcoatl and Kukulkan.

As the early human with whom they came in contact considered these travelers gods, the concept that they might be humans who had come from another planet was lost. Human rulers could be overthrown by the oppressed masses, but gods were to be worshipped. From this concept came the idea that Kings ruled by "divine right".

LANDING PLACE OF THE GODS

If, in fact, the early gods were spacefarers, then where did they land? Is there any evidence that early man knew from whence came the gods? Surprisingly enough, there is a great deal of evidence to support a conclusion that the gods of pre-history came from the vast unknown areas that make up the still little known continent of Asia.

The evidence of which I speak can be found in the early languages of the first known civilizations. The continent of Europe took its name form the early Hebrew oreb or ereb, meaning "evening, or "west" or from the ancient Greek europe, which means "dark place"[169]. Moses referred to Europe as the Island of Nations and other early writers referred to this continent as Japetia. Europe being considered a westerly country would only be logical if it was being referred to by those living in Asia.

The word Asia derives from the ancient Phoenician asir, which means central. Asir is said to derive from the ancient Scandinavian word ase, which means "god". There is a great deal of evidence supporting this word derivation sequence as the Phoenicians are said to descend from the Pelasgians, the ancestors from the north. The gods of the Pelasgians were called Ases.

The Phoenician, Phrygians and Assyro-Babylonians gave their gods and goddesses names in which the Celtic-Scandinavian root appears, such as Astarte, Astarot, Asmodeus, and Asherah. The Egyptian name for the god Osiris was Asar and the Babylonian name for Marduk was Asari. So it would appear that this language approach supports the belief that the gods came from somewhere in Asia. I might also point out that the legendary Garden of Eden was also supposed to be located somewhere in the Middle East.

---

[168] Ibid
[169] Ibid

THE CONQUEST OF MAN

So did advanced entities landed on earth and established control over the existing human race? It would certainly seem that this is a distinct possibility. There is a large body of evidence that a world wide civilization existed sometime in pre-history, through it does not indicate whether this world wide civilization was established prior to the landing of the invaders or as a result of the invaders. However, there is no doubt that once in power, the so called gods ruled the human race with a firm hand, sometimes using them as playthings. But then something happened and the gods withdrew completely from the affairs of man.

As theorized in The Occult Connection: UFOs, Secret Societies and Ancient Gods[170], the ancient gods lost their control after a devastating civil war that reduced the earth to a barbaric, prehistoric level. After this point, without much of their advanced technology that gave them their incredible power, these former gods were forced to rule from the shadows through "front men" such as High Priests and Kings. Additionally, it would appear from legends that the ancient gods left agents behind to carry out their plans. These agents may well be the "Men in Black" referred to previously.

I am not the first writer to observe that there seems to be an intelligence that delights in toying with humans to the point of tormenting them. The contacts between humans and this entity are always clothed in trapping directly related to the age in which the contact is taking place. For example, in the middle ages, people in Ireland expected, and therefore saw, Leprechauns and other "wee" people. Highly religious people expected to see Angels and as a result saw these ethereal beings.

In the 20th century, as a result of movies, television shows about alien invasions, humans expected to see aliens and little green (or grey) men from outer space and as a result, this is what they saw when in contact with this intelligence. Is it possible that the Men In Black" (MIB) are the 20th century (or 21st century) version of Little Green Men and Leprechauns? The general description of these MIBs is somewhat interesting to consider.

The very first modern report of the mysterious Men in Black dates from the year 1955, and was made by a young man named Albert K. Bender, a teenage UFO buff, who went on to become a very well known researcher of this strange phenomena[171]. Bender claims that he was approached by three men clad in black suits who ordered him to abandon his UFO research if he wanted to stay safe. As a result of this visit, Bender did abandon his early research.

---

[170] Hudnall, Ken, THE OCCULT CONNECTION: UFOs, Secret Societies and Ancient Gods, Omega. Press, El Paso, Texas 79912. 1996.
[171] Berlitz, Charles, Charles Berlitz's World of Strange Phenomena, Fawcett Crest, New York. 1988.

However, when a large number of reports are reviewed, there are some similarities that become evident. Folklorist Peter Rojcewicz[172] notes that the visitors in a classic Men In Black visitation often dress in black clothing that may appear soiled and generally unkempt or unrealistically neat and wrinkly free. On occasion, the three figures display a very unusual walking motion, moving about as if their hips were on a swivel joints, their torso and legs at odds with one another. Some display a preference for driving black Cadillacs or other large dark sedans. In fact there are a large number of reports involving these large older cars.

I would also point out that no less an authority than the Holy Bible discusses a Men In Black visitation when it talks about the Three Kings from Orient Are, also known as the three wise men that were present at the birth of Jesus. No one has been able to identify these three mysterious individuals or even what countries they came from and they were described as appearing to be Oriental. Certainly, their scanty descriptions had a great deal in common with the classic Men in Black.

Some MIBs show unusual hair growth as their heads had been cut closely and then allowed to grow back sort of haphazardly. The appearance of the figures indicate that almost all races and complexions, have been seen in these visitations, though the figures are uniformly male in gender and generally appear to have a Asiatic cast to their features. Once they have carried out their mission, the three very real figures seem to vanish. Legends from many races report such visitations, though not in the UFO context.

THE END OF THE FIRST CIVILIZATION

The myths of the early days prior to the beginning of our history give a large number of hints about the possibility that there was a world wide cataclysmic war which destroyed the earliest civilizations. From the translations that Zacharia Sitchin of early Sumerian works, it would appear that this early war was as a result of political factions among the gods. The human race was merely caught in the crossfire of this war of the gods and reduced to barbarism. Like innocents caught in every war throughout history, the Human Race had no say, but faced the brunt of the damage.

Support for this premise can be found in Genesis, the first book of the Christian Bible. In the King James Edition of the Bible, the first sentence of Genesis has been translated to say "In the Beginning God created the heaven and the earth.[173]" However, there is another translation for the familiar opening words. The Hebrew Scholar J.M. Vasehalde attributes the accepted translation to the "divine complex" that has always affected translators of the Bible. He believes that an alternate translation would be "with what remained from the past", referring not

---

[172] Ibid

[173] Genesis, Chapter 1, verse 1.

to the beginning of creation, but rather to a reconstruction after a world wide cataclysm[174].

From this time forth, during the reconstruction of the civilization of the world, the gods slowly lost their historical dominance over the human race and were forced to rule from the shadows. According to legends, the first Kings to rule over the human race, called demi-gods, were the products of mating between the gods and human women and placed on their thrones by the gods, themselves. Even the Holy Bible wrote of these matings between gods and humans when it stated that "the sons of God came unto the daughters of men and they bare children to them, the same became mighty men which were of old, men renown[175].

Though these physical rulers, descended from these matings, were basically human, the power that protected their thrones was from beyond the stars. There is no doubt that the gods felt themselves to be far above the human race and desired to protect the prerogatives of the gods. History is full of examples of the gods striking out to destroy anyone that challenged their power.

However, there was always the possibility that the human race would once again regain the ability to challenge the gods, who were now somewhat weakened as a result of the civil war that raged before time. To guard against this, an ambitious program was put into operation to suppress all scientific learning among humans. This recreation of the world through the power of God is certainly supported by recent scientific findings, but is there any support for a calculated attempt to suppress the advancement of knowledge? Actually there is, as we shall see.

---

[174] Charroux, Robert, Masters of the World, Berkley Publishing Company, New York. 1967.

[175]Holy Bible, Book of Genesis, Chapter 6, verse 4.

CHAPTER SIXTEEN

WAS THERE A HISTORICAL CONSPIRACY TO SUPPRESS KNOWLEDGE?

Throughout our long history as a race, at least since the beginnings of recorded history, that has been an almost criminal attempt to suppress early knowledge. Every reference to flying machines and advanced activity were expunged from early Christian writings. The books that made up the early Christian Bible that have come down to us were carefully reviewed to insure that there were no "confusing" thoughts in them. The entertainment of a thought that was not in the accepted Christian writings was considered a sin worthy of a death sentence by the leaders of the early Church.

It would also seem that the political differences between the various factions of the gods still continue as a great deal of effort was put into depicting the benevolent gods as diabolical, lewd and cruel. The "modern" religions, without exception went to great lengths to supplant and eradicate the very existence of earlier religions. The efforts to suppress early knowledge went to such basics as denying that the earth was round.

But let us look even closer at the learning of the common man over the last two thousand years of human history. At the time that Columbus sailed for the new world, the general belief was that the earth was flat. Galileo was forced to proclaim that the Earth was motionless as stated in the Bible[176], though Copernicus had earlier taught that the Earth revolved around the Sun.

At the same time accepted doctrine stated that the Earth was flat, the Greek Historian Musaeus, 1400 B.C., wrote a treatise entitled The Sphere[177]. This treatise

---

[176] He was a victim of the Inquisition, a Church organized attempt to stamp out thought contrary to Church doctrine.

[177] Charroux, Robert, Masters of the World, Berkley Publishing Company, New York.

discussed the Earth being round as an established fact. I would point out that Musaeus was a high priest of the Eleusinian mysteries and an initiate in their higher mysteries. He would have had access to knowledge not available to the average man.

Aratus of Soli, a Greek physician and poet of the third century B.C. wrote an astronomical treatise in which eh described the spheres so precisely that there could be no doubt about the roundness of the earth. Aratus was not an unknown, but rather a very famous man for his time associating with Ptolemy Philadelphus, King of Egypt. His work was also translated by Eratosthenes, Hipparchus, Cicero, Caesar, Ovid and many others.

The early Hindus, Mayas and Incas left records showing that they had very sophisticated, advanced knowledge regarding cosmological knowledge. In 450 B.C. Pythagoras learned from the initiates of Egypt that the earth rotated on its axis and revolved around the Sun.

In a work entitled Meadows of Gold and Mines of Gems, Masudi, a 10th century Arabian historian wrote that "the sphere revolves around two points or poles, which can be likened to the pegs of the carpenter or turner who makes balls, bowls and other wooden objects[178]."

In the year 1000, Sylvester II, the reigning Pope demonstrated that the earth was round and revolved around the Sun. If the Pope, the head of the Catholic Church was aware that the earth revolved around the Sun, why did the Church continue to persecute those who held this position?

TINY MEN AND BIG IDEAS

There is evidence of the existence of advanced knowledge dating back to at least the time of the Incas that is very solid. As an example, the moons of Mars were not discovered until 1877 when astronomer Asaph Hall first saw them in the night sky. This was the first recorded sighting of these two satellites of Mars. However, Jonathan Swift, the author of Gulliver's Travels, wrote about the moons of Mars very specifically, long before Hall first saw them[179].

Jonathan Swift wrote Gulliver's Travels in 1726, some 151 years before any astronomer had even laid eyes on the moons in question or even had any idea that any planet in the solar system besides Earth was orbited by moons and yet Swift very accurately stated their proportions and orbits. Swift even wrote about some oddities of the moons of Mars, such as their specific orbits. There is no way he could have known this information, and yet he did. Even more oddly, he wrote

---

1967.

[178] Ibid

[179] Berlitz, Charles, Charles Berlitz's World of Strange Phenomena, Fawcett Crest, New York. 1988.

about the retrograde orbits of these two satellites, which leads researchers to think perhaps these moons are hollow. Is it possible that the satellites of the Planet Mars are artificial moons[180] placed in orbit by some earlier civilization? Was author Jonathan Swift able to draw upon some repository of information that he incorporated into Gulliver's Travels?

PROOF OF ADVANCED ANCIENT CIVILIZATIONS

Perhaps Swift was simply psychic; maybe he made a lucky guess. It would be very revealing if solid proof of advanced knowledge could be shown that could not be explained away by an uncaring scientific community. It will surprise many to learn that there is such incontrovertible evidence available that shows advanced knowledge on the part of early man.

It seems that approximately 10,000 years ago, some unknown civilization very carefully mapped the entire surface of the planet Earth. When the civilization that prepared these unusual maps ended, the maps themselves survived and were copied and recopied and then passed from one age to another[181]. Any knowledge regarding those who prepared these unusual documents was lost from the memory of man. Left behind by this mysterious early civilization are ancient, deserted massive cities of stone that were hoary with age when early man cautiously explored them.

In 1929 these unusual maps were obtained by a U.S. diplomat from one of those that participated in the looting of the former Imperial Palace of the Sultan of Constantinople. The set of maps in the possession of the looter clearly had been part of a larger volume of maps that could not be found no matter how diligently the diplomat searched. Finally, upon returning to the United States from his duties abroad, this worthy gentleman eventually turned these maps over to the care of the Library of Congress where they remained forgotten for many years.

Eventually, copies of these ancient maps, dated 1513 A.D., came to the attention of Captain Arlington H. Mallory. To most who had viewed these unusual documents they appeared to be nothing more than a garbled, stylized view of the ancient world. However, Captain Mallory saw something else. Working with the U.S. Hydrographic Office and the Weston Observatory of Boston, Captain Mallory developed a grid system that surprisingly brought the maps into sharp focus and dropped them in the middle of a major mystery. The modern Mercator grid system was not developed until the year 1559, but when Captain Mallory applied his newly developed grid system to these confusing maps, he discovered that they were as detailed and as accurate as the most modern maps prepared with the aid of aerial photographs.

As an example of the accuracy of these unique maps, called the Piri

---

[180] Ibid

[181] Keel, John A., Our Haunted Planet,Fawcett Publications, Greenwich, Conn., 1971.

Re'is[182] Maps, the continent of Antarctica was not discovered until Captain Cook reached it in 1773. However, this icy wasteland was not explored until the 1950s so there was little information on this desolate part of our planet available to modern mapmakers. To everyone's surprise, on these ancient maps the continent of Antarctica is presented with almost pinpoint accuracy, to include mountain ranges not even discovered until 1952. Other aspects of these ancient maps made it clear that the originals upon which these copies were based were prepared prior to the last Ice Age.

Professor Charles Hapgood, a scientific historian, turned the study of these unique maps into a class study project at Keene State College. After detailed study, Professor Hapgood's students found that these ancient maps were never more than 5 degrees off and this difference was probably due to land movement that occurred after the maps were drawn.

MORE EVIDENCE

Archeological evidence has also added much to our knowledge of this early unknown civilization. Approximately 50 years ago, science believed that man had migrated to the North American continent no more than 5,000 years ago and the level of civilization on the North American continent had not progressed beyond that of a primitive hunter until the arrival of the Europeans in the 1500s. Then a discovery was made in 1952 that drastically changed this belief[183].

Mexico City is built upon a dried lake bed and is the modern incarnation of an earlier Aztec City that had existed on the same spot for many years prior to the arrival of the Spanish Conquistadors. In 1952, Dr. Paul Sears of Yale University was excavating a spot where it was believed that the remains of early man could be found. At the level of 240 feet below the surface of the dried lake bed, Dr. Sears found some ancient grains of maize pollen. Maize is the most highly developed agricultural plant n the world and one of the most mysterious, since scientists have never been able to trace its original ancestors. However, according to radiocarbon testing, the pollen grains found by Dr. Sears beneath the dried lake bed beneath Mexico City were at least 25,000 years old[184].

Based upon these test results, someone or some civilization was harvesting domesticated maize in what is now Mexico at least 20,000 years before our science believes anyone in the Americans was doing anything more than hunting local game. The domestication of maize would have required a fairly well developed culture that we have been taught did not exist in the Americas at that time.

---

[182] Piri Re'is was a Turkish Admiral.
[183] Steiger, Brad, Overlords of Atlantis and the Great Pyramids, Inner Light Publications, New Jersey, 1989.
[184] Ibid.

HOUSE OF THE DEAD

There are many secrets concealed within the jungles of South America. Secrets that, if revealed could change how we look at human development on this planet. For example, when the Empire of the Incas was at its peak over 600 years ago, there existed the remnants of a massive city known as Tiahuanaco, also known as the City of the Dead. Even 600 years ago, this city was so old that there were not evens legends as to who built it. Pottery found within the deserted city has been dated to over 20,000 years old. There are other experts, however, who believe that the city dates from over 40,000 years ago and that rather than always being at an altitude of 13,000 feet, centuries ago, it was much closer to see level. So the question is who could have built such a city 40,000 years in earth's past, or even 20,000? Even with our modern equipment, we would have trouble building such a massive city today.

However, one thing that is very interest is that the Calassassayax, or House of Worship, found within Tiahuanaco is almost a replica of the Egyptian Temple of Karnak. According to established science, the Ancient Incans and the Ancient Egyptians did not have any direct contact, so how is it possible that each built an important religious center that had the same design?

ADDITIONAL EVIDENCE OF EARLY ADVANCEMENT

In addition to the vanished civilization that built the megalithic structures, there is also evidence of other early civilizations previously unknown to science. For example, in 1965, while examining the ruins of the Starcevo settlements, a Neolithic civilization first identified in the early 1930s, Yugoslav archaeologist Draodlav Strejovic found statues of round eyed household gods dating from a much older, unknown civilization[185]. This excavation, situated on the banks of the Danube River has produced tools and other implements dating back to 7000 BC. The complexity of the layout of the ancient town and the various artifacts discovered indicate that the early inhabitants of this site were very advanced as craftsmen and were very artistic and religious as well. However, to this date, no one has any idea who these people might be, nor where they originated.

It is interesting, however, to consider that though this site is dated back to approximately 7.000 BC, the statues of their gods dated to a much earlier period. Our history teaches that earlier than 7,000 BC, man on earth was extremely primitive. So who were the round eyed entities around at this early period in the history of man that could be considered a god?

In the early 1950s, Dr. J. Louis Giddings, Jr., of the University of Pennsylvania, conducted a study of ancient Arctic ruins that produced solid evidence of a culture that had circled the entire top of the world during prehistoric

---

[185] Ibid

times. In spite of the unbelievable achievements that this culture had achieved, it vanished into the pages of history. However, once again, no one has any idea what this culture might be, nor where it originated[186].

However, an even more interesting question is why in the last years of the 20th century with learning as wide spread as possible, why have these mind blowing discoveries not been trumpeted from the rooftops?

ANOTHER VIEW OF CREATION

Each religion believes that its religious teachings are inspired by God. However, with each modern religion, there is evidence that its teachings are based upon the teachings of an earlier religion. It is believed that the records upon which the Biblical Book of Genesis was based was the book Phoenician History written by Sanchuniathon long before the Biblical Old Testament was ever though of by the Biblical patriarchs. This Phoenician History and its first century translation by Philo Byblius have both mysteriously vanished, though there is a large body of secondary evidence making it clear that this unique work did, at one time, exist.

In the third century, a controversy arose between the Greek Porphyry and Eusebius, Bishop of Caesarea. In his attack on Porphyry's arguments, Eusebius first quoted from the Phoenician History and then stated that Sanchuniathon had never existed and that Philo had written the book as an attack on Christianity. Truth was the real victim in this disagreement as several ancient authors had written of Sanchuniathon.

Faced with the proof that Sanchuniathon was real and that his work did predate Genesis, Eusebius then switched tactics and tried to completely confuse the issue. Eusebius wrote the well known Historia Ecclesiastica, and despite his exalted position, he has a very dubious reputation for accuracy. Eusebius worked diligently on behalf of his patron Constantine in supporting Christianity and tearing down anything that appeared to question the new religion. In fact, Eusebius even wrote in Evangelical Demonstration that it was "permissible to use falsehood as a remedy for those why may be converted by that means[187]." So clearly, the early Church had an approved program of suppressing anything that would tend to "confuse" possible converts.

EXAMPLES OF ATTEMPTS TO SUPPRESS KNOWLEDGE[188]

As James Bond remarked, once is happenstance, twice is coincidence, but

[186] Ibid

[187] A tactic still used today by many religions to gain converts.

[188] Charroux, Robert, Masters of the World, Berkley Publishing Company, New York. 1967.

three times is enemy action. A single destruction of an early depository of ancient knowledge would be understandable, but the following list contained a large number of "major" assaults upon learning. There can be no doubt that these incidents were not all accidents.

330 BC The troops of Alexander the Great burned the Persepolis Library.

240 BC The Chinese Emperor Shih Huang Ti destroyed all books regarding science and history.

75 BC The Sibylline Books of the priests of Apollo perished in the burning of the Capitol.

48 BC Julius Caesar burned the Alexandrian Library.

A.D. 1 Augustus destroyed more than 2,000 volumes of predictions of the Oracle.

54 Saint Paul, at Ephesus, burned all books dealing with "strange things".

296 Diocletian burned the Christian libraries, with a large number of Egyptian and Greek documents.

3rd Century AD The Christian emperors of the West burned and destroyed many wonders of the ancient world, including the Temple of Diana at Ephesus and the archives contained within the Temple.

390 Theodosius burned the Books of Sibyl.

390 The forces of Christianity burned the Alexandrian Library for the second time.

405 Stilicho destroyed copies of the Sibylline Books.

410 Alaric pillaged and burned the libraries of Rome,

7th Century Irish monks burned 10,000 runic manuscripts written on birch bark, containing the history of the Celtic civilization.

641 The Caliph Omar ordered the third burning of the Alexandrian Library, saying that if what was in the Library was in the Koran then it was unnecessary and if it was not in the Koran than it was heretical and needed to be destroyed.

728	Leo the Isaurian burned 300,000 manuscripts in Byzantium.
789	Acting on the decrees of the Councils of Arles, Tours, Nantes and Toledo, Charlemagne forbade the worship of trees, stones and springs and ordered the destruction of all objects and documents related to pagan rites.
1221	Genghis Khan burned books of the ancient city of Bamian, the Thebes of the Orient.
13th Century	The Catholics destroyed the books of the Cathari.
14th and 15th Centuries	The Inquisition burned heretical manuscripts.
16th Century	The Christian conquistadors of Bishop Diego de Landa destroyed nearly all of the sacred books of the Aztecs.
	The books of Garcilaso de la Vega were burned by the Inquisition.
1566	Francisci Toledo, Vicery of Peru, destroyed an immense collection of Incan cloths and painted tablets relating to the ancient history on civilization in the Americas.
18th Century	In Ouardan, in Egypt, Father Sicard burned a "papyrus dovecote covered with magic characters."
1709	In Lisbon, Portugal, the Inquisition burned Gusinso's scientific documents.
20th Century	The ancient Hindu astronomical tables known as the Tirvalour Tables were sequestered in Paris and may well have been destroyed.
1926	Through rumor and innuendo, the credibility of Glozel, the world's richest archeological deposit was fraudulently undermined.
1937	The prehistoric library of Lussac-Ics-Chateaux was sequestered.

None of these disgraceful events of destruction were committed by accident, but rather on the explicit orders of some leader during each time period. While the actual amount of destruction seemed contained to the locale where the records in question were found, each of these incidents tore huge holes in our knowledge of a possible early civilization. There can be no doubt that each of these shameful incidents was part of a very carefully crafted plan to suppress any existing knowledge regarding earlier civilizations.

With all of these blatant attempts directed at destroying the amassed early knowledge of the ancient world which were directed by the then rulers of the known world, there can be no doubt that there was a concerted plan to control the spreading of this knowledge. Early Occult teachings tell that many Secret Societies arose to protect and hand down suppressed early knowledge. Though many of these disgraceful incidents of destruction were at the orders of early Church officials, the question would be who ultimately directed this destruction of early knowledge. The answer to this question would certainly be very revealing.

ADDITIONAL EVIDENCE OF EARLY ADVANCED KNOWLEDGE

In 1953, Dr. Samuel A. B. Mercer, professor emeritus of Semitic and Egyptian languages at Trinity College, University of Toronto, finished translating the hierographics carved into five small pyramids near Sakkara, Egypt[189]. These hierographics then considered to be the oldest written records of mankind's history, revealed that 3,600 years before Columbus accidentally bumped into America, Egyptian children were being taught that the world was round. Additionally, Egyptian students were being routinely taught history, astronomy, medicine, engineering, agriculture and other subjects we would consider "modern."

Frankly, knowledge of the existence this rather advanced educational system in ancient Egypt, supports the belief among many researchers that the Egyptian civilization appeared at its peak of advancement and then slowly disintegrated over time. This would certainly be in keeping with the theory that a civil war led to the collapse of the first civilization and that the survivors spread out to try and rebuilt what had been.

In 1952-53, John Brown, the leader of the Thirstland Expedition to the southern and central Africa's desert zones sent back an account of cave art found in the Mountains of Fire[190]. In some of these truly remarkable cave paintings, the central figure was a pretty white woman[191], young and graceful with her hair bobbed in the style of Ancient Egypt. She wore a beaded head-dress, a garment that resembled a modern jersey blouse, shorts, gloves, girdle and shoes similar to those worn in modern Mediterranean countries[192]. To my way of thinking, this is fairly

---

[189] Steiger, Brad, Atlantis Rising, Dell. New York. 1973
[190] Ibid
[191] The figure in question possessed classic Caucasian features.
[192] Steiger, Brad, Atlantis Rising, Dell. New York. 1973

convincing evidence of an advanced early civilization existing on earth and interacting with primitive cultures long before it is believed to be possible.

What happened to this early advanced civilization and its knowledge? We may never know, but certainly, as shown above, an effort was made to suppress knowledge of this early civilization as much as possible. Even more importantly, even though this early civilization has long vanished, what happened to its residents, did they all die? Or did some continue to live; influencing events in our world from the shadows?

Unfortunately, those who support contemporary scientific knowledge would say that one example is not sufficient to prove anything. However, there are a number of examples of various anomalies that support the idea of an existing early advanced civilization as we shall see in later chapters.

CHAPTER SEVENTEEN

PHYSICAL EVIDENCE OF OLDER RACES

"What has happened will happen again, and what has been done will be done again, and there is nothing new under the sun. Is there anything of which one can say, "Look, this is new?" No, it has already existed, long before our time. The men of old are not remembered and those who will follow will not be remembered by those who follow them."

Ecclesiastes 1:9-11

Now that I have presented evidence that the physical remains of an ancient civilization exists on this planet alongside our own civilization, the next question would be to ask if there is any physical evidence of another race existing here besides our own. Prior to the appearance of Homo Sapien there was, of course, Cro-Magnon and Neanderthal man. Science tells us that only Homo Sapien survived the rigors of the ancient world as Darwin postulated in his Theory of Evolution. At the same time, science also says that modern man is not directly related to Neanderthal or Cro-Magnon man.

So the question would be how three separate species of man arose on this one planet. However, such an extensive study is not the mission of this text; rather the question is was evidence ever found that showed that a totally unrelated race of creatures once walked the surface of our world. The short answer is that there actually is a great deal of evidence that another race did inhabit our planet and may well still be here.

Supporting the hypothesis that there were earlier races possessing even greater potential for advancement than our own was the English Chemist Frederick Soddy, winner of the Nobel Prize in 1921. Dr. Soddy stated the view that traditions provide justification for believing that there were once human races, now vanished that not only reached our level of knowledge but also possessed powers which we do not yet have[193]. Taking this position as a starting point, as we shall see, it would also appear that there were earlier races that were not necessarily human.

LEGENDS OF EARLIER CIVILIZATIONS

Did earlier civilizations pre-date our own in the planet Earth? Soviet professor J. B. Federov believes that all civilizations on earth originated in a mother civilization that existed at the beginnings of time, lost to us as a result of a major disaster[194]. French author Monsieur de Longueville Harcouet wrote[195] that the Chinese had legends of a world older than our own that had existed for several hundred thousand years.

Even the ancient Hindu's speak of an advanced world wide empire, called MU[196] that existed at the dawn of time, destroyed when the continent upon which it existed sank in a great cataclysm. With the destruction of the motherland, only the colonies, such as Egypt remained. Other legends maintain that even mythical Atlantis was a more recent remnant of the earlier civilization. Assuming that there is any validity to these legends, there should be evidence of extremely ancient advanced civilizations. Surprisingly enough, there is a large body of evidence, most of which has never been openly discussed.

As an example, in 1969, Soviet Professor Leonidov Marmajaijan led an expedition underwritten by the Universities of Leningrad and Ashkhabad into central Asia. In one large cave, the researchers discovered perfectly preserved skeletons that have been dated as being in excess of 100,000 years old[197]. A report[198] discussing the discovery was presented to the Soviet Academy of Science in November, 1969. Of course, little mention of this momentous discovery was made in the West.

Most interesting of all, the researchers discovered evidence of the removal of the center area penetrated by a trephination. Even more astonishing, they also discovered traces of a surgical operation on the bones bordering the chest cavity. The ribs on the left side of the skeletons had been cut and an opening had been made and widened by retraction to permit the operation. Since the bones around the opening were covered with periosteum (a fibrous membrane that covers bones and enables callus to form) the Soviet scientists concluded that "after the success of this major operation, the patient recovered and lived at least three to five years, as

---

[193] Charroux, Robert, Forgotten Worlds, Popular Library, New York. 1973.
[194] Ibid
[195] Histoire des personnes qui ont vecu plusieurs siecles et qui ont rejeuni, 1735.
[196] Churchward, Frank, Children of MU.
[197] Charroux, Robert, Forgotten Worlds, Popular Library, New York. 1973.
[198] Report of the Marmajaijan Scientific Expedition in Soviet Central Asia in 1969 on Behalf of the Turkmenistan Anthropological Society.

shown by the thickness of the periosteum." In other words, these skeletons in question demonstrated that approximately 100,000 years ago several successful heart operations had been performed by supposedly primitive man. According to accepted science, 100,000 years ago was the time of Pithecanthropus and the beginning of Neanderthal man, neither of which had the capability to perform such delicate operations[199].

As if the discoveries in 1969 were not enough to upset the accepted pronouncements of accepted science, evidence of similar operations had been found in the Middle East, dating from over 50,000 years ago. From where did the advanced medical knowledge come to make such operations possible? After all, such knowledge had to have developed over a long period of time and be supported by a fairly advanced civilization[200].

Support for the existence of such advanced knowledge can also be found in the records of ancient Egypt. According to a papyrus found in the library at Alexandria, Egypt, written in Coptic, but based upon an older text, a member of Pharaoh's guard received a wound in the heart. A surgeon had the idea of replacing the man's heart with that of a bull. The operation was reported to have been successful.

It is also interesting to note that brain surgery was known to have been practiced among the ancient Incas, with the patients generally surviving the procedure. These advanced medical procedures took place at a time when the most advanced civilization on earth was alleged that of Europe in the middle ages when witches were being burnt at the stake.

Of a more practical nature, gynecology was an unknown science until the latter half of the 19th century, however, according to the October 20, 1900 issue of Scientific American, ancient medical implements found in the Temple of the Vestal Virgins, buried by the eruption of Mount Vesuvius in A.D. 79, demonstrated that the science of gynecology was flourishing at a very high level at the time of the eruption[201]. Where did the ancient Romans get such advanced medical knowledge? The medical instruments found are almost absolute duplicates of those used in the most advanced medical facilities and the workmanship demonstrated in the manufacture of the instruments found in the Temple is as fine as anything produced in the 20th century.

As if this were not enough, rock paintings have been found in Europe of the Ice Age creature called the Diprotodon, a rhinoceros sized animal which became extinct over 6,000 years ago. However, researchers were stunned to find similar paintings in Australia at a rock shelter north of Cairns in Queensland. The rock painting in question shows a Diprotodon with a rope around its neck suggesting that the creature not only lived in Australia, but that early inhabitants of

---

[199] Ibid

[200] Ibid

[201] Steiger, Brad, Mysteries of Time and Space, Dell, New York. 1973.

this continent had also domesticated the creature. Such domestication certainly predates accepted scientific beliefs of when early man began to domesticate the animals around him[202].

I will give one last example of advanced knowledge before moving on. In 1956, a solid sheet of glass weighing approximately 8.8 tons was found in an ancient cistern. This unusual sheet of glass was 3.40 meters long and 1.95 meters wide. It was not until the mid 20th century that modern man was able to successfully manufacture the largest glass object every created, the 200 hundred inch reflecting mirror in the Hale Telescope at Mount Palomar. However, the solid glass sheet referred to above was manufactured at Beth She'arim, an ancient center of Jewish learning in southwestern Galilee. From where did the advanced knowledge of glass work come from to allow such an accomplishment thousands of years ago[203]?

There have been other discoveries that make it clear that an advanced civilization existed in the Artic regions. In June 1940, archaeologist Magnus and Froelich Rainey discovered a buried city almost a mile long and at least a quarter of a mile long. Within this city were over 200 houses that showed a remarkable state of advancement. Elaborate and sophisticated carvings found at the site proved that the inhabitants of the buried center were not related to the Eskimo cultures but rather came from some other advanced cultural center[204].

With the proof on the table that there existed very advanced medical knowledge among those thought to be very primitive, and that man began to domesticate members of the animals kingdom far earlier than previously believed, we must next ask ourselves is their proof that other races predated our own? Surprisingly enough there is such proof.

GIANTS

I remember when I was very young hearing a number of fairy tails involving wicked giants interacting with normal humans. While the stories of giants roaming the earth are found in the legends of almost every civilization, most of us relegate such stories to the realm of fantasy. However there is a large body of evidence that holds that giants once did roam our planet and may well have interacted and warred with Humans.

In 1898, Ed Earl Repp was present when H. Flagler Cowden and Charles C. Cowden, scientists specializing in the study of desert antiquity uncovered the remains of a giant female in the Death Valley region that they believed was a

---

[202] Berlitz, Charles, Charles Berlitz's World of The Odd and The Awesome, Fawcett Crest, New York. 1991.

[203] Ibid

[204] Ibid

member of the race of unprecedented large primitives which vanished from the face of the earth over 100,000 years before. The age of the remains, which were estimated to be over seven and one half feet tall, was determined through measuring the amount of silica in the soil and by the state of petrification of the skeletal remains[205]. Further examination revealed that there were several extra buttons at the base of the spine and there was every indication showing that the people were endowed with a tail-like appendage. Her canine teeth were twice the size in length of those of modern man.

In 1874, workmen opening the way for the railroad between Weldon and Garryburg, North Carolina broke into a catacomb containing a large number of bodies of "a strange and remarkable formation[206]." According to a story reported in the Daily Independent of Helena, Montana on April 4, 1984,

"*The skulls were nearly an inch thick, the teeth were filed sharp, as those of cannibals, enamel perfectly preserved; the bones were of wonderful strength, the femurs being as long as the leg of an ordinary man, the stature of the body being probably as great as eight or nine feet.*"

On July 30, 1974, the Dallas Morning News[207] carried a story regarding the discovery of the remains of a woman estimated to be seven feet tall. According to Frank Tolbert, Dr. Ernest Adams, an attorney in Somervell County and an amateur archaeologist, found the bones sealed in a cave at the crest of a mesa near Chalk Mountain. Dr. Adams believed that the woman was of average size for her race.

On May 4, 1912, no less an authority than the New York Times[208] reported that several gigantic human skeletons were found while an ancient mound was being excavated at Lake Delavan, Wisconsin. According to the report, the heads were much larger than the heads of any race which inhabit America today.

At Gargayan in the Philippines a human skeleton over 17 feet tall was discovered and in southeast China, human remains over ten feet tall have also been discovered[209]. It was determined that these remains were over 300,000 years old. At Agadir, in Morocco, a French Captain discovered a cache of hunting weapons, some of which weighed over 17 ½ pounds. Due to the size of these ancient weapons, it was estimated that those that wielded them had to be over 13 feet tall.

In addition to the remains that have been found, there are a number of literary references that confirm the existence of the giants. Greek mythology talks of the Titans and the Cyclops. The Titans, of course, were not only described as giants, but were the original gods who were overthrown by Zeus and his followers.

---

[205] Steiger, Brad, Overlords of Atlantis and the Great Pyramid, Inner Light Publications, New Jersey, 1989.

[206] Ibid.

[207] Dallas Morning News, July 30, 1974.

[208] New York Times, May 4, 1912.

[209] Kolosimo, Peter, Timeless Earth, Bantam Books, New York. 1975.

This sounds very similar to my theory of a revolt among the so called gods that resulted in destruction of the original mother civilization on this planet.

As if this was not enough support of the existence of giants, no less an authority than the Holy Bible spoke of these huge humanoids. In the Book of Genesis, Chapter 6, the Bible specifically states that "there were giants in the earth in those days". In the Book of Deuteronomy, Chapter 3, Verse 11, it was written that "only Og king of Bashan remained of the remnant of giants". Confirming his giant size was a description of his bed, being 9 cubits by 4 cubits (13.5 feet by 6 feet). Like most people, I like a big bed, but one that is 13 feet long is a bit excessive for a normal sized person. Then there was Goliath, of biblical fame who was described in the 1st Book of Samuel, Verse 17 as being six cubits and a half tall or 9 ¾ feet tall.

In addition to these references, there are also references to giants to be found in the Book of Joshua, Chapters 12, 13, 15 and 17 as well as the second Book of Samuel, Chapter 21; 1st Chronicles, Chapter 20; the Book of Job, Chapter 26; the Book of Baruch, Chapter 2 and in Revelations, Chapter 20. With so many references from so many diverse Books, there is no doubt that there once existed a race of giants that interacted with man. Saurat also makes the observation that giant size and longer life also appear to go hand in hand and could well be the reason that the giant gods and the concept of immortality are so closely associated. Who is to say that there may not be remnants of this race of immortal giants that may be living even today? This would certainly explain why they must operate from the shadows through agents or through secret societies.

Could these giants be the last remnants of an earlier civilization that developed the unbelievably advanced medical knowledge that allowed heart and brain surgery over 100,000 years ago? Perhaps, however, there is also evidence that there were other races that existed here besides the giants.

LITTLE PEOPLE

In addition to giants, there is also evidence that the many stories of chance encounters with the "wee folk" may not be simply a fairy tail or a hallucination brought on by too much drink. Not only were such reports common in Europe, but there were also reports from the so called New World.

In the year 1828 in the great state of Tennessee, several newspapers reported the discovery in Sparta, White County, Tennessee, of burial several mysterious burial grounds. When several of the apparent graves were opened, they were found to contain tiny stone coffins. Inside the coffins were the remains of very small people, the tallest of which was approximately 19 inches tall. The graves were only two feet deep and the small corpses were burred on their backs with their heads to the east. Buried with each tiny skeleton was a pint vessel made of ground stone or shell. Each of these tiny vessels contained two or three shells. In 1853, in a work entitled The Romance of Natural History referred to tiny stone coffins being found in Kentucky and other parts of Tennessee[210].

In the old country, in the 12th century, Giraldus Cambrensis, the Welsh chronicler told of an unusual story he had heard from his uncle, David II, the Bishop of St. David's. The Bishop told of an old priest named Elidor who, as a young child, spent some time with a small race of people that inhabited a hidden land beneath the earth. According to the old priest, these mysterious folk spoke a language similar to Greek, ate no meat, but subsisted on milk, butter and cheese mixed with saffron[211]. Eventually, Elidor's greed resulted in his banishment from the underground kingdom.

The Celts and Germanic countries of Europe stories of small races go back literally thousands of years. According to legend, these wee people lived below ground and only ventured to the surface at night. In England, they were called Fairies or Elves, in Ireland they were called the Sidhe or Gentry and in Scotland, they were called the Sith or the Good People.

According to legend, the Fairies were thought to be divided into two races, the Fair Folk or Light Elves and the Dark Elves, which were described as swarthy, squat, and often hairy beings that seemed to have an affinity for places deep beneath the earth. Included in the classification of Dark elves were the Brownies, Kobolds, Gnomes, Dwarfs, Trolls and a virtual army of cavern and mine spirits[212].

In Central America, dwarf like humanoids are known as ikals and wendis. Legends of the local inhabitants have long held that the ikal paralyzed and kidnapped Indian women, who were then taken back to their caves and impregnated as often as once a week, giving birth to black off-spring that were taught to fly. Some of these stories are very similar to those told by abductees regarding small humanoids that paralyze, probe and impregnate their captives. Could these small humanoids be somehow related to the small UFO occupants[213] seen by so many of those who have reported that they have been abducted by unknown entitles?

The evidence shows that both the giants as well as the little people had existed in the distant past, it is also possible that other, unknown races have existed that perhaps looked enough like man to exist among us unnoticed. This theory would explain many of the mysterious visitations written about in ancient works.

In Peru is the ruined complex of Sacsahuaman, built of dressed stones,

---

[210] Steiger, Brad, Overlords of Atlantis and the Great Pyramid, Inner Light Publications, New Jersey, 1989.

[211] Kafton-Minkel, Walter, Subterranean Worlds: 100,000 years of dragons, dwarfs, the dead, lost races & UFOs from inside the Earth, Loompanics Unlimited, Port Townsend, Washington, 1989.

[212] Ibid.

[213] Bertliz, Charles, Charles Berlitz's World of Strange Phenomena, Fawcett Crest, New York. 1988.

some of which weighed 20,000 tons[214]. Such technology is beyond our own best efforts today, so how did so called primitive man work with such huge stones? However, even stranger than the huge stones of which the vast fortress is constructed, was a maze of tunnels with miniature staircases that were carved out of the solid rock. Investigation revealed that the entire fortress was honeycombed with these tiny tunnels that were so small that even midgets and small children would have trouble moving through them.

At Raica, Chile, a vast, ancient, ruined city built specifically for a tiny race of humanoid beings has been found[215]. There is no information available regarding this ancient tiny race. There is, however, little doubt that they were numerous based on the size of the ruins.

In Exeter, New Hampshire, an area well known for UFO activity, another ancient maze of tiny tunnels has been discovered. Were the Americas once home to a tiny race of beings now unlike the "wee people" of legend? It would appear that this may well have been the case.

Further evidence supporting this unusual theory can be found in the ruined pyramids and temples at the Monte Alban site in the Oaxaca region of Mexico. Archeologists have long believed that these monumental ruins were built by the Zapotec culture, but there are some problems with this conclusion. Primarily, the legends that exist in this part of the world maintain that these ruins were ancient when the earliest culture first moved into the area. If these legends are true, then who built such monumental structures and where did the builders go?

EVEN MORE EVIDENCE OF CONTACT

The concept that early man was visited by more advanced individuals is given even more support by other Hindu traditions. This tradition relates that men from the great white star[216] took up their abode on the island in the Sea of Gobi in the year 18,617,841 B.C. According to the ancient writings, these advanced visitors built a fortress and a vast city on the island, linking it to the mainland by a maze of large tunnels. The suggested date above may certainly be in error, but the story of an advanced race settling in the Gobi is supported by a number of unrelated writings.

Some decades ago, a map of the heavens was found in a cave in Bohistan in the Himalayas. This map was confirmed to be very accurate by modern astronomers, who also noted that this unique map showed the stars as they would have been seen more than 13,000 years ago. It was also noted in a related story in

---

[214] Andrews, George C., Extra-Terrestrials Among Us, Llewellyn Publications, St. Paul, Minnesota. 1993.
[215] Ibid.
[216] Thought to be the planet Venus.

the National Geographic that there were lines drawn on the map connecting the earth and the planet Venus. Some researchers suggested that these lines represented the path that space craft took from the Planet Venus to their landing site in what is now the Gobi Desert.

In the year 1778, Jean-Sylvain Bailly, the Mayor of Paris and the French Astronomer Royal, was puzzled by some ancient maps of the heavens that were brought back to France from India. The maps, acquired by Missionaries allegedly seeking to save souls but instead looking for treasure, were found to be thousands of years old and showed stars which could not have been visible from the supposed place of origin in India. It appeared to Bailly that the maps had been drawn from some location in the Gobi Desert[217]. So now the question is what race lived in the Gobi Desert that was advanced enough to make extremely accurate maps of the heavens? There was no doubt in Bailly's mind that the maps had been found by explorers and taken to India long after the demise of the advanced race that had drawn them.

It should also be noted that this region that we call the Gobi Desert was once the heartland of the Empire of MU, the first civilization. The ancient Hindu legends of the space visitors that landed on the Island in the Gobi Sea and the evidence supporting the existence of MU seem to be gelling together in a remarkable fashion[218].

ANCIENT TEACHERS

Many civilizations have legends of benevolent teachers who came from some unknown place to teach early man the basics of civilization. However, it would certainly be a surprise to many to know that one of the most ancient civilizations known to modern man was the result of visits by such advanced teachers.

The early civilization known as Sumerian rose to great heights of learning in Mesopotamia several thousand years ago. Their advancement seemed to have been nothing short of miraculous in a number of areas of learning. However, the Sumerians wrote that their speedy advancement from primitive tribesmen to city builders was the direct result of teaching that they received from the Apkallu, whose leader, Oannes, had a body that resembled a great fish and a head that combined the features of a fish and a human[219].

According to records left by the ancient Sumerians, the Apkallu descended from the heavens in a star and transformed the Sumerians, who were living like the beasts in the field into people well versed in the working with metals, ceramics and all of the other skills needed to build a civilization.

---

[217] Kolosimo, Peter, Timeless Earth, Bantam Books, New York. 1975.
[218] Ibid.
[219] Bell, Art and Brad Steiger, The Source, Paper Chase Press, New Orleans, Louisiana. 1999.

Under the guidance of Oannes and his followers, the Sumerians not only built permanent cities, but also created the first love song, the first school system, the first consolidated listing of pharmaceutical concoctions, the first codified system of laws and the first parliamentary system of government[220].

As if these achievements were not enough, at the peak of the Greek civilization, the highest number used was 10,000. Any sum above that number was referred to as infinity. However, according to a tablet found in the Kuynjik Hills in what was ancient Sumeria, the Sumerians were working with 15 digit numbers. On the table unearthed from a ruined structure, the number 195,995,200,000,000 was used. I think that anyone would have to agree that for a civilization that modern science considers primitive, working with 15 digit numbers would be considered quite an accomplishment[221].

In keeping with the discussion of unknown teachers and suppressed knowledge, there have long been legends regarding one or more rooms hidden beneath the Sphinx and tunnels running from the Sphinx to the Great Pyramid. Well, according to authors Graham Hancock and Robert Bauval in their book *The Message of the Sphinx*[222].

OTHER UNKNOWN RACES

Is there substantial evidence that there exists a race, which I shall refer to as para-humans, that lives alongside us and yet is apart? It may surprise many to discover that there does in fact exist such a body of evidence. In fact, no less a body of work than the Holy Bible of the Christian religion give support for the belief that there exists another race that has the appearance of man. In the book of the Bible known as Hebrews, Chapter 13, verse 2, it is written "Be not forgetful to entertain strangers, for thereby some have entertained angels unawares." Very clearly, this verse is sating that there exists another, more advanced race, that looks enough like man to be considered an ordinary human.

Human looking members of such an unknown race could easily fool those less advanced with whom they came in contact and explain many events that are still considered mysterious. For example, Chinese archaeologists discovered the oldest, most complete mummy ever found in China. The baffling aspect to this otherwise momentous discovery is that the mummified woman is not Chinese; rather she is clearly Caucasian and died over 4,000 years ago, at a time when there were no known European visits to China[223]. The unknown woman was described as

---

[220] Ibid.

[221] Ibid.

[222] Hancock, Graham and Robert Bauval, The Message of the Sphinx , Three Rivers Press; 1st Pbk edition (May 27, 1997)

[223] Berlitz, Charles, Charles Berlitz's World of The Odd and The Awesome, Fawcett

being about five feet tall, with reddish brown skin and long blonde hair. Working within the parameters of known scientific discoveries, researchers decided that the woman was a member of the nomadic Uigur, the forerunner of the modern Turks. However, no one was able to explain how this supposedly primitive woman died with high levels of cholesterol in her muscles and traces of the silvery white element antimony in her lungs.

Other discoveries in the Taklamaken Desert in the late 1970s only added to the confusion. Dozens of mummies, known as the Tarim Basin people, were discovered, perfectly preserved by the areas alternately hot, dry desert air of the summer and the frigid temperatures of winter. The perfectly preserved bodies of the Tarim Basin people were found to have dark blond, reddish or yellow-brown hair, deep set eyes and long limbs. After years of study, even the most die hard Chinese scientist had to admit that there was no question that these mummies were Caucasian. Ancient legends had spoken of a Caucasian race that had arrived at the dawn of time and established a very advanced civilization that thrived for over 1,500 years[224].

Thus far, over 1,000 mummies have been found and new sites are found continually. As of yet, the scientists excavating what seems to be the center of the Tarim Basis civilization have yet to determine either the extent or the actual level of advancement of this unknown culture[225]. Where did such an advanced culture originate?

Then there are the stories of a god-king known as Quetzalcoatl (or the Plumed Serpent) who is said to have come to Mexico with a group of companions from a far off land the to the east[226]. Quetzalcoatl was described as

"*a fair and ruddy complexioned man with a long beard. He was a mysterious white man with strong formation of body, broad forehead, large eyes, and a flowing beard, who came from across the sea in a boat that moved by itself without paddles. He condemned sacrifices, except of fruits and flowers. He was known as the god of peace.*[227]"

The teachings of this mysterious white, bearded figure is surprisingly like the teachings of Christianity, though no one has ever identified this mysterious individual or what country he may have come from. Though this mysterious figure is associated with the Mayans, even the ancient Olmecs spoke of visits from Quetzalcoatl some 3,500 years ago. This early date would actually predate the birth of Jesus and the beginnings of the Christian religion. More than 2,000 years ago

---

Crest, New York. 1991.

[224] Hart, Will, The Genesis Race, Bear & Company, Rochester, Vermont. 2003.

[225] Ibid.

[226] Hancock, Graham and Santha Falla, Heaven's Mirror: Quest for the Lost Civilization, Crown Publishers, Inc. New York. 1998.

[227] Ibid.

work began at Cholula in central Mexico on a gigantic monument dedicated to the mysterious Quetzalcoatl. How could this mysterious being teach Christianity before this religion was ever first mentioned by the one known as The Christ?

It might also be noted that the Aztecs believed that their race had originated in a womb-like cave in the heart of a mountain in Aztlan, which they said existed on an island to the east. They also believed that their race had been ordered to leave this first homeland by the god Huitzilopochtli[228]. Though well versed in the arts of war by their gods, the Aztecs also admitted that they received their rather surprisingly advanced knowledge in one piece from the god-king Quetzalcoatl and his followers.

Though accepted scientific learning has held that there were no Caucasians in the Americans prior to the arrival of Columbus, newly discovered evidence makes it clear that this is not the case. In fact, it would now appear that the Americas were regularly visited by so called primitive man long before Columbus bumped into North America. In 1997, skeletons were unearthed in several western states that began to upset the established teachings that the first inhabitants of the Americans were of Asian descent[229]. The skeletons' skulls had features similar to those of Europeans, suggesting that Caucasoid people were among the earliest humans to come to the Americans more than 9,000 years ago. In fact, a mummified body of a Caucasoid man that died approximately 9,300 years ago was found near what is now Kennewick, Washington. The appearance was so close to modern man that at first the body was mistaken for that of a colonial settler. It was only later that scientific dating techniques made it clear that the remains were incredibly old.

These disturbing discoveries raise a large number of questions about the possible identity of Quetzalcoatl and the secret existence of survivors of an earlier civilization who looked enough like modern man to be able to pass as one. There was no doubt that Quetzalcoatl demonstrated knowledge far in advance of the norm and more in keeping with a member of a more advanced civilization. Perhaps, he was working as a missionary, so to speak. Could he have come from some last remnant of the mother civilization in order to try and raise the level of the vast majority of the inhabitants of the world? There is evidence that would tend to support such a theory.

I would also point to the discoveries of the world famous anthropologist Richard Leakey. In November, 1972, Dr. Leakey discovered a fragmented skull near Lake Rudolf in Kenya, estimated to be at least 2.5 million years old and "almost certainly the oldest complete skull of early man." He also said that while the skull appeared different from that of Homo sapiens, it was also different from all other known forms of early man and thus does not fit into any of the presently

---

[228] Ibid

[229] Washington Post, April 15, 1997.

held theories of human evolution[230].

If man, or something like man, existed over 2.5 million years ago, then it would certainly be very possible that such an ancient race could have given birth to an equally ancient civilization of which we known nothing. If Homo Sapiens were intelligent enough to build a highly advanced civilization then why would we expect less from a race that clearly existed over 2 million years ago? This is a long time to expect a race to exist and accomplish exactly nothing. The fact that the skull discovered by Dr. Leakey was different from that of Homo Sapien made it clear that this skull may have come from a totally different race that inhabited this planet but who predated the arrival of early man. Could this skull be that of one of the exalted Annanaki of legend?

More evidence of this mysterious advanced civilization can be found in the writings of the early Spanish Conquistadors who invaded and destroyed the Incan civilization. There was no doubt that the Incas were barbaric descendants of or inheritors of knowledge that belonged to a much earlier civilization. The Spaniards were totally unconcerned with gaining knowledge, being on a hunt for gold. The Incas had gold in large amounts and this ignited a greed that still burns today. In their lust for the riches of the Incas, Pizarro and his follows not only murdered the last Incan Emperor, but tens of thousands of his followers. However, what they were able to steal amounted to only a small fraction of the riches that were available.

The wife of the last Incan Emperor had consulted the oracles and learned that the Spaniards were going to murder her husband no matter what ransom was paid in order to ensure that he would not be able to organize a revolt against their precarious rule. She decreed that all of the massive treasure still possessed by the Incas would be hidden in secret caves and ancient hidden tunnels that had been built by a mysterious, highly advanced race that had once populated their country. The secret to recovering this treasure would be passed on to only one member of her people in each generation[231].

Many think that this story of lost and hidden Incan treasure is just a myth, but actually there is a great deal of evidence that it may be true. Explores have discovered that there is actually a maze of tunnels that run through the South American continent. In fact, the best known part of this tunnel system is the portion that runs from Lima to Cuzco, Peru, the ancient Incan capital. From Cuzco, the tunnels run south-eastward to the Bolivian border. According to legend, one of these hidden tunnels contains a royal tomb containing vast riches.

It is fairly well agreed that the Incas did not and could not have created this tunnel system. It is much more likely that the Incas merely used what they found already in existence, much as they did the larger portion of their somewhat advanced knowledge. There is no knowing what secrets would have been revealed

---

[230] Steiger, Brad, Mysteries of Time and Space, Dell, New York. 1973.

[231] Kolosimo, Peter, Timeless Earth, Bantam Books, New York. 1975.

to us in the Incan records, had not the early Christian Missionaries who accompanied the Spanish Conquistadors on their invasions into the Americas burned all of the written history of the Incas believing that it was evil since their gods were not those of the Christians.

AN ANCIENT WORLD WIDE CIVILIZATION?

How about the possibility that this earlier civilization was world wide and that its survivors continued to travel from continent to continent long after the mother civilization was reduced to dust in an attempt to resurrect past glories? Sounds outlandish, but let us look at some possible evidence that supports this hypothesis of a globe trotting group of individuals who left some impossible things behind them when they disappeared.

There is no doubt that the sophisticated tunnel system found in the jungles of South America can be found in almost every part of the world. This may well have given rise to the legends of a hollow earth. Hidden, little known tunnels are found in California, Virginia, Hawaii, Oceania, Asia, Sweden, Czechoslovakia, the Balearics and the Island of Malta[232]. There is one huge tunnel that runs between Spain and Morocco of which a little over thirty miles has been explored. We do not even have legends about the civilization that constructed this remarkable tunnel system, but it would seem that it extends to most parts of our planet.

Historians have long taught that early man was very primitive and did not travel much outside his familiar areas. Certainly there was not travel to the new world until around the 1400s. However, if this was the case, then how can the following anomalies be explained?

- Roman coins have been unearthed in early Amerindian burial mounds as far west as Illinois and yet according to our accepted history there was no way that Romans could have come to the New World;

- An iron fork was found in a prehistoric Indian site near Eddyville, Kentucky;

- Japanese pottery from the Jomon period of 3,000 B.C. was found in Ecuador in 1966;

- Ancient Viking rune stones have been found throughout the Untied States and Canada;

- Colossal stone heads scattered in the jungles of Veracruz, Mexico display

---

[232] Ibid.

obvious Negroid features and yet our accepted history maintains that no representatives of this race traveled much beyond the borders of Africa;

- A clay tablet found along the Susquehanna River near Winfield, Pennsylvania bears a cuneiform inscription that describes a short term loan of an Assyrian merchant in Cappadocia around 1900 B.C.;

- In 1910, a boy playing in some 800 year old Indian ruins along the Animas River in Flora Vista, New Mexico dug up two slabs of carved rock showing an unknown language and two elephants[233];

- In July 1945, Waldemar Julsrud, of Acambro, Mexico discovered more than 30,000 artifacts that totally overturn many preconceived scientific notions. The figures are more than 6,500 years old, but a large number of them depict dinosaurs and plesiosaurs, others depict grotesque dragons and monster like creatures while others represent strange fish faced humans. Some of the creatures so depicted passed into extinction over 12,000 years before the unknown artisan made the artifacts and the dinosaurs died out millions of years ago.

There is no way to determine from where these unusual items originated. Is it possible that there actually did exist some world wide civilization that now exists only through the efforts of a few survivors? How does an iron fork come to be found at a prehistoric Indian site? How can an unknown artesian fashion a statute of a dinosaur that became extinct millions of years before the statue was fashion?

Even more interesting are some of the monuments left behind by earlier unknown civilizations. For example, in the state of Paraiba in eastern Brazil, there is a ruined fortress with walls over 80 feet high and over 16 feet thick. The inner hall of this mysterious building is 164 yards by 50 yards. This fortress is so old there are not even legends about the builders, but what ancient civilization had the technology to building something so massive?

If this structure is not large enough to raise a number of questions, then consider the stones of Baalbek, an ancient ruined city in the country of Lebanon. The builders of this ancient monument were able to transport and left into position blocks of solid stone over 750 tons in weight. This feat was accomplished at a time when we are told everything had to be done by hand and with sheer strength. As if this amazing accomplishment was not enough, in the quarry approximately ½ mile from this ancient city is the largest cut stone in the history of the world, weighing

---

[233] Elephants have not existed, if they ever did, in the Americas in thousands of years. So how did the ancient artist draw the accurate pictures of creatures that he or she had never seen?

over 2,000 tons and beyond even our capabilities to day to lift and transport. However, apparently the ancient builders felt that they could work with such a huge stone. What civilization was capable of working with such building materials?

Finally, I would also point to some little known Russian discoveries that seem to upset our well ordered beliefs regarding both the development of the human race as well as the rise of civilization. Today, we are taught in our schools that the Phoenicians invented the alphabet from which that of Greece as well as our own were derived. More recent discoveries have shown that the Phoenicians actually appropriated the alphabet from the ancient Egyptians.

To further upset those who swear by existing theories regarding the rise of civilization, a Russian archaeologist by the name of Petr Kozlov (1863-1935) was exploring the ruins of Karahoto, an ancient city in the Gobi Desert. In this ruins of this ancient city he found an ancient tomb in which there was found a very beautiful mural that was dated as being in excess of 18,000 years old. The mural represented a young ruler and his consort. Their emblem was a circle divided into four quadrants. In the center was a sign corresponding to the Greek letter mu, which we know as the letter M. What early unknown civilization was represented by the young ruler and his consort depicted in the mural found by Dr. Kozlov? We know of no advanced civilization of this ancient age.

CONFUSING DISCOVERIES

As further proof that not only mankind is much older than presupposed but that civilization was much further advanced during ancient times than we now believe possible, I would point to several other discoveries in the field of archeology that have not been given much air time.

On January 18, 1998, the Egyptian museum in Cairo, Egypt added an ancient metal statue to one of its exhibits. The statue had been case over 4,000 earlier for the Pharaoh Pepi I, a little known ruler from the Sixth Dynasty. According to the Egyptian and German archeologists who worked to restore the statute, this was not only a rare work of art, being made of hammered copper, but it was also one of the oldest known metal statues ever found[234]. Who was capable of working with copper in this manner over 4,000 years ago?

In March of 1998, Reuters News Service reported that a richly colored wall fresco had been found that was believed to date from more than 2,000 years ago. Such news would be interesting but not earth shaking were it not for the fact that the fresco showed a panoramic view of the ancient city of Rome as seen from the air[235].

---

[234] Bell, Art and Brad Steiger, The Source, Paper Chase Press, New Orleans, Louisiana. 1999.

[235] Ibid.

Finally, on April 26, 1998, the London Times carried a story regarding the discovery of a number of buildings found underwater off of the coast of Japan. According to archeologists, these buildings had been constructed over 8,000 years ago by a previously unknown civilization using building techniques that showed a high level of knowledge[236].

Clearly these three discoveries make a strong case for the existence of an unknown civilization whose very existence has been lost in the mists of time. Or was the knowledge of this unknown advanced civilization purposely hidden by descendants of the survivors of this advanced civilization?

ANCIENT SECRET SOCIETIES

Perhaps the answers to these and many other unanswered questions can be found in the teachings of some of our earthly secret societies. Supporting the idea that more advanced civilizations existed prior to our own are the hidden teachings of various of the ancient secret societies. For example, though Masonry can traced back more than 5,000 years to even earlier ancient Egyptian Secret Societies, there are those who claim that this very well known Secret Society is even older that 5,000 years. There are those that claim that the Masonic Order is older than any existing religion and that it originated in remote antiquity[237]. According to General Albert Pike, head of the American Masonry in the late 1800s,

"With her traditions reaching back to the earliest times, and her symbols dating farther back than even the monumental history of Egypt extends . . .it is [still the same as] it was in the cradle of the human race, when no human foot had trodden the soil of Assyria and Egypt."

I should also point out that Albert Pike was a man with a number of connections to various secret orders and perhaps was an agent of the Eternal Conspiracy. He was one of the founders of the Knights of the Golden Circle and one of those who helped bring about the American Civil War. He served as a General in the Confederate Army, but was never punished by the victorious North as were so many Confederate leaders.

Author Manley P. Hall, a thirty-third degree Mason, even claims that the secret society that we known as Masonry actually originated in the mythical kingdom of Atlantis. He wrote:

"*The age of the Masonic school is not to be calculated by hundreds or even thousands of years, for it never had any origin in the worlds of form. It is a shadow of the great Atlantean Mystery School, which stood with all of its splendor in the*

---

236 Ibid.

237 Still, William T., New World Order: The Ancient Plan of Secret Societies, Huntington House Publishers, Lafayette, Louisiana. 1990.

ancient City of the Golden Gates, where now the turbulent Atlantic rolls in unbroken sweep[238]."

Most believe that the Craft is only a fraternal organization with certain traditions; however, Hall has gone on record that Masons are the guardians of the ancient secrets of life, collected and practiced by history's greatest philosophers and adepts known as "the Mysteries". However, what were these mysteries that had to be protected with such secrecy?

It is also interesting to discover that every ancient civilization seemed to have its own version of secret societies. In fact, secret societies have been found to have existed since the beginnings of recorded history[239]. Primitive secret societies have been found to have existed among African tribes, in Eskimo populations, throughout the East Indies and northern Asia, among American Indian Tribes, in China, India and even among that tribes that lived in what is now the Middle East.

These many secret societies maintained their wall of secrecy in order to prevent condemnation and prosecution from those who were not among the "elite", as well as to safeguard the very existence of the organization itself. The organization was the mechanism for the perpetuation of secret policies, principles or systems of learning known only to those specially chosen. Though most have laughed at the idea, the teachings of these primitive secret societies are further proof that there was once a civilization that spanned our globe. As further proof supporting this theory, 32nd degree Mason John Loughran recently found what he called an ancient Indian Masonic Lodge at an Anasazi Indian archeological site in New Mexico[240].

According to Mr. Loughran:

"*The furniture was placed the same way, and the area where the main rituals took place seemed eighty percent identical to the Masonic lodges in America now. The only difference was that these temples were round. Then I did some research and found out that in northern Africa the Masonic temples were round.*"

In the ancient Anasazi Lodge, Mr. Loughran was able to decipher symbols left by the Anasazi Masons that led him to a locator device. This device, in turn, led him to a hidden library containing fifty rock and clay tablets which he dated to an era between 1000 and 1200 A.D. According to Mr. Loughran, these tablets were written in a language that appeared to be Arabic, noting that the very name Anasazi is translated as "ancient ones." Could the ancestors of the mysterious Anasazi culture have come from the Middle East? If this most ancient of American

---

238 Ibid.
239 Ibid.
240 Ibid.

civilizations had its beginnings in the Middle East, then how did it get to the American Southwest? What brought it down and removed almost every trace of it except for Chaco Canyon in New Mexico?

ORIGINS

Can it be that it was from remnants of this ancient civilization that even the name "America" derived? We are taught that the name America was selected for the New World based on the name of Amerigo Vespucci, an early explorer and writer, but perhaps this is not the case. According to an 1895 edition of a magazine called Lucifer, published by the Theosophical Society, the supreme god of the Mayan culture of Central America was known as Amaru and the territory over which he ruled was called Amaruca.

According to author James Prye, the word America is derived from the Mayan word Amaruca, which translates as "Land of the Plumed Serpent[241]." The Plumed Serpent, of course, was another name for Quetzalcoatl, the mysterious white figure who brought peace and learning to the ancient cultures of the Americas. It is also interesting to note that since the serpent is usually looked at as a symbol for Lucifer, the rebellious Angel thrown down by God[242], then perhaps The Land of the Plumed Serpent may also be known as the Land of Lucifer.

In many secret societies, Lucifer is depicted as a benevolent peace loving god with nothing but the best intentions for the human race. In Greek mythology he was Prometheus, the titan who defied Zeus and the other gods to bestow the gift of fire upon the human race. For his transgression against Zeus and the laws of the gods, he was cursed to be tortured for all eternity[243].

Among those who worship Lucifer, God is seen as an evil being that is trying to keep knowledge away from the human race. Remember that in the story of the Garden of Eden, God punished Adam and Eve for eating of the Tree of Knowledge after being tempted to do so by the serpent. Does this not seem to be in keeping with the idea that the gods had a policy of keeping man in a state of blissful ignorance? Perhaps this explains the continued targeting and destruction of ancient places of learning by later rulers.

It is also interesting to note that there are many depictions of Lucifer and his followers as being beasts with horns on their heads as well as forked tails. Clearly such beings cannot exist, or do they?

El Paso, Texas is a place with a number of mysteries of its own, such as the deadly Chupacabra and a number of UFO sightings. However, in addition to the Chupacabra and mysterious lights in the sky, there have been a number of other

---

[241] Ibid.

[242] This is very much in keeping with my theory of a civil war amongst the Gods. Perhaps Lucifer was a leader of one sect of the Annunaki.

[243] Still, William T., New World Order: The Ancient Plan of Secret Societies, Huntington House Publishers, Lafayette, Louisiana. 1990.

little publicized mysteries unearthed in the El Paso area. For example, early in the last century, a 30 + year old male skeleton was unearthed in a mining area of the El Paso area. The Skull had two small horns protruding from the forehead area. Witness of this unusual event was a Texas Ranger investigating another murder case.

There was never any explanation about what happened to the owner of this unusual skull. It would seem to be that if in fact this skull was of recent origin, then surely someone would have noticed a man or woman wondering around with two horns growing out of their forehead. Of course, perhaps the skull was much older than it seemed and belonged to an ancient resident of the El Paso area[244].

It is when one digs deeply into legend and attempts to penetrate the mists of time that the first faint hints of a master race begins to become apparent. There are many legends and myths that claim that it is as a result of the terrible civil war when their weapons of mass destruction were turned on their fellow gods and their human followers that the Mother civilization was destroyed. Now they must rule from behind the scenes in an attempt to control a rebellious human race. But even more than this, they have occasions interfered in human affairs directly, though this has always been written off as legend. But in the next chapter, let us see if in fact we can find a pattern of involvement by "greater" beings.

---

[244] Hudnall, Ken and Sharon Hudnall, Spirits of the Border III: The History and Mystery of the Rio Grande, Omega Press, El Paso, Texas 2005.

CHAPTER EIGHTEEN

EVIDENCE OF DIRECT INTERACTION WITH THE HUMAN RACE

Having presented a strong case for the existence of an earlier, unknown civilization, I think it is now incumbent upon me to show that some members of this earlier civilization may well have survived its destructions. These survivors became known to the less advanced Humans of the day as the gods. It would be interesting if we were able to also show a direct intervention with the actions of the Human Race by some unknown group. This would certainly be solid support for my theories were some unknown group shown to be operating in the shadows. Surprisingly enough, there is both indirect evidence of such meddling in Human affairs as well as a body of direct evidence.

IN THE GARDEN

Probably the most famous account of the interaction of advanced entities with early man is the story of the Garden of Eden. According to the Book of Genesis, God said, "Let us make Man in our image, after our likeness." The creation of Adam was probably the most direct intervention with the Human Race that one can think of. It has also long puzzled Biblical researchers that God used the phrase "Let us make man in our image." The question arises was, or is, there more than one God? We may never know. However, there is no question that from the moment of creation, God continually interacted with Man for eons after the creation event. The question is how detailed and extensive was that involvement?

According to the text, God would walk in the Garden with Adam and Eve. Clearly from the context of this story, God was demonstrating the characteristics of a flesh and blood man. The text also raises some other interesting questions. For example, if God is all knowing, then why, when Adam and Eve hid from him after eating of the Tree of Knowledge; he had to call out and ask them where they were and why they were hiding from him[245].

Of course, to the horror of most members of orthodox religion, in looking for proof that the gods have interacted with mere mortals, there is no more believable source than the Holy Bible. One of the most blatant interferences with the Human Race may well have been the destruction of the ancient cities of Sodom and Gomorrah.

Many members of the Soviet scientific community have demonstrated a much more open mind than western trained scientists about such things. Some very prominent Soviet scientists are convinced that the ancient Hindu tale of visitation by advanced entities from Venus and have conducted extensive explorations into the almost inaccessible Gobi Desert.

One such scientist is Professor Mikhail Agrest, a very prominent mathematician and physicist. Professor Agrest has long expressed the conviction that the destruction of Sodom and Gomorrah was caused by a nuclear explosion. The Bible does not given any dates for many events that are recorded and it is possible that this destruction of two earthy cities happened many eons ago. The Bible does record that the inhabitants of these two cities were found to be evil in the eyes of God and as punishment for their evil activities, the cities were destroyed by a rain of fire and brimstone that came from the heavens[246].

The Bible further records that God sent two of his Angels to warn Lot, one of the few in either city who had remained true to the religious teachings. As stated in the Book of Genesis, Chapter 19, verse 1[247] "Now two angels came to Sodom in the even, as Lot was sitting in the gate of Sodom. When Lot saw them, he rose to meet them and bowed down with his face to the ground." His actions make it clear that Lot recognized these two strangers as being of the gods, hence his bowing down as if to a ruler.

The Bible makes no statements as to the Angels being spiritual creatures, rather from every available description, they appear very substantial in both description and to those with whom they interact. In fact, they were substantial enough to become targets for a mob that which to assault them. The two Angels were menaced by a crowd of citizens until Lot came to their rescue, giving them shelter in his home. These two beings were real enough that the men of Sodom came to Lot and said in verse 5 "Where are the men who came to you tonight? Bring them out to us so that we may have relations with them."

In fact, according to verse 3 of the same Book and chapter, "So they turned aside to him and entered his house; and he prepared a feast for them, and baked

---

[245] Sitchin, Zecharia, Divine Encounters, Bear & Company, Rochester, Vermont. 1995, 2002.

[246] The Holy Bible, The King James Edition.

[247] Ibid.

unleavened bread and they ate." Why would spiritual beings either need or be able to eat solid food? There would seem to be little doubt that these two beings were as real and as solid as any Human being that we might meet in the street.

By all accounts the two beings were able to fly and yet they had no wings and they demonstrated unbelievable power as shown in the Book of Genesis, Chapter 19, Verse 11 by striking the unruly mob blind before they could overrun Lot and enter the house to take the visitors by force. After demonstrating their power over lesser Humans, the two beings warned Lot of the punishment to come to the City and urged him to take his family and flee into the hills. So it was that as a result of the warning of two Angels, only Lot and his family were spared this Heavenly punishment.

Unfortunately, Lot's wife disobeyed God's instructions not to look back and looked back toward the city as they fled. She was immediately turned into a pillar of salt as punishment. As can be seen here with the punishment of Lot's wife, there has long been a belief among humans that to disobey the orders of God, or the gods depending on your belief system, brings immediate severe punishment.

Turning once again to the Holy Bible, we see in the Second Book of Kings, verses 8-23, that God took a direct hand in the war between Syria and Israel. This particular incident resulted in a major change in the balance of power in the Middle East. Had the King of Syria defeated Israel, the entire history of the world would have changed. However, the desires of the King of Syria were not in keeping with the master plan of the Lord of Hosts[248]. Thus, it is clear that to ensure the success of his plan, the Lord of Hosts will take a direct hand if necessary.

THE GODS RULE

According to the Holy Bible, China was ruled by Emperors for over thousand years who were supposed to be direct descendants of the Gods. For this reason, the Chinese Emperor was referred to as the "Son of Heaven." According to David Hawkes, who has written extensively about the Chinese Emperors, when the Chinese were still living in a tribal state, their primary god was referred to as di[249]. According to the Shang tribe, di impregnated a virgin who gave birth to the zu, the first ancestor, of the tribe. This legend sounds much like the birth of The Christ Child as told in the Holy Bible. It is very surprising that a similar myth can be found in almost every ancient race on the planet.

As the Shang's knowledge of the world around them widened, it became clear to them that there must be a number of sky gods who were subordinate to a senior God. It is also very surprising that the Chinese di is very similar in pronunciation with the Latin deus. This similarity also reinforces the fact that

---

[248] Andrews, George C., Extra-Terrestrials Among Us, Llewellyn Publications, St. Paul, Minnesota, 1993.
[249] Ibid.

almost every royal family had a legend that their early ancestors were descendants of the gods.

These many stories of the rulers of various countries being direct descendants of the ancient gods make it clear that the ancient gods had total control over early man, or else how could they have appoint the Kings? It is also said that the early gods started the various religions in order to instill in mankind a system of controls that would be very basic to their make up. These transgressions against the "gods" were punished very severely, memories of which have come down to us in the form of legends of great death and destruction. At the same time the gods appeared to withdraw from daily contact with man, the secular rulers and the chief priests appointed by the gods became extremely powerful, having a directly pipeline to God so to speak.

Assuming for a moment that the "gods" were in fact, extremely intelligent visitors to this planet who were so far about the native inhabitants that they appeared as awe inspiring beings, then we are left with a quandary in determining the nature of these creatures. There is no doubt that in spite of the Biblical reference as Adam being the first man, there were clearly others living on this planet of ours. Where did they come from?

There is also no doubt from the various references in the Bible that the "Sons of the gods" interbred with human females to create a hybrid race with powers and abilities far beyond those of mortal man. It was these hybrids who were appointed to be the first generation of priest-kings to rule over their fellow mans.

THE WARS OF THE GODS

There is a large body of information regarding the involvement of the ancient gods in the wars of man, both as direct field commanders and as advisors from the sidelines. The Priest-Kings who became the rulers of man appeared to have many of the flaws to be found in the human race, such as greed and jealousy. As a result, they began to quarrel among themselves, leading those humans they ruled in wars of conquest over each other.

As a result of the many wars and other wrongs committed by these appointed rulers, the gods, decided to destroy the human race and star over as shown in the Book of Genesis, Chapter 6, verse 7. However, some of those early offspring of the gods still had the ability to sway their creators. One individual that was held in particular favor was Noah, as shown in Genesis, Chapter 6, verse 8. As a result of his relationship with the gods, he was warned in time to enable himself and others to survive the flood.

Another source that might surprise many would be an ancient Indian text which relates how a mysterious being called Sanatkumara[250] visited our planet from

---

[250] This name translates as everlasting youth, perhaps referring to an immortal being.

the planet we know as Venus. Since there is no record of the ancients writing science fiction, then we much give these ancient writings a serious study.

According to the description of the arrival

"Thundering down from unspeakable heights, and wreathed in flames that filled the heavens with tongues of fire, came the chariot of the Sons of Fire and the Lords of Flame from the Resplendent Star. It alighted on the White Island of the Sea of Gobi, a green, marvelous expanse of fragrant flowers."

According to the ancient Indian text, Sanatkumara and his companions came to earth and awakened the intelligence of mankind, teaching our ancestors the arts of tillage and bee-keeping and many other ways to improve their lives. In other words, this is an earlier tale of advanced being coming to teach the primitive humans.

Could this somewhat far fetched tale be true? To be sure, modern scientists have dismissed this text as pure fantasy, but no one has answered the important question, how could ancient Indian scribes so accurately describe the fiery exhaust of a landing spaceship? This is not the only text that very clearly describes the use of aircraft and space ships in ancient India.

Many legends emanating from Central Asia related to the mysterious area we now refer to as the Gobi Desert. There is a large body of physical evidence that supports the belief that the Gobi Desert may well have been a great sea eons ago. If the ancient tales about this fables sea are true then can the other stories about the islands that once existed in this mysterious body of water by so quickly dismissed?

Further support for the ancient tales emanating from India can be found in ancient Chinese stories that tell of an island that existed in this ancient sea peopled by "white men with blue eyes and fair hair[251] who descended from heaven and imparted the arts of civilization to their fellow-men, including, as some believe, the inhabitants of ancient MU[252], who thus attained a high degree of culture some 75,000 years ago."

THE LAND OF THE RISING SUN

Another country in the mysterious east which has legends of other races co-existing with man is Japan. In fact, the legends surrounding these alleged alien visitors are so detailed and wide spread that there has been serious study undertaken as to whether or not strange beings might actually have arrived in Japan from outer space and lived there until about the year 3,000 B.C.[253]. In support of this theory,

---

[251] Kolosimo, Peter, Timeless Earth, Bantam Books, New York. 1975.

[252] MU was supposedly an ancient civilization, in fact the mother civilization, that existed on a continent located in the Pacific Ocean. This continent was destroyed much as is supposed to have happened to Atlantis.

[253] Kolosimo, Peter, Timeless Earth, Bantam Books, New York. 1975.

Professor Komatsu Kitamura, an archaeologist and historian, wrote that he was led to this theory by a print illustrating an old work on the history of the Kappas or "men of the cane brake" who inhabited Japan in the Heian period, (the 9th to 11th century A.D.). The Kappas are described as web-footed bipeds with three hooked fingers on each hand, the centre digit being much longer than the others. The skin of these creatures is described as being brown, smooth, silky and lucent; their heads are elongated, with large ears and strange eyes of a triangular shape[254].

According to all the available reports, these creatures wore a hat with four needles in it; their nose was like a proboscis and was connected to a casket shaped hump on their backs. To me this description sounds like a biped wearing a survival suit or a scuba suit, the four needles being antenna allowing them to communicate with each other and their headquarters and the long proboscis being an air tube running to an air supply worn on their backs.

Such descriptions of possibly amphibious creatures or at least beings using the oceans as for protection against the natives, interacting with local cultures can be found around the world. Are these legends actually descriptions of various aspects of a world wide training program designed to raise man above the beasts of the field?

---

[254] Ibid.

CHAPTER NINETEEN

ANGELS: REAL BEINGS OR SPIRITUAL CREATURES?

There has been much written over the centuries regarding the existence or non-existence of Angels. In fact, there is no doubt that on a number of occasions, so called Angels have acted just like men, though demonstrating powers far beyond anything of which a mere man would be capable.

The word for "Angel" in Biblical Hebrew is mal'ak . Its main meaning is "messenger". It's the same name given to the prophetic book that is the last of the Prophets. That book's author has no name, just the title of Messenger. He could've been the editor who gathered the Prophetic books together so that his people could remember and prepare for what was to come. Some angeliphiles think Malachi is an angel, but the book's content and its presence among the Prophets make it certain that Malachi is a human messenger, a prophet.

But this raises a question that has puzzled man for centuries: can we always tell this difference when we find the word 'messenger' in the Scriptural reports or the traditions? Angels are definitely not humans, especially not dead humans who 'earn wings'. (That idea was not invented by Frank Capra for Clarence in "It's A Wonderful Life". Its roots go back at least as far as *The Martyrdom of Polycarp*, 1:39, early 2nd century AD.)

It is generally believed that Angels don't even have sex, though they are pictured as having gender (and earth-style body forms) so we can relate to them better. However, if we are dealing with entities associated with God in every case then what about the Biblical verse about the “Sons of God, fining the daughters of men fair and taking unto them wives”? Clearly these being had sex because their children became men of great renown.

Most Biblical writers felt that the ancients couldn't picture anything in the 'pure' world of heaven as being female or neuter, so they called them by what they felt was greatest -- male. Maybe we're getting over that myopia. Angels are pictured as having feathered wings. The ancients believed the angels flew, so they pictured it through the only means of flying they knew for large beings: birdlike feathered wings. However, there is no doubt that in many of the ancient stories, the Angels flew without wings.

It's a fine line between the main task of an angel and the task of a prophet, an evangelist, or a poet or storyteller, or just anyone who brings us a divine truth that's hard for us to take. The Christmas "herald angels" of Jesus' birth and resurrection, or the figure that wrestled with Jacob, were certainly supernatural. But sometimes it's not so certain, maybe these entities are only one normal human step from the prophets.

According to the scriptures, the main task of an Angel is to tell a truth that communicates God's will to some person(s), leaving the results to the people who hear it and the Holy Spirit at work among them. Since Christians are all given the charge of spreading the good report on Jesus Christ to others who don't know or understand, then in a way every Christian and every Christian church is a 'messenger', a mal'ak. So it may well be, by this same definition that not every entity that communicates with man is an angel in the sense of a divine being, nor a replacement for such divine beings.

Putting this in plane English, it may be that there exists a race somewhere between the “gods” of the ancients and humans. This race may have powers and abilities far beyond those of mortal men, but be much less than gods. Such a description would certain be true in the case of a 21st century American dealing with a primitive tribe such as the Cargo Cult of the South Pacific. This native tribe was caught in the middle of World War II and looked at what dropped from the sky, be it cases of Coca Cola or airplanes as being gifts from their gods. Today, they still pray for the gods to return. Are we the Cargo Cult equivalent in comparison with these “Sons of God” who still see the daughters of man and find them fair?

GOOD VERSUS EVIL

It seems to be a basic truth in nature that everything must be balanced. This is also a great truth taught by many eastern systems of training. If this is true than if there are good Angels, there must also be evil Angels. It should be remembered that the Bible teaches that when Lucifer rebelled against God, he took with him a large number of Angels who are now working against the interests of God. Thus, if the teachings of the Bible are to be believed these anti-God Angels are what we know of as Demons.

There are tens of thousands of people in asylums and prisons who have committed crimes that they claim were caused by outside influences that took control of their bodies to carry out the events for which they are imprisoned. There are some who believe that such things as possession are truly possible.

In fact, according to Father Malachi Martin, a Jesuit scholar and a leading authority on demons and exorcism, there is a spiritual war going on about us every day of which only a few of us are aware[255]. In fact, he has gone to far as to maintain that over 50% of persons suffering psychiatric problems are really possessed by demons. He also claims that many multiple personality disorders have been shown to be cases of demonic possession.

Referring again to the possibility that the forces that would keep the Human Race confused and under control, suit the nature of their approach to the expectations of the victims, I would point to several instances where the scriptures state that God took a prophet to heaven without the necessity of the death of the body. This sounds suspiciously like the alien abductions that fill the modern literature. Where once man believed that God walked the earth many people now believe in the possibility of aliens from outer space. It is the same conduct, just the trappings are different.

I also think that it is very interesting that both the gods that once walked the earth as well as the benevolent Space Brothers who are said to visit with unsuspecting people bring similar messages about spiritual growth. Additionally, both have also warned their "contactees" about the power of the evil ones. Is this a coincidence or something else? Taking the similarities a step further, many contactees have claimed that the benevolent Space Brother that contacted them resembled pictures of Jesus Christ that the contacteee has seen before.

As I pointed out in the first volume of this series[256], there are a number of statements attributed to some of the benevolent Space Brothers that the aliens created religion as a control mechanism to keep the Human Race under control. It is certain that for many of us, our religions have an unusual amount of control over our actions. Perhaps religion actually was created by those who are now forced to work from the shadows as a mechanism to keep us under control.

The beliefs in demons and possession have become so wide spread that these ideas have begun to be found in many criminal events. During the 20th century there were even a number of murders carried out by individuals who claimed to have been carrying out the orders of some higher being or who heard voices that gave them instructions. The young New Yorker convicted as the Son of Sam killer is an example of such a situation. David Berkowitz claimed that the neighbor's dog gave him his orders mentally. Perhaps such things do happen. Just a medium can alleged speak to the dead, perhaps there are those who are, unknowingly, tuned in on the wave length of some other person or entity. Modern science does not have an answer for everything.

---

[255] Bell, Art and Brad Steiger, The Source, Paper Chase Press, New Orleans, LA. 1999

[256] Hudnall, Ken, The Occult Connection: UFOS, Secret Societies and Ancient Gods, Omega Press, El Paso, Texas 1994.

MENTAL MANIPULATION

There are many who have theorized that alien abductions as well as deeply moving religious experiences many not be real, but rather implanted in the mind of the one targeted for the experience. This would explain many aspects of the abduction phenomenon that currently baffle science.

Neuroscientist Michael Persinger not only believes that these incidents are artificially induced, but he claims that he has created a mental/technical device that came simulate the experiences that have been claimed by those who believe that they have been abducted by aliens[257]. Dr. Persinger has tested his device on a number of volunteers at his laboratory at Laurentian University, in Sudbury, Ontario, Canada. Using the manipulation of magnetic fields, he claims to induce within the mind of the subject perceptions of aliens, angels, demons and a number of other monsters from the Human Id.

Dr. Persinger contends that the human brain is highly sensitive to information produced by complex or irregularly pulsed magnetic fields. Through the manipulation of these fields, Dr. Persinger reported that he has been able to induce almost identical phenomena to that experienced by those who claim to have been abducted by aliens. It is certainly interesting to note that in many UFO incidents that involve motorized vehicles, the ignitions of the vehicle have been effected by the electromagnetic fields alleged to be produced by the purported UFO.

It has also been proposed that alien abduction experiences are actually mental indoctrination programs disguised as a kidnapping. Those who have been indoctrinated are subject to the control of those who modified the victim's thought processes. It is certainly true that after such an event a number of those who claim to have been abducted by aliens demonstrate completely different personalities than they did before the alleged abduction experience. If there is a group working from the shadows to gain control of segments of the human race, perhaps mental programming would suit their needs and help them gain followers. It would certainly make sense from the point of view of a small group trying to dominate a large group and fit the known facts.

PATTERNS

In any study such as this, it is important to isolate patterns of behavior that appear to be similar in incidents that take place over a long period of time. With the advent of the alleged alien abduction phenomenon there has emerged a pattern that seems to hold true in almost every event.

First, the "victim", for want of a better term, reports having seen an

---

[257] Bell, Art and Brad Steiger, The Source, Paper Chase Press, New Orleans, LA. 1999.

unidentified flying object and has some type of experience that results in physical contact between the observer and the "alien" presence. In some cases, this physical contact results in unconsciousness of the observer and the famous "lost time" phenomenon.

In other type of cases, the observer/victim has no previous contact, but is alone when visited by the "alien" presence. This type of contact usually results in a period of "lost time".

Then there is the group of individuals who manage to remain conscious throughout the incident and retain what they believe to be clear memories of everything that transpired. In these incidents, it is communicated to the observer/victim that they have been selected for a particular mission that is of tremendous importance to the human race. This selection, they are told, has been made because the victim/observer is someone very special. Quote often, the victim/observer is told that they are the actual reincarnation of someone very famous or important from either the Earth's past or the alien race. Others are led to believe that they are actually a crossbreed between humans and the alien race put here on earth as a very small child. Whatever may be the story, the person being indoctrinated is led to believe that they have a special relationship with their abductors, a sort of galactic Stockholm Syndrome.

In most cases, the victim/observer is given a liquid and told to drink it. If there is any hesitation, then the abductors convince the victim/observer that they have ingested this particular liquid before, either as children or during their previous existence as a member of the alien race.

All of this stage dressing is designed to make the person abducted feel that they are a very special person who has been carefully selected for an important mission upon which the lives of millions may hang. Such a build up naturally leads to the victim/observer feeling a certain attachment to the abductors. Playing to the ego of anyone can lead to feelings of attachment between the abducted and the abductor.

After the event, the "selected" person is returned to their normal environment where they all tend to go through a period of restlessness, irritability, and experience very unusual dreams during the short time they are able to sleep. It is as if the mind is struggling to absorb and internalize new programming. Perhaps the indoctrination process needs a few days to "take" to the point that normal behavior is influenced. It is after this period of restlessness that the victim/observer begins to preach the wonders of the space brothers.

It is also interesting to note that almost every one of these contactees begins to look forward to the return of their space brothers and most begin to remember that they have been "abducted" numerous times over their lifetime as their space brothers "prepared" them for their mission. This is very similar to the physical and sexual abuse cases where adults "suddenly remembered" that they were abused by their parents as small children. In these instances, the so called memories are so vivid that no one can convince the "victim" that the abuse never took place.

Once the contactee begins to preach the wonders of the aliens, family and close friends report that their personalities undergo complete changes. No loner are they the person that he or she might have been prior to the event. Many of these advocates of the wonders of the space brothers become so obsessed with their "mission" that they totally forget about their own personal safety or taking care of their own families. The only thing that is important to them is the needs of the space brothers.

To me, all of the personality changes shown by those who have been contacted by the space brothers, or the Greys of any other advanced race sounds very much like standard brainwashing that has been around and used very effectively by our own government since the 1950s.

CHAPTER TWENTY

SO WHERE DID THEY GO?

So, if my theory is true that there existed, or perhaps, still exists an advanced race of beings that once ruled over the human race as gods, then where did they go? Clearly, this is the weakness of any theory such as mine for we have yet to find the grave of a Zeus or a Thor to prove that the Norse gods were real beings. However, at the same time, man has searched for the fabled elephants' graveyard for centuries, but no one would argue that the elephant does not exist.

However, to get back to this particular mystery, there is perhaps, strong evidence pointing to where the gods went they were forced to leave earth. Man was allegedly made in God's image so I will assume that man and God have much the same outlook on things, at least for this purpose. This being the case, when have you ever known anyone to give up absolute power voluntarily? I can't think of or find a single time this has been done. Therefore, I do not think that the gods are too far away, assuming that they still exist[258].

In a very interesting book entitled, *We Discovered Alien Bases on the Moon*[259], former NASA engineer Fred Steckling sounded the alarm that mankind was not being given the full story about what NASA had found on the moon. Mr. Steckling made it very clear that there was solid evidence that there is an alien presence on earth's satellite. Then David Hatcher Childress made his own strong case for an alien presence on the Moon in his fascinating book Extraterrestrial Archaeology[260].

Adding to the strong body of evidence that things were taking place on the moon that NASA was not talking about was Cynthia Turnage's book, Extraterrestrials Are on the Moon and Mars: The Photographic Evidence[261]. Ms.

---

[258] For those quick to jump to conclusions and criticize those of us who have the daring to ask questions, I would point out that when I use the word god (small g) I am referring only to that mysterious race of beings that once walked the earth and ruled mankind.

[259] Steckling, Fred, We Discovered Alien Bases on the Moon, Light Technology Publications. (July, 1997)

[260] Childress, David Hatcher, Extraterrestrial Archaeology, Adventures Unlimited Press (February 11, 2000).

[261] Turnage, Cynthia, Extraterrestrials Are On The Moon and Mars: The Photographic

Turnage goes a step further, however, and makes the case that there has been an intentional wall of silence erected by NASA and our government concerning any potential concrete evidence of extraterrestrial life that has been captured on film.

Supporting the theory that there is someone else on the Moon, astronomers have, for centuries, seen what appear to be buildings, lights and activity on the Moon. These sightings began long before it was even remotely possible to put a man on the Moon. So who was up there looking down at us?

It was no less than the late Carl Sagan who conjectured that if extraterrestrial being came to earth, that would quite likely establish bases on the Moon and place their most important installations on the dark side of the Moon to keep earth eyes from watching the activity. He even theorized that if there are alien bases on the Moon that they have probably been there for thousands, if not millions, of years.

The Crater Aristarchus is the single brightest spot on the Moon and since the earliest of telescopes was developed in the early 1600s by Galileo a wide variety of flares, lights and other activity has been seen in this area. Luminous triangles and grids of lights have been consistently seen at a location named Plato, the darkest spot on the Moon.

Other astronomers, as early as 1832, have seen lights that blink as if sending signals from the Moon. Even more interesting was the determination in 1873 by the Royal Society of Britain that the irregular blinking of lights seen on the Moon were intelligent attempts by an unknown race on the Moon to send signals to Earth.

Then in 1953, astronomer John J. O'Neill was studying the eastern edge of the Mare Crisium and saw what has been described as a large artificial bridge some twelve miles long and 500 feet high. He had looked at this same area previously and the bridge had not been present. This very unusual sighting was confirmed on a public television program by English astronomers Dr. H.P. Wilkins and Patrick Moore. So who is on the Moon?

NAZI MOONMEN?

Of course the idea that some mysterious group is based on our moon is nothing new. Vladimir Terziski, President of the American Academy of Dissident Sciences[262]. According to Dr. Terziski, Nazi Germany made a Moon landing in 1942 as shown in the following article[263],

---

Evidence, Timeless Voyager Press (May 1, 1998).

[262] The American Academy of Dissident Sciences believes that the accepted sciences work to keep much from society. Vladimir Terziski, President,- American Academy of Dissident Sciences, 10970 Ashton Ave. #310, Los Angeles, CA 90024, phone and fax: USA-(310)-473-9717.

[263] http://www.v-j-enterprises.com/moonger.html

HALF A CENTURY OF THE GERMAN MOON BASE (1942 - 1992)

From: rkrouse@netcom.com (Robert K. Rouse)
Newsgroups: alt.paranet.ufo,alt.alien.visitors,alt.conspiracy
Subject: Moon and Mars Bases
Date: 24 Aug 93 16:20:45 GMT

The Germans landed on the Moon as early as probably 1942, utilizing their larger exoatmospheric rocket saucers of the Miethe and Schriever type. The Miethe rocket craft was built in diameters if 15 and 50 meters, and the Schriever Walter turbine powered craft was designed as an interplanetary exploration vehicle. It had a diameter of 60 meters, had 10 stories of crew compartments, and stood 45 meters high. Welcome to Alice in Saucerland. In my extensive research of dissident American theories about the physical conditions on the Moon I have proved beyond the shadow of a doubt that there is atmosphere, water and vegetation on the Moon, and that man does not need a space suit to walk on the Moon. A pair of jeans, a pullover and sneakers are just about enough. Everything NASA has told the world about the Mood is a lie and it was done to keep the exclusivity of the club from joinings by the third world countries. All these physical conditions make it a lot more easier to build a Moon base.

Ever since their first day of landing on the Moon, the Germans started boring -and tunneling under the surface, and by the end of the war there was a small Nazi research base on the Moon. The free energy tachyon drive craft of the Haunibu-1 and 2 type were used after 1944 to haul people," materiel and the first robots to the construction site on the Moon. When Russians and Americans secretly landed jointly on the Moon in the early fifties with their own saucers, they spent their first night there as guests of the .... Nazi underground base. In the sixties a massive Russian - American base had been built on the Moon, that now has a population of 40,000 people, as the rumor goes. After the end of the war in May 1945, the Germans continued their space effort from their south polar colony of Neu Schwabenland. I have discovered a photograph of their underground space control center there.

Is it possible that the many missing Nazis that the allies searched for at the end of World War II actually went to a hidden German base at the south pole and then to the Moon? There have been a number of stories about this south pole base and an equal number of stories about moon bases. It would be fascinating to know if any of these stories are true. What follows are some more articles from the same website mentioned above that continue this theory.

GERMAN-JAPANESE MILITARY R&D COOPERATION:

According to Renato Vesco again, Germany was sharing a great deal of the advances in weaponry with their allies the Italians during the war. At the Fiat experimental facility at lake La Garda, a facility that fittingly bore the name of air martial Hermann Goering, the Italians were experimenting with numerous advanced weapons, rockets and airplanes, created in Germany. In a similar fashion, the Germans kept a close contact with the Japanese military establishment and were supplying it with many advanced weapons. I have discovered for example a photo of a copy of the manned version of the V-1 - the Reichenberg - produced in Japan by Mitsubishi. The best fighter in the world - the push-pull twin propeller Domier-335 was duplicated at the Kawashima works. (There is also) a photo of Japanese high ranking Imperial navy officers inspecting the latest German radar station.

A Japanese friend of mine in Los Angeles related to me the story of his friend's father, who worked as technician in an aircraft research bureau in Japan during the war. In July of 1945, two and a half months after the war ended in Germany, a huge German transport submarine brought to Japan the latest of German inventions - two spherical wingless flying devices. The Japanese R&D team put the machines together, following the German instructions, and... there was something very bizarre and other-earthy standing in front of them - a ball shaped flying device without wings or propellers, that nobody knew how it flied. The fuel was added, the start button of this unmanned machine was pressed* and it .... disappeared with a roar and flames without a in the sky. The team never saw it again. The engineers were so frightened by the unexpected might of the machine, that they promptly dynamited the second prototype and choose to forget the whole incident.

GERMAN-JAPANESE FLIGHT TO THE MOON AND MARS IN 1945-46:

According to the authors of the underground German documentary movie from the Thule society, the only produced craft of the Haunibu-3 type - the 74 meter diameter naval warfare dreadnought - was chosen for the most courageous mission of this whole century - the trip to Mars. The craft was of saucer shape, had the bigger Andromeda tachyon drives, and was armed with four triple gun turrets of large naval caliber (three inverted upside down and attached to the underside of the craft, and the fourth on top of the crew compartments).

A volunteer suicide crew of Germans and Japanese was chosen, because everybody knew that this journey was a one-way journey with no return. The large intensity of the electro-magnetogravitic fields and the inferior quality of the metal alloys used then for the structural elements of the drive, was causing the metal to fatigue and get very brittle only after a few months of work of the drive. The flight to Mars departed from Germany one month before the war ended - in April 1945.

It was probably a large crew, numbering in the hundreds, because of the low level of automation and electronic controls inside the saucer. Most of the systems of the craft had to be operated like these on a U-boat of that time -

manually. Because the structurally weakened tachyon drives were not working with full power and not all the time, the trip to Mars took almost 8 months to accomplish. An initial short trust towards Mars was probably used the strong gravitational field close to Earth, after that the craft was "coasting" for 8 months in an elliptical orbit to Mars with its main drives turned off. Later trips to Mars by the joint Soviet - American craft in 1952 and by the Vatican craft of the Marconi project from Argentina in 1956 reached Mars in only 2 - 3 days, because their drives were working during the whole flight: accelerating in the first half and decelerating in the second. Smaller Kohler converters were probably used to power the systems and life support equipment on board. I do not have any information at the present time about any artificial gravity capability on board the craft, but that could have been easily done with the large antigravity drives of the ship.

After a heavy, almost crashing landing, the saucer slammed to a stop, damaging irreparably its drives, but saving the crew. That happened in the middle of January 1946. The crash landing on Mars was not only due to the crippled tachyon drives of the craft - it was also due to the smaller gravitational fleld of Mars generating less power for the tachyon drives; and also due to the thinner atmosphere on Mars, that could not be used as effectively for air breaking as the Earth's atmosphere could. The craft was shaped as a giant saucer - a form that is very efficient as an air brake, when it is entered into the atmosphere with its luge cross section perpendicular to the trajectory of descent.

One question, that I have not answered yet in the affirmative is how were the Germans able to regenerate the air inside the craft for 8 months for this big crew. Quite probably they were using advanced life support systems, developed initially for their larger Walter turbine and free energy submarines, that were cruising the oceans without resurfacing.

The radio message with the mixed news was received by the German underground space control center in Neu Schwabenland and by their research base on the Moon.

So this is the story told by Dr. Terziski. If true, then some of the activity that has been seen on Mars and on the Moon may be the operations of Nazis or Japanese settlers. I will submit that based upon some of the Nazi research that has come to light since the war it is not outside the realm of possibility that they may well have had he technology to launch the mission discussed above.

But let us continue with our review of the evidence that there are or have been others to colonize the Moon or Mars.

THE FACE ON MARS

There has long raged a controversy that has a direct impact on this book. In 1976, NASA's Viking Probe began to send back photos of the surface of Mars. While passing over the area of Mars called Cydonia, a series of photos were taken that had an earth shaking impact on those who were privy to the information. The photos showed what appeared to be a large face and a ruined city on the surface of a supposedly dead planet. NASA discounted this evidence of habitation as being natural formations distorted by shadows.

However, Richard Hoagland discovered these photos and as outlined in his book The Monuments of Mars[264], he conducted detailed studies of these and other photos that NASA had simply filed away in its archives and concluded that the formations shown in the photographs were not natural formations, but evidence that an alien race had constructed a city on Mars.

According to Hoagland's book, NASA's Viking probe had taken 100,000 pictures of Mars and he was told that a second picture of the Cydonia area a few hours later confirmed that the apparent face was just a trick of lighting. At the time he took the word of the NASA scientist who made this statement and no one asked to see the second picture. However, when he saw the picture being discussed sometime later, there was no question that the two photos sowed the presence of a ruined city.

In Hoagland's very interesting book, he makes a strong case for there not only being a giant face on Mars but several four and five sided pyramids as well. He also states that when NASA's Mars Global Surveyor sent back pictures in 1998, they were taken at such close range that the surface looked like a giant sandbox, making it impossible to really see the face. However, what was shown beyond a shadow of a doubt in this somewhat bungled attempt to cover up the existence of the face were very clear pictures of the City of Cydonia. Hoagland is quoted in the Mary 11, 1998 issue of USA Today as saying the photos sent back by the Mars Global Surveyor were photos of ancient, ruined architecture. He also maintains that NASA is hiding photos that would clearly confirm the premise that, at least at one time, Mars was inhabited.

It would seem logical to me that if the gods were forced to leave this planet, for whatever reason, that either the Moon or Mars would be logical destinations. In fact, if there was a civil war as I hypothesize then one faction could have gone to the Moon and the other to Mars.

---

[264] Hoagland, Richard, The Monuments of Mars: a City On The Edge of Forever, North Atlantic Books; 5th edition (September 9, 2001).

EPILOGUE

It was U.S. President Franklin D. Roosevelt who said "Nothing in politics ever happens by accident. If it happens, you can bet it was planned that way." As someone who was clearly connected with the "insiders" he knew exactly what he was talking about.

Decades earlier Benjamin Disraeli, famed as the Victorian-era Prime Minister of Britain, wrote: "The world is governed by people far different from those imagined by the public." He was another leader who seemed able to effortless hang onto power even during the most trying of times. He too, knew what he was talking about.

Taken together, these two statements illustrate the basic premise of the Occult Connection series and which underlies all of the Dr. Peter Beter AUDIO LETTER tape reports[265]. This premise is that major events in politics, economics

[265] Professional credentials: The things made public by Dr. Beter are extraordinary--but so is the professional background which preceded his public visibility. He practiced general law in Washington, D.C., from 1951 to 1961, becoming a member of the U.S. Court of Military Appeals in 1952 and the U.S. Supreme Court in 1964. Many of his cases were against the federal government, all of which he won--including one case in which he caught none other than the U.S. Department of Justice burning records in an attempt to defeat him. The resulting decision--Farley vs. U.S., 131 C. Cls. 776 (1955), 127 F Supp.
562--made new law.

In 1961 President John F. Kennedy appointed Dr. Beter Counsel to the U.S. Export-Import Bank, the largest government-owned bank in the Western world, where he served until 1967. After leaving the Ex-Im Bank, Dr. Beter became an international financial and legal consultant, as well as one of the chief developers of private international business in the Republic of Zaire. He is a member of the Judicature Society, the Bankers' Club of America, the Royal Commonwealth Society of London, and the United States and international relations are the products of deliberate moves by largely unseen power factions in the world. All of these factions seek to increase their influence over us, the general population of the world. Each one also wishes to increase its own power at the expense of the other power factions.

Any real student of history will confirm that there is very little doubt that there has been a cooperative effort among a small group of people who many times profess to be the worst of enemies to control the money flow of society as far back as one care to research. This same small group has cooperated to bring down entire governments, to include the United States government on more than one occasion, and change the balance of power in the world at large. Amazingly, at no time have any of these endangered governments dared to strike back at these conspirators. What type of power must these people have?

These people who would be masters of the rest of us also tend to operate through ancient secret societies in order to mask not only their identities but their intentions as well. Even though the operate in the shadows, these faceless power brokers have been known to select those to rule over the rest of us as shown by some of the hidden deals that have elected US Presidents. This is also evident to anyone who has taken the time to rally study the actions of the prominent and the powerful.

The study of what I call the Hidden Race is one that takes the researcher down some very strange roads. However, at the end of the search there is no doubt that these faceless people operating in the shadows feel no kinship to the rest of us. The worship strange gods and have agendas that certainly do not benefit the human race. So who are they? They are the chosen ones who have ruled over and controlled the human race since before history began – they are the Hidden Race.

Naval Institute. He is listed in biographical reference works such as Who's Who in the East, the Blue Book of London, and 2000 Men of Achievement (London).

INDEX

C

D

E

F

G

H

I

J

K

L

M

N

O

T

U

V

W

X

Y

Z

www.ingramcontent.com/pod-product-compliance
Lightning Source LLC
Chambersburg PA
CBHW031242290426
44109CB00012B/395
* 9 7 8 0 9 7 5 4 9 2 3 7 6 *